THE COMMUNIST EXPERIMENT

REVOLUTION, SOCIALISM, AND GLOBAL CONFLICT IN THE TWENTIETH CENTURY

ROBERT STRAYER

Professor Emeritus
State University of New York, College at Brockport

Adjunct Professor
University of California, Santa Cruz

Adjunct Professor
California State University, Monterey Bay

Mc
Graw
Hill

Boston   Burr Ridge, IL   Dubuque, IA   Madison, WI   New York
San Francisco   St. Louis   Bangkok   Bogotá   Caracas   Kuala Lumpur
Lisbon   London   Madrid   Mexico City   Milan   Montreal   New Delhi
Santiago   Seoul   Singapore   Sydney   Taipei   Toronto

The **McGraw·Hill** Companies

Mc Graw Hill **Higher Education**

THE COMMUNIST EXPERIMENT: REVOLUTION, SOCIALISM, AND GLOBAL
CONFLICT IN THE TWENTIETH CENTURY

Published by McGraw-Hill, a business unit of The McGraw-Hill Companies, Inc., 1221
Avenue of the Americas, New York, NY, 10020. Copyright © 2007 by The McGraw-Hill
Companies, Inc. All rights reserved. No part of this publication may be reproduced or
distributed in any form or by any means, or stored in a database or retrieval system,
without the prior written consent of The McGraw-Hill Companies, Inc., including, but
not limited to, in any network or other electronic storage or transmission, or broadcast
for distance learning.

Some ancillaries, including electronic and print components, may not be available to
customers outside the United States.

This book is printed on acid-free paper.

2 3 4 5 6 7 8 9 0 DOC/DOC 0 9

ISBN: 978-0-07-249744-1
MHID: 0-07-249744-0

Vice President and Editor-in-Chief: *Emily Barrosse*
Publisher: *Lyn Uhl*
Senior Sponsoring Editor: *Jon-David Hague*
Editorial Coordinator: *Liliana Almendarez*
Marketing Manager: *Katherine Bates*
Managing Editor: *Jean Dal Porto*
Project Managers: *Catherine R. Iammartino and Margaret H. Leslie*
Art Director: *Jeanne Schreiber*
Designer: *Srdjan Savanovic*
Interior Designer: *Karen LaFond*
Photo Research Coordinator: *Natalia C. Peschiera*
Art Editor: *Katherine McNab*
Senior Production Supervisor: *Janean A. Utley*
Composition: *10/13 Palatino by GTS—India*
Printing: *45# New Era Matte by R.R. Donnelley & Sons*

Credits: The credits section for this book begins on page 197 and is considered an
extension of the copyright page.

Library of Congress Cataloging-in-Publication Data

Strayer, Robert W.
    The communist experiment: revolution, socialism, and global conflict in the twentieth
century / Robert Strayer.—1st ed.
       p. cm.
    ISBN–13: 978-0-07-249744-1
    ISBN–10: 0-07-249744-0 (softcover: alk. paper)
    1. Communism—Soviet Union—History—20th century.
    2. Communism—China—History—20th century. 3. Communism and culture—Soviet
Union—History—20th century. 4. Communism and culture—China—History—20th century.
1. Title.
HX313.S735 2007
335.43′09′04—dc22

                                                                                    2005050493

The Internet addresses listed in the text were accurate at the time of publication. The
inclusion of a Web site does not indicate an endorsement by the authors or McGraw-Hill,
and McGraw-Hill does not guarantee the accuracy of the information presented at these
sites.

www.mhhe.com

CONTENTS

MAJOR EVENTS IN THE
◀ HISTORY OF COMMUNISM ▶

1911:	Overthrow of the Qing Dynasty
1917:	Russian Revolution
1918–1921:	Russian Civil War
1919:	Zhenotdel established in Soviet Union
1919:	Comintern established
1919:	May Fourth Movement: China
1921–28:	New Economic Policy in the Soviet Union
1921:	Chinese Communist Party founded
1927:	Massacre of Chinese Communists
1928–32:	Collectivization of agriculture in Soviet Union
1929:	Stalin's rise to power
1935:	The Long March: China
1936–38:	The Terror in the Soviet Union
1937:	Japanese invasion of China
1939–45:	World War II in Europe
1945–50:	Beginning of the Cold War; Soviet control of Eastern Europe cemented
1949:	Communist victory in China
1950–53:	Korean War
1953:	Death of Stalin
1956:	Hungarian Uprising
1958:	Great Leap Forward: China
1962:	Cuban Missile Crisis
1964–73:	American War in Vietnam
1966–69:	Cultural Revolution: China
1968:	Prague Spring: Soviet invasion of Czechoslovakia
1969:	High point of Soviet/Chinese conflict
1976:	Death of Mao Zedong
1978:	Beginning of Chinese reforms

A NOTE FROM THE SERIES EDITORS

World history has come of age. No longer regarded as a task simply for amateurs or philosophers, it has become an integral part of the historical profession and one of its most exciting and innovative fields of study. At the level of scholarship, a growing tide of books, articles, and conferences continues to enlarge our understanding of the many and intersecting journeys of humankind framed in global terms. At the level of teaching, more and more secondary schools as well as colleges and universities now offer, and sometimes require, world history of their students. One of the prominent features of the world history movement has been the unusually close association of its scholarly and its teaching wings. Teachers at all levels have participated with university-based scholars in the development of this new field.

The McGraw-Hill series—Explorations in World History—operates at this intersection of scholarship and teaching. It seeks to convey the results of recent research in world history in a form wholly accessible to beginning students. It also provides a pedagogical alternative to or supplement for the large and inclusive core textbooks which are features of so many world history courses. Each volume in the series focuses briefly on a particular theme, set in a global and comparative context. And each of them is "open-ended," raising questions and drawing students into the larger issues that animate world history.

This particular volume, written by one of the series editors, deals with a major global phenomenon of the twentieth century—communism. Rooted in nineteenth-century patterns of European industrialization and Marxist socialism, communism erupted onto the world stage with the Russian Revolution of 1917. In its global dimensions, communism intersected with and shaped most of the dominant trends of twentieth-century world history—revolution, world war, empire, feminism, nationalism, the global cold war, and more. But communism was surely not a singular movement. The quite different shapes that it took in the Soviet

Union and in China illustrate the deep divisions and variations in the "communist experiment." This book explores the global impact of communism, while developing a comparative approach to its Soviet and Chinese expressions. In doing so, it provides a unique window on the world history of the twentieth century.

Robert Strayer
Kevin Reilly

◀ ACKNOWLEDGMENTS ▶

A thoughtful Buddhist meditation exercise asks participants to examine their own hands, a piece of food, or a beloved object and to imagine all the people and circumstances that have contributed to its current state. It is, of course, intended to evoke a sense of profound interdependence and connectedness to a wider and complex web in which we are all embedded. The publication of a book provides yet another useful occasion for such an exercise. Even a modest book such as this is the outcome of a long chain of relationships, stretching well into the past as well as the product of a collective enterprise. It is wholly fitting to acknowledge publicly at least a bit of dense network that generated this book.

My own interest in communism took shape as a young child of the cold war, playing anti-communist games in the early 1950s. Gradually, through association with various teachers, with my own students, with many friends in Russia, and with colleagues in the "peace movement," that interest took new shapes. I am grateful to the institutions in which I have taught while working on this book—SUNY College at Brockport, University of Canterbury in Christchurch, New Zealand, CSU Monterey Bay, and UC Santa Cruz. All these people and places are a part of the process that generated the book because they have shaped its author.

More directly involved in the publication process have been the good folk at McGraw-Hill—Lyn Uhl, Jon-David Hague, Allison Rona—who have encouraged and supported at every point. Kevin Reilly, my co-editor for the World History series, has been a wonderful companion and collaborator at a distance. Reviewers who made many helpful comments include Nathaniel Weston of Seattle Central Community College, Oscar Lansen of University of North Carolina at Charlotte, Hubert P. Van Tuyll of Augusta State University, and Jim Strandberg of McGraw-Hill.

In a different category altogether is my wife, Suzanne Sturn. She had little to do with the book directly, though she kindly allowed me to read her passages from it and always praised them highly. But she had everything to do with the making of an enormously rich personal life which has been for 13 years the context from which this book and everything else of value in my modest sphere has flowed. I am grateful beyond measure.

THE COMMUNIST
EXPERIMENT

REVOLUTION, SOCIALISM, AND GLOBAL
CONFLICT IN THE TWENTIETH CENTURY

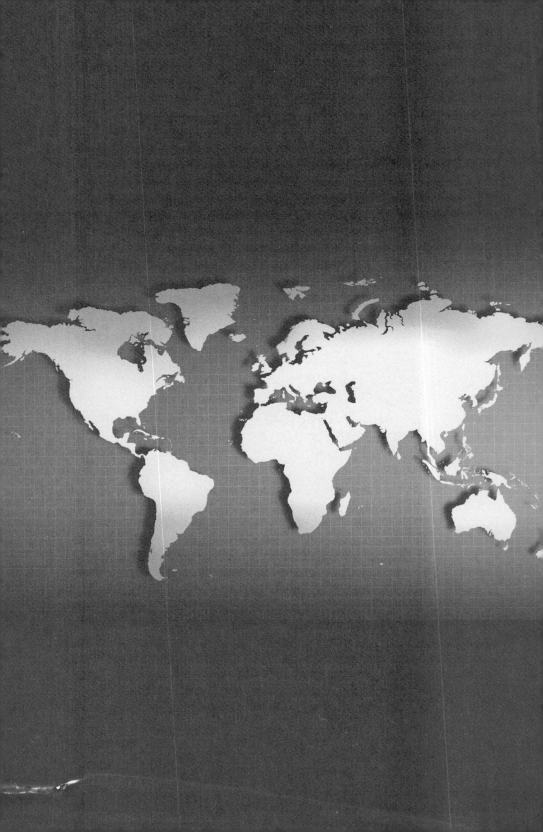

 CHAPTER ONE

COMMUNISM IN CONTEXT

GETTING STARTED ON CHAPTER ONE: When and where did communist parties come to power in the twentieth century? What earlier precedents and patterns contributed to the rise of communism in the twentieth century? To what else in the twentieth century world history has communism been connected? With what else might we compare the communist movements?

"Excuse me, sir, but what exactly is the big deal about communism and the Cold War?" This was an honest question from a serious student in my World History class in the fall of 2000 as we were discussing the major events and processes of the twentieth century. She had grown up in a post-communist world from which the Soviet Union had disappeared and in which China was viewed as a growing market or a human rights problem rather than a communist country. To her generation communism was history and her question a reminder of just how rapidly our collective memories fade. But to the several generations that preceded her, all across the world, communism had been far more than an academic question. Communist efforts to create new, socialist, and modern societies, without the exploitation and inequalities that had burdened humanity to date, had generated enormous hopes and spurred great movements in many parts of the world. Many others, however, felt those efforts as a sharp threat to the existing ways of life, and the many brutalities spawned by communist states created deep and enduring fears of a new dark age in the making. The global rift between the communist world and the rest of the world was among the most serious divisions and the most dangerous conflicts of the twentieth century. And struggles over communism created deep divisions and extensive

3

violence within many countries as well. Seldom in human history had a political idea generated such passion.

This book is a modest attempt to answer that young woman's question. It focuses primarily on the experience of the Soviet Union and China as by far the most important expressions of twentieth-century communism. Briefly we will examine and compare the revolutionary upheavals in these two countries that brought communist parties to power in Russia in 1917 and in China by 1949. Then we will explore, also comparatively, their efforts to build new societies that were both socialist and modern. The international impact of communism, especially during the Cold War, represents a third major theme of this book. And finally, we will turn the spotlight on both Soviet and Chinese attempts to reform their communist systems in the 1980s and beyond—efforts which brought the communist experiment to an inglorious end, though with very different outcomes in the two countries. But first, we will outline briefly the extent of the communist experiment and place this dramatic twentieth-century phenomenon in the larger context of world history.

COMMUNISM AS A GLOBAL PHENOMENON

It began in the Russian Empire, the land of the tsars, the world's largest country. There in early 1917, amid the carnage of World War I, the tsarist system collapsed, and just nine months later, to the amazement of almost everyone, a small fringe socialist party called the Bolsheviks seized power. "It makes my head spin," remarked Lenin, the Bolshevik's charismatic leader. He was not alone. Few people expected this fragile toehold of socialism to last, but the Bolsheviks consolidated their power after a bitter civil war, renaming themselves the Communist Party. They also renamed their country the Union of Soviet Socialist Republics (the Soviet Union) after the "soviets" or grass-roots councils that had sprung up in 1917 to assume local power as the tsar's authority melted away. For 30 years, the Soviet Union remained the sole world outpost of the socialist alternative.

Then in the aftermath of World War II, in which the Soviet Union had suffered so terribly and contributed so much to the defeat of Nazi Germany, communist regimes took shape in much of Central and Eastern Europe. It was the first real extension of communist power beyond the Soviet Union. While communism in the Soviet Union was associated with an internal revolutionary upheaval, in Eastern Europe it was in large measure imposed by Soviet military forces that had liberated these areas—eastern Germany, Poland, Czechoslovakia, Romania, Hungary, Bulgaria—from Nazi rule. The Soviet leadership determined that after repeated invasions from the West, their country badly needed a security buffer zone in Eastern Europe, consisting of governments under their control. But the local communist parties that the Soviets installed in power also had some popular support deriving from their commitment to reform and social justice and from their role in resistance to the Nazis. However, in Yugoslavia and Albania, communist parties genuinely independent of the Soviet Union also came to power. In the late 1940s, the communist world was enlarging.

A far more significant extension of communism took place at the same time but on the other side of the world. In 1949, Mao Zedong, leader of the Chinese Communist Party, marked the communist victory in an epic, decades-long struggle by declaring that "the Chinese people have stood up!" As in the Soviet Union, Chinese communists had ridden to power on a vast wave of social revolution, but the process was far more extended. In Russia, only nine months separated the collapse of the tsarist system and the communist seizure of power, whereas in China, the old imperial state of the emperors dissolved in 1912, followed by 37 years of intense struggle before a new stability under communist rule was achieved. But when it happened, the world's most highly populated nation had joined the world's largest country as the twin centers of global communism, and a vast stretch of territory from central Europe to East Asia was governed by communist parties.

Further, though much smaller, extensions of communism followed. After Japan's defeat in World War II, its Korean colony was partitioned with the northern half coming under Soviet, and therefore communist, control. In Vietnam, a much more locally based communist movement under the leadership of Ho Chi Minh battled Japanese, French, and later American invaders and established communist control first in the northern half of the country and after 1975 throughout the whole country. The victory of the Vietnamese communists spilled over into neighboring Laos and Cambodia, where communist parties took power in the mid-1970s. In the Caribbean, Fidel Castro led a revolutionary nationalist movement against a repressive and American-backed government in Cuba; on coming to power in 1959, he moved rapidly toward communism and an alliance with the Soviet Union. Finally, a shaky communist regime took power in Afghanistan in 1979, propped up briefly only by massive Soviet military support. At its maximum extent in the 1970s, communist rule encompassed perhaps a third of the world's population.

Beyond the countries formally governed by communist parties lay other kinds of communist influence. In postwar Europe, communist parties played important political roles in Greece, Italy, and France. In the United States, a small communist party became in the 1950s the focus of an intense wave of fear and political repression called McCarthyism. Revolutionary communist movements threatened existing governments in the Philippines, Malaya, Indonesia, Bolivia, Peru, and elsewhere. A number of African states in the 1970s declared themselves Marxist for a time and aligned with the Soviet Union in international affairs.

The creation of the communist world had lasted from 1917 into the 1970s, and then with amazing suddenness, almost the entire fabric of world communism dissolved during the last two decades of the century. Beginning in 1978, China progressively abandoned communist economic practice in favor of private farming, foreign investment, and the market, even while maintaining Communist Party control of politics. In 1989, popular movements swept away the widely despised communist governments of Eastern European countries and tore down the Berlin Wall, long the symbol of Cold War antagonisms. But the centerpiece of communism's collapse was the disintegration of the Soviet Union as a country along with its state-run economy, its Communist Party, and its socialist ideology as Mikhail Gorbachev's efforts to reform the Soviet system badly backfired and led to its demise in 1991. Elsewhere as well, signs of the end of the communist era proliferated. Vietnam, Laos, and Cuba, like China, undertook substantial economic reforms while maintaining communist governments. In Yugoslavia and Czechoslovakia, as in the Soviet Union, nationalism proved more powerful than communism as both split apart into separate ethnically based countries. Soviet troops and communism were chased out of Afghanistan, where an Islamic fundamentalist party called the Taliban took power in the 1990s. Every African country that had proclaimed itself a Marxist state now repudiated that commitment. As world communism faded away, so did the Cold War. Although tensions remained between Russia and the United States, the ideological hostility was gone, and the two former enemies agreed on military reductions and other forms of cooperation. As the twentieth century passed into history, so too, it seemed, had communism.

COMMUNISM AND WORLD HISTORY

The rise and fall of world communism has been a distinctive feature of the twentieth century, but that experience connected to other broad trends of the century and has roots in even earlier patterns of historical change. How then can we situate the history of the communist experiment in the larger context of world history? To what does it connect and with what might it be compared?

MARX AND INDUSTRIALIZATION

Communists everywhere claimed to base their actions on the ideas of a nineteenth-century German intellectual, Karl Marx, and often referred to themselves as Marxists. It was one of the major cultural "exports" that the West transmitted to the rest of the world, along with European languages, Christianity, modern science and technology, nationalism, and much more.

THE MARXIST VISION.   Marx had lived (1818–1883) during the early stages of that enormous transformation of European life known as the Industrial Revolution, and he did more than anyone else to give a certain meaning to that process. On the one hand, he celebrated in almost lyrical terms the productive virtues of capitalism and industrialization, creating for the first time the real possibility of an abundant and humane life for all. The wonderful new science, machines, and factories of industrial Europe could produce more than enough of this world's goods to end permanently the ancient scourge of poverty and with it the class conflicts that scarcity had always bred. But the fatal flaws of capitalism—private property, growing inequalities, bitter class conflict, worsening cycles of economic expansion and recession, competitive and individualistic values—prevented the realization of those marvelous possibilities. Instead, they generated a savage process, described by Marx as "naked, shameless, direct, brutal exploitation."[1] Here was an economic system that could produce enough for everyone through the wonders of industrial technology but was absurdly unable to distribute to its workers the fruits of their own labor. No wonder capitalism would be swept away in revolutionary upheaval featuring the urban proletariat, exploited industrial workers who Marx saw as the "gravediggers" of capitalism. Then the vast productive potential of a modern economy would be placed in service to the whole of society in a rationally planned and egalitarian community. In such a socialist commonwealth, degrading poverty, conflicting classes, contending nations, and human alienation generally would be but fading memories. From the ashes of capitalism, Marx wrote, there will emerge a socialist society in which "the free development of each [person] is the condition for the free development of all."[2]

To Marx, this general direction of historical change—from a class-ridden and exploitative capitalism through a working-class revolution to an abundant and humane socialism—was not only preferable, but inevitable. It was inscribed in the laws of historical development that he had discovered. Capitalism would self-destruct through its own internal contradictions; workers were ground down and exploited, not because capitalists were bad people, but because the competitiveness of the system required factory owners to pay them very little. Thus, capitalism generated its own "gravediggers" in the factory working class who would someday rise in revolutionary action to redistribute in a new socialist society the vast wealth their labor had created.

MARXIST MOVEMENTS.   Marx's ideas inspired socialist movements of workers and intellectuals amid the grim harshness of Europe's industrialization in the second half of the nineteenth century. Socialists established political parties in most European states and linked them together in international organizations. These parties recruited members, contested elections as they gained the right to vote, agitated for reforms, and in some cases plotted revolution.

THE FAILURE OF MARXISM IN EUROPE.   But no socialist revolution occurred, and socialists achieved power nowhere in Europe during the nineteenth century, thus failing to fulfill Marx's prediction. In part, it was because Marx's understanding of capitalism was itself flawed. Improving standards of living rather than growing impoverishment characterized Europe's industrializing societies in the later nineteenth century. An expanding democracy and trade unions allowed workers to improve their conditions within a capitalist system far more open to reform than Marx had ever imagined. As a consequence, many socialists abandoned revolution, seeking to achieve their goals through education, reform, and the ballot box. Furthermore, the growth of mass nationalism bound workers to their country rather than to an international working-class movement as Marx had expected. In one of the grand ironies of world history, socialism triumphed not in the most advanced industrialized countries as Marx predicted, but in Russia and China, where capitalism and industrialization were far less developed.

THE APPEAL OF MARXISM.   Despite the industrial backwardness of their societies, small groups of revolutionary intellectuals in Russia, China, and elsewhere found Marxism attractive. It was a modern and Western set of ideas at a time when modernity and the West had enormous prestige. Yet it was directed against the most offensive feature of Western life—capitalism. Furthermore, Marxism claimed to be "scientific" at a time when science seemed to many almost a new religion. To believers, it was based on careful research, and it revealed laws of historical development that were as sure as Newton's laws of motion. Beleaguered revolutionaries working in discouraging conditions could now believe that their revolutions were inevitable. They found in Marxism a moral certainty and a rock-hard confidence that derived from being on the right side of history.

ADAPTING MARXISM. But these revolutionaries gave Marxist ideas their own spin and adapted them to local conditions. They argued that it was not necessary to wait for the full development of capitalism before launching a socialist revolution. Communist states almost everywhere were forced to actually construct a modern industrial society largely from scratch rather than merely to take over one already made, as Marx had imagined. Particularly in Asia they relied very heavily on a revolutionary peasantry in the countryside rather than the urban working class that Marx had foreseen. And Lenin in particular argued that capitalism generated imperialism. This meant that the struggle against capitalism was at the same time a blow against colonial rule and European domination from which so many Asian and African peoples had suffered.

Thus, Marxism as it took root in China, Russia, Vietnam, Cuba, and elsewhere was an adapted western ideology. This process of importing and changing foreign ideas has been a recurring pattern in world history as Buddhism took root in China; Christianity in Europe, the Americas, and Africa; and Islam throughout the Afro-Eurasian world. Thus the actual construction of communist societies was a kind of "experiment," for Karl Marx had provided no detailed blueprint as to how a revolution should be conducted or what would happen in its aftermath. The Russian and Chinese cases, highlighted in this book, illustrate two variations of this fateful experiment.

HEAVEN ON EARTH: COMMUNISM AND UTOPIA

UTOPIAN VISIONS. Twentieth-century communists also participated in a tradition even more deeply rooted than Marxism—utopianism. Human societies the world over have generated movements and ideas that imagined, and sometimes sought to realize, the perfect or ideal society, free from oppression and injustice, informed by freedom, equality, abundance, and community. The ancient Hebrew prophets spoke of a time "when justice would roll down like the waters and righteousness as an ever-flowing stream." Millenarian movements in Asia, Africa, and Europe have projected communities of abundance and equality from which evil has been banished. In the late-eighteenth and early-nineteenth centuries, utopian thinkers in Europe became more secular and rational, basing their ideas on the new possibilities of modern science and technology, and sometimes urging political action to bring them into reality. The Marquis de Condorcet, an eighteenth-century radical thinker of the French Enlightenment, imagined a future in which major inequalities had vanished, all diseases disappeared, life spans became indefinite, gender inequality ended, and war was considered a monstrous crime. "Progress" he wrote, "can have no limits."[3] Early nineteenth century followers of several "utopian socialists" such as Charles Fourier and Robert Own created small short-lived communities which attempted to put the detailed visionary dreams of their founders into practice.

MARXIST UTOPIANISM.   Karl Marx strenuously denied any connection with the utopian tradition, believing his ideas to be scientifically and historically based. Nonetheless, his writings and his imagination had a strongly utopian cast. On the far side of revolution and after an extended period of transition called socialism, Marx foresaw nothing less than the end of history as it had been lived thus far: no more poverty as the abundance of industrial society provided for all; no more class conflict as a rational planning evened out the distribution of material wealth; and no more war or violence as the coercive power of competing states, no longer needed to prop up privileged elites, withered away. This was communism. It would ensure the emergence of wholly new men and women, free from ancient constraints and finally able to realize their full human potential. What could be more utopian than Marx's capsule description of the new order?—"from each according to his abilities; to each according to his needs."

SOVIET UTOPIANISM.   Despite their hard-headed scientific pretensions, twentieth-century communists too have often spoken and acted in utopian ways. Lenin, like Marx before him, imagined an eventual society of communism in which the released energies and skills of the masses would replace an authoritarian state and bureaucracy. More concretely, he viewed electricity as almost magical. It symbolized "heat and shelter in a land of arctic climes; light and knowledge in a land of darkness and bigotry, energy and economic growth in a land of poverty and sloth."[4] In the decade following the Revolution of 1917, utopian expectations and projects proliferated explosively. Orchestras without conductors symbolized the equality and cooperation of the new age. Communes sprang up by the thousands as workers, students, and peasants sought to put socialist principles into practice. Revolutionary science fiction featured technological and urban utopias on a global scale. "We will remake life anew—right down to the last button of your vest," wrote one of the revolution's major intellectual champions.[5]

THE UTOPIAN DEBATE.   The utopian aspects of communism have generated a great deal of controversy. Some have viewed them positively, arguing that utopianism drove efforts to reduce ancient inequalities of gender or class, that it raised a standard by which its own failures—and those of other social systems—might be measured, and that it injected joy, enthusiasm, and spontaneity into an often violent and brutal revolutionary process. But on the other hand, communist utopian dreams, when joined to unrestrained political power and pursued on a huge scale, generated some of the most chilling barbarities of the twentieth century. China's Great Leap Forward in the 1950s, a visionary scheme intended to generate rapid economic growth and an immediate move to full communism, in fact produced an economic crisis and massive famine that cost millions of lives. Even more horrendous were the efforts of Cambodian communists, led by Pol Pot in the 1970s, to implement communism almost overnight. This came to involve the emptying of the cities, the abolition of money, total collectivization, the elimination of entire groups of people such as property owners, businessmen, and intellectuals, and the killing of perhaps a quarter of the country's population—all in the space of several years. Visions of human happiness and social perfection, no less than the drive for power, can motivate and justify the most appalling means of achieving these utopian dreams.

THE REVOLUTIONARY TRADITION

AMERICAN AND FRENCH REVOLUTIONS.   Another global context in which twentieth-century communism may be situated is that of revolution, for in both Russia and China, communism emerged out of vast social and political upheavals. But these revolutions take their place alongside earlier revolutions of which the American and especially the French are the most prominent. The American Revolution was, of course, directed against the growing interference of the British government in the affairs of 13 increasingly prosperous colonies located an ocean away from the mother country. The result was independence for the new United States of America. And accompanying its independence was a self-conscious effort to create a "new order for the ages" based on a republican constitution and at least partially democratic principles. The French Revolution of 1789, on the other hand, began as an internal affair, taking aim at a domestic monarchy and the ruling class of aristocrats who supported it. In its most radical phase, that revolution executed a king and queen, abolished the ancient privileges of the nobility and the Catholic clergy, confiscated much of the church's land, and unleashed a reign of terror against suspected enemies of the revolution, sending about 40,000 of them to the guillotine. In its efforts to create a new society, French revolutionaries tried to replace Christianity with a secular "cult of reason" and even promoted a new calendar for a new age. It was a far more revolutionary process than the Americans had undertaken.

But revolutionaries in both countries shared a novel idea derived from eighteenth-century European thinkers—that it was both possible and desirable for people to reconstruct their societies in a deliberate and self-conscious way. This notion flew in the face of conventional thinking in almost all of the world's large-scale agrarian societies. Human societies, it was widely held, were hierarchical, consisting of distinct, fixed, and unequal groups in which individuals would live and die. These societies, and the kings or emperors who ruled them, were ordained by God, an idea expressed in Europe as the "divine right of kings" and in China as the "mandate of heaven." Against this conception of society, American and especially French revolutionaries hurled their ideas of freedom from traditional beliefs and practices, the equality of all persons, and popular sovereignty, which meant that the right to rule derived from the consent of the people.

COMPARING REVOLUTIONS.   The communist movements of the twentieth century quite self-consciously drew on the mystique of the French Revolution, as an opening to new and better worlds. It had happened once and could happen again. Communist revolutionaries, like their French predecessors, ousted old ruling classes and dispossessed landed aristocracies. They, too, believed that human societies could be deliberately reshaped by human hands and found their vision of the good society in a modernizing future, not in some nostalgic vision of the past. They worried lest their revolutions end up in a military dictatorship like that of Napoleon following the French Revolution. And all of them involved vast peasant upheavals in the countryside and an educated leadership with roots in the cities.

But the communist revolutions were distinctive as well. They were made by highly organized parties guided by a Marxist ideology, were committed to an industrial future, pursued economic as well as political equality, and sought the abolition of private property. In doing so they mobilized, celebrated, and claimed to act on behalf of society's lower classes—exploited urban workers and impoverished rural peasants. The middle classes, who were chief beneficiaries of the French Revolution, numbered among the many victims of the Russian and Chinese upheavals.

BECOMING MODERN AND CATCHING UP

THE DILEMMA OF BORROWING.   Europe's growing military and economic power, demonstrated most clearly in its Industrial Revolution and its expanding imperial reach during the nineteenth century, gave rise to an increasingly common dilemma: how could other societies gain access to the sources of European power and wealth while protecting their own independence, cultural distinctiveness, and elite privileges? How could they catch up with Europe and defend themselves against European aggression at the same time? That dilemma drove the reforms of Peter the Great and his successors in imperial Russia, animated the modernizing efforts of the Ottoman Empire, Egypt, China, Japan, and others in the nineteenth century, and confronted the nationalist movements of Europe's Asian and African colonies in the twentieth. It was a dilemma that communists faced as well. Like the others, they found an answer in selective borrowing and adaptation. Communists would take what was most advanced in Europe—its scientific world view, its industrial technology, and its Marxist ideology—but they would reject, decisively, Europe's capitalist framework, its individualistic middle-class values, its parliamentary democracy, and its religious traditions.

A BETTER WAY?   Put into practice in communist-governed states, this amounted to a claim to have discovered an alternative, and a superior, route to modernity. Through the use of state power and guided by their communist parties, the Soviet Union and China would mobilize their people and their resources to construct in record time thoroughly modern industrial societies. And by substituting a rationally planned economy for private property and the market, they would do so without the painful consequences of the capitalist path—the instability of repeated recessions and depressions, the gross exploitation of women and children as well as men in industrial sweatshops and urban slums, endemic conflicts between rich and poor, and economic rivalries that led to war and imperial aggression. In some ways, they did it. In both the Soviet Union in the 1930s and China in the 1950s, industrial growth rates were astonishing. Iron, steel, and coal production leaped ahead. New cities and industries boomed, and the urban work force expanded rapidly. Education and upward social mobility were available to ordinary people to a degree unknown before the revolutions. During the 1930s, the contrast between a rapidly growing Soviet economy and the Great Depression in the capitalist countries was particularly striking. By the end of that decade, the Soviet Union was clearly one of the world's modern industrial states—an achievement that went a long way in explaining that country's victory over Nazi Germany in World War II. Centralized planning by an authoritarian state seemed to work, and many people—some intellectuals in the West and some political leaders in European colonies—saw communism as the wave of the future and capitalism as exhausted and moribund.

But over the long haul, that very claim to superiority, both economic and moral, was also the rock on which communist systems foundered. It became apparent by the 1970s that communist economies could not outperform capitalist economies and that Soviet economic growth in particular had slowed dramatically. Furthermore, Stalin's Soviet Union and Mao Zedong's China had generated some of the most appallingly brutal and repressive states that a bloody twentieth century had witnessed. Thus, both the economic and moral failings of communism contributed to its demise. The communist path to modernity, it turned out, was a road to nowhere.

COMMUNISM AND FEMINISM

Among the most remarkable developments of the twentieth century was the vast transformation in the lives and the consciousness of women and in thinking about the role of women. Many millions of women all around the world joined the paid work force, became literate, took part in public life, and established a more equal relationship with the men in their societies. These changes, though highly uneven, incomplete, and frequently challenged, represent one of the most genuinely revolutionary dimensions of twentieth-century world history.

Communist societies also took part in that revolution of feminism in the twentieth century. In fact, in many respects they led the way, pioneering forms of "women's liberation" that only later were adopted in the West. Furthermore, communist feminism was state directed, with the initiative coming from the top rather than from grassroots movements. In the West, by contrast, feminism bubbled up from below in the form of popular movements that subsequently pushed governments, laws, and cultural norms to change. No sooner had the communists come to power in Russia than they issued a series of laws and decrees regarding women. They declared full legal and political equality for women; marriage became a civil procedure among freely consenting adults; divorce was legalized and made easier, as was abortion; illegitimacy was abolished; women no longer had to take their husbands' surnames; pregnancy leave for employed women was mandated; and women were actively mobilized as workers in the country's drive to industrialization.

SOVIET FEMINISM. In 1919, the Communist Party set up a special organization called *Zhenotdel* (Women's Department), which pushed a decidedly feminist agenda in the 1920s. Its activist leaders organized numerous conferences for women, trained women to run day-care centers and medical clinics, published newspapers and magazines aimed at a female audience, provided literacy and prenatal classes, and encouraged Muslim women to take off their veils. Much of this encountered opposition from male communist officials and from ordinary people as well, and Stalin abolished *Zhenotdel* in 1930. But while it lasted, it was a remarkable experiment in women's liberation by means of state action, "animated by a magical sense of the limitless possibilities of a revolutionary new world."[6]

CHINESE FEMINISM.   Similar policies took shape in communist China. The Marriage Law of 1950 was a direct attack on patriarchal and Confucian traditions as it decreed free choice in marriage, relatively easy divorce, the end of concubinage and child marriage, permission for widows to remarry, and equal property rights for women. A short but intense campaign by the Chinese Communist Party in the early 1950s sought to implement these changes, often against strenuous opposition. As in the Soviet Union, women became much more actively involved in production outside the home and by 1978, 50% of agricultural workers and 38% of nonagricultural laborers were female. "Women can do anything" became a famous party slogan in the 1960s.

But communist-style women's liberation had definite limits. Stalin declared the women's question "solved" in 1930, fearing that it would detract from his emphasis on production. Little direct discussion of women's issues was permitted in the several decades that followed. In neither the Soviet Union nor China did the Communist Party undertake a direct attack on male domination within the family. Thus the "double burden" of housework and child care plus paid employment continued to afflict most women. And women appeared only very rarely in the top political leadership of either country.

THE TRIUMPH OF THE NATION

Communism represented a challenge not only to capitalism and to patriarchy, but also to the nation as the primary focus of political loyalty and cultural identity in the modern world. After all, the entire socialist tradition highlighted class as the most fundamental division among people everywhere. The rich and the poor, those with property and those without, the haves and the have-nots—it was class struggle, Karl Marx argued, that drove historical change. It made sense then for communists to believe that the workers of the world would unite across national boundaries. When the Russian Revolution brought the Bolsheviks to power, most of their leaders believed that their revolution was only the trigger for a larger Europe-wide upheaval that would issue ultimately in a worldwide socialist commonwealth, leaving nations and national antagonisms in the trash heap of history. And even when that dream proved illusory, Soviet leaders openly anticipated the "merging" of nations and the creation of a new "Soviet" identity within their own vast and multinational country.

But "nation" trumped class in the twentieth century, and this dimension of the communist challenge, like its claim to outproduce capitalism, also failed. It failed to spark communist revolutions in the developed industrial countries as well as in most of the "new nations" of the Third World. Even within particular communist countries it failed to transcend national or ethnic loyalties, as the disintegration of the Soviet Union, Czechoslovakia, and Yugoslavia so dramatically demonstrated. And it even failed to create friendly relations among communist countries, each of which developed a unique national style of communism. Many eastern Europeans, living in communist countries, thoroughly despised and feared their Russian neighbors. The Soviet Union and China came to the brink of war over territorial disputes, ideological differences, and rivalry for communist leadership. China and Vietnam, neighboring communist countries, did in fact go to war in 1979, as did Vietnam and Cambodia. Precisely why the claims of nationality or ethnicity have proven so much more compelling than those of class and communism is among the great questions of twentieth-century world history.

DEMOCRACY AND TOTALITARIANISM

DEMOCRACY ON THE RISE.   The nineteenth-century history of western Europe and its outposts in North America, Australia, New Zealand, and elsewhere had witnessed the slow growth of democratic practice as the vote was gradually extended to larger groups of citizens and parliamentary institutions assumed a more prominent role in political life. These were limited democracies, and only very gradually and with much struggle did poor men, people of color, and women gain voting privileges. Nonetheless, the progress of democracy by the early twentieth century and the victory of the most democratic countries in World War I persuaded many that democracy was the wave of the future, "a natural trend," as one observer put it.[7]

DEMOCRACY CHALLENGED.   But the 1920s, 1930s and early 1940s witnessed instead the sharp contraction of democracy. In Italy, Germany, Spain, and much of Eastern Europe, fascist or right-wing movements came to power as the chaos of war and depression undermined new, fragile, and often corrupt democracies. The military victories of the Nazis put an end to many others, such as those in Austria and Czechoslovakia. In Nazi thinking, democracy was associated with their country's defeat in World War I, with the punitive Treaty of Versailles that ended the war, with political division and mediocrity in government, and with an emphasis on individualism that undermined a strong state. The triumph of communism in Russia following the revolution of 1917 likewise ended the modest democratic innovations that the tsar had only recently established as a highly authoritarian and repressive state, dominated by its Communist Party, monopolized political power in the country. To communists, western style parliamentary democracy was an illusion, benefiting only people of property while leaving the working classes and peasantry at their mercy. Nazi success in overcoming the terrible unemployment of the Great Depression in Germany and Soviet success in promoting rapid industrialization in the 1930s seemed to confirm the effectiveness of authoritarian states and to underline the weakness and fragility of the remaining democracies.

TOTALITARIANISM.   Viewing communism and fascism as similar challenges to democracy has triggered a great deal of controversy. Soviet communists in particular bitterly resented any comparison with Hitler's Germany because their country had bled almost to death in a heroic struggle against the Nazis in World War II. But many western scholars saw striking similarities. Both communism and fascism repudiated the middle-class democracy and liberalism of European practice. Both were genuinely revolutionary in seeking to overthrow existing societies and to transform them in line with an ideological vision—racial purity in the case of Nazi Germany and Marxist socialism in the Soviet Union and China. Both were embodied in mass political parties, claimed an exclusive truth, were led by a single dominant leader, and were unwilling to permit political opposition. Both imposed an unprecedented degree of repressive state control over the societies they governed and in doing so gave rise to the novel notion of a "totalitarian" system. And both engendered state-directed terror and mass murder on a scale never seen before, although in Germany this was implemented as an effort to eliminate racially defined inferiors and in the Soviet Union to root out class-based enemies of socialism. A controversial book published in the mid-1990s argued that communism on a worldwide basis was in fact far more destructive of human life than Nazism, claiming some 100 million lives, roughly four times that of the Nazi's victims.[8]

TRANSITIONS TO DEMOCRACY?   The collapse of fascism in Germany and Italy and militarism in Japan was followed by the creation of successful and apparently lasting democracies in those countries. Similarly, the demise of communism in the Soviet Union and Eastern Europe brought to power a number of at least semidemocratic governments. These have been most fully developed in Poland and the Czech Republic and less certainly in Russia and many of the other states of the former Soviet Union. Whether these countries that have recently abandoned communism will evolve toward fully democratic systems remains an open question of the twenty-first century.

A GLOBAL RIFT

Beyond its challenge to capitalism, nationalism, and democracy, communism was linked to many of the twentieth century's other major patterns. It was born amid the flames of World War I in Russia and World War II in China. It drew strength from the global crisis of capitalism known as the Great Depression. It attracted attention in many of the "new nations" that emerged from European colonial rule in Asia and Africa. It contributed much to the further spread of industrial society and the growing human impact on the environment that industrialization generated. In a century rich in promises of liberation—class, national, democratic, feminist—communism offered, at least for a time, greater hope for women, workers, peasants, and oppressed people generally. But it also furthered another twentieth-century trend—the vast extension of state power over the lives of individuals and social groups.

EAST AND WEST. But the primary world-historical significance of communism lies in the great divide that it caused in the world of the twentieth century. Beginning with western and Japanese intervention in Russia's Civil War (1919–1921) and expressed most clearly in the Cold War, that global rift decisively shaped much of twentieth-century world history. It gave rise to sharp ideological antagonisms that imbued the Soviet/American superpower rivalry with a sense of total threat on both sides. In that respect it resembled the Muslim threat to Christian Europe in the sixteenth century. To many Europeans the powerful Ottoman Empire seemed to bear not only the prospect of military defeat or territorial loss, but also a threat to an entire civilization, a way of life, and a system of values. Even in distant England, the writer Richard Knolles in 1603 referred to "the glorious empire of the Turks, the present terror of the world." The Catholic/Protestant hostilities of early modern European history as well as the ideological threat posed by the ideas of the French Revolution represent perhaps still other possibilities for comparison with the East/West divide of the twentieth century.

Beyond the contest of ideologies, the Cold War divided Europe, Germany, Korea, Vietnam, and China and sparked rivalries for political influence among the emerging nations of the Third World. It also produced an ever-escalating arms race and the wholly unprecedented threat of nuclear holocaust which, according to sober scientists, might well render human life on earth extinct. That very threat, however, helped to ensure that this bitter rivalry never once gave way to an actual shooting war between the principal protagonists.

Within the western capitalist nations, especially the United States, the struggle against communism had a profound impact. It greatly increased the power of the American president at the expense of Congress, for the threat of a sudden nuclear attack seemed to require the capacity for rapid decision making; it enhanced the influence of the defense establishment, better known as the "military-industrial complex," as preparation for war became a pervasive concern; it narrowed the range of political debate because anything vaguely "socialist" was subject to attack; and especially during the Vietnam War, it provoked deep divisions within American society.

NORTH AND SOUTH.   This global rift—the East/West divide—intersected with that other great division of the twentieth century—the so-called North/South conflict between the rich and the poor nations of the world. Patterns of colonial exploitation and impoverishment provided an opening for communist influence in the Third World, for it allowed both the Soviet Union and China to represent themselves not only as proponents of communism, but also as defenders of the poor nations seeking to extricate themselves from the grasping clutches of the rich and powerful. Communist leaders argued that the class struggle operated not only between the rich and the poor within particular countries, but also at the international level between the wealthy industrialized capitalist nations and impoverished former colonies of Africa, Asia, the Middle East, and Latin America. In this way, the message of Marxism, originally designed for the most advanced industrialized societies, became for a time more relevant to the vast majority of humankind living outside of that charmed circle.

CONCLUSION: COMMUNISM AND THE TWENTIETH CENTURY

Clearly, communism was a distinctive feature of the twentieth century, but it was related to much else that shaped that tumultuous era—world wars, nationalism, totalitarianism, mass murder, democracy, feminism, and much more. It also connected to earlier patterns of world history such as utopianism, industrialization, Marxism, and scientific views of the world. Communism, in short, decisively shaped the world of the twentieth century, but it was in turn shaped by the larger patterns of modern world history.

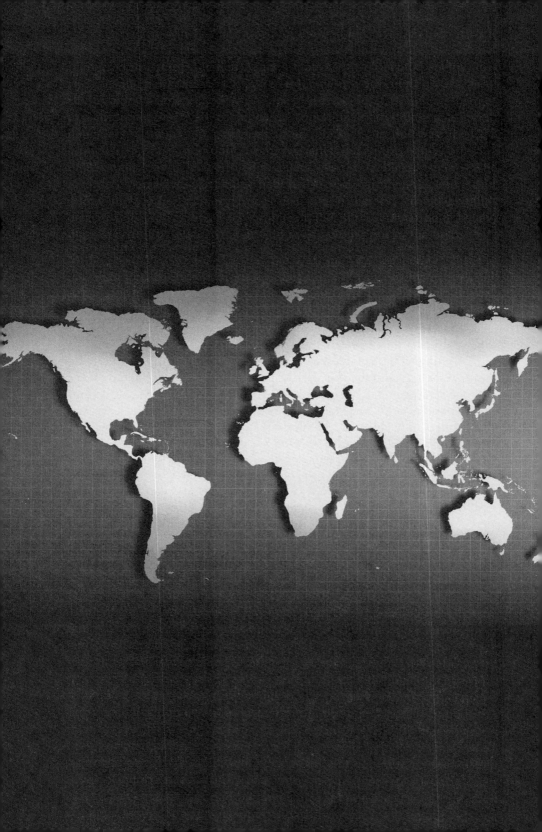

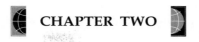

CHAPTER TWO

REVOLUTION AND THE BIRTH OF COMMUNISM

GETTING STARTED ON CHAPTER TWO: Why did Russia and China experience vast revolutionary upheavals in the twentieth century, whereas many other societies, likewise under the pressures of war and modernization, did not? Why did those revolutions bring communist regimes to power rather than more liberal and democratic orders? What similarities and differences can you observe between these two revolutionary processes?

Revolutions are rare in human history, especially those that involve a vast, rapid, and violent social upheaval as well as a change in government. Russia and China represent the largest and most important revolutions of this kind during the twentieth century. Explaining these revolutions has been a major task for historians, and it has involved two separate but related questions. First, why did the old regimes—tsarist Russia and imperial China—collapse? And second, how were initially quite small communist parties able to emerge among many contenders for power as the successors to these old regimes in both countries?

WHY REVOLUTION?

Because of their importance in world history, revolutions have attracted considerable attention among scholars, prompting a major debate as to why revolutions occur.[1] Some have emphasized circumstances of various kinds that might render a given society vulnerable to revolutionary upheaval. One common-sense notion is that misery, poverty, and oppression breed revolution as desperate people seek an alternative way of life. But human misery has been far more widespread than revolution,

21

leading some to argue that slowly improving conditions and rapidly rising expectations may be more important in generating revolution than suffering itself. Other scholars have focused attention on weaknesses in the state, arguing that revolutionary possibilities increase when existing authorities lose their grip. Military defeat by a foreign enemy, for example, might undermine the credibility of a government. Or a state might lose the support of key groups, such as the military, intellectuals, the aristocracy, or the middle class, and thus diminish its capacity to control the population. Still other scholars have looked for the source of revolution in class conflict and the conditions of the masses. High taxes or rent and the lack of access to land of their own have been frequent grievances of peasants in many societies, and the high cost of food and unemployment have often fueled popular uprisings in the cities. Karl Marx, and those who followed his ideas, saw revolution growing out of the class struggles of modern capitalism as a small but wealthy bourgeoisie, owning industrial property, confronted a large, growing, and impoverished factory working class with "nothing to lose but their chains."

And yet, do such circumstances by themselves produce revolution? Critics of this approach often believe that it neglects the intentions, plans, and actions of particular individuals or groups in society and presents the historical process as the impersonal and inevitable outcome of these conditions. Might the particular policies of state authorities, for example, be decisive in generating or avoiding revolution? Governments that resist or repress change and refuse to permit some wider participation in political life may unwittingly create social pressures that explode in revolution. Alternatively, governments that sponsor limited reforms may generate escalating expectations that escape their control. And what of revolutionaries themselves? Most societies, after all, have tensions, problems, and conflicts. Perhaps it is the presence of organized revolutionaries, dedicated to the cause and able to fan the flames of ordinary discontent into explosive action, that accounts for revolutions. Or should we focus on ordinary people in both rural villages and urban settings? Their grievances, their cultures, and their ability to act—sometimes even without the leadership of revolutionary elites—have often played a critical role in the unfolding of revolutionary upheavals. In this view, the choices of government authorities, of revolutionary groups, and of peasants and workers are the decisive factors in explaining the outbreak of major revolutions. Because different choices were always possible, this point of view highlights the unexpectedness of the historical process.

These two approaches to explaining revolutions—circumstances and deliberate actions—are hardly incompatible. But they reflect an enduring tension in all historical understanding. Do people make their own history through deliberate and self-conscious action, or is history made by larger and impersonal forces such as "modernization," population growth, fluctuations of the economy, or class conflict? Both approaches will be useful in examining the birth of communism in the Russian and Chinese revolutions.

THE COLLAPSE OF OLD REGIMES: RUSSIA

In the second decade of the twentieth century, two long-established monarchies collapsed—that of China in 1911 and Russia in 1917. Both were large—Russia was the world's largest state in size and China was the largest in population. Both were overwhelmingly agricultural societies. Both were backward in technology and modern industry compared with the more highly developed countries of western Europe, North America, and Japan, at whose hands they suffered military defeats in the nineteenth century. Neither, however, had been formally colonized, as had India or most of Africa. And in both countries, communist parties subsequently came to power to continue the transformations that the collapse of the old systems had begun. The spectacular demise of these ancient and enduring states set the stage for some of the most significant events of the twentieth century. How should we understand their collapse? And how might we compare them?

In early March of 1917, as World War I raged in Europe, Nicholas II, the tsar of the Russian empire, abdicated the throne. That act brought an end to the Romanov dynasty, which had governed the empire for almost three centuries, to an imperial tradition that had endured even longer, to a state that had been of great significance to Europe, Asia, and the Middle East, and to a distinctive society and a way of life. It opened the door to a vast and revolutionary transformation of that country and to a new shape for world history in the twentieth century. How had it happened? How far back in the historical process should we look for the roots of this Russian Revolution?

LEGACIES OF OLD RUSSIA

PEASANTS AND NOBLES.   Perhaps the revolution was rooted deep in Russian history—in its ancient inequalities, oppressions, and divisions. One of those legacies was the sharp divide between the vast peasant majority of the country and its small landowning nobility. Russia's peasants, legally serfs until the mid-nineteenth century, lived precarious lives at best, for they worked with a primitive technology largely untouched by more modern agricultural innovations. Furthermore, they owed substantial rent or labor obligations to their landlords and taxes to the

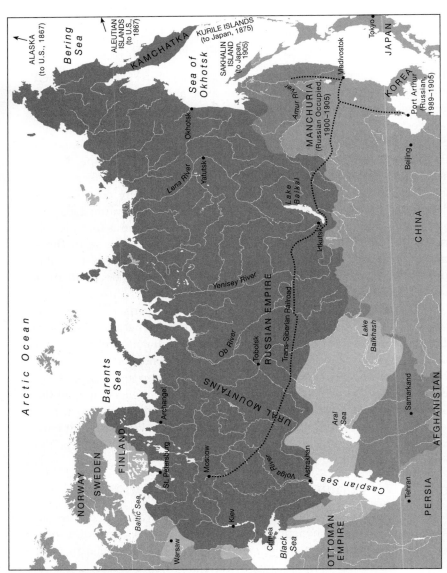

RUSSIAN EMPIRE, 1914:
By the early twentieth century, the Russian empire stretched from Eastern Europe to the Pacific Ocean, incorporating dozens of peoples, cultures, and nationalities. Russians made up only about half of the empire's population.

state. Local landowners could order their serfs to marry, could flog them at will, could exile them to Siberia, or send them to the army. Within their villages, however, Russian peasants had some independence, for the village commune or *mir*, consisting of the male heads of households, had collective responsibility for local affairs. The commune divided village land into strips for individual families and periodically redistributed these strips to ensure a rough equality. Village culture reflected the prominence of the Russian Orthodox Church with its many holidays, feasts, and rituals, but elements of pre-Christian culture—fables, folktales, spirits, and spells—persisted as well.

A vast gulf separated these peasants from the nobility who dominated their lives. In peasant eyes, the nobility were parasites who had no legitimate right to the huge estates they owned, for land rightly belonged only to those who actually worked it. And by the eighteenth century many of the nobles had become highly westernized, sometimes speaking French better than Russian. To them, peasants were the "dark people"—superstitious, backward, lazy, quarrelsome, and often hostile. Periodic peasant rebellions reflected this deep and pervasive class antagonism.

THE NOBILITY AND THE STATE.   But if the nobility dominated the peasantry, they were themselves controlled to an unusual degree by the Russian state. Any independence that the Russian nobility may have once possessed had been crushed long ago by ruthless tsars such as Ivan the Terrible and Peter the Great. Russian nobles were granted land and serfs by the tsar, and their estates were often scattered across different regions of the country to prevent the accumulation of local power. They were expected to serve the state in the military or the civil service. And increasingly, as time went by, many nobles became impoverished and indebted. Unlike their Chinese counterparts, the Russian landed nobility was heavily dependent on the power of state authorities.

RUSSIANS AND THE REST.   A further division in the Russian Empire— and one with potentially revolutionary implications—was ethnic or national. Beginning around 1550, the Russian state expanded from a core area around Moscow to incorporate a huge territory covering about one-sixth of the earth's land. It stretched from Poland across Siberia to the Pacific, and from the Arctic Ocean in the north to Central Asia and the Black and Caspian Seas in the south. Although the empire was largely a Russian creation, Russians represented only about 45% of its population in 1900. The rest comprised a veritable museum of ethnic and cultural diversity including Poles, Finns, Ukrainians, Jews, Georgians, Armenians, Turkic speaking Muslims, Latvians, Lithuanians, and dozens of smaller peoples. Until the later nineteenth century, however, a sharp sense of ethnic or national identity was rare, and most people thought of themselves in terms of regional, village, religious, or class identities.

When the revolution exploded in 1917, these national and class tensions of old Russia came into play. Peasants revolted against their landlords and non-Russian peoples sought autonomy or independence. But these enduring divisions in Russian society were surely not the direct cause of the revolution, for they had been present in Russian life for centuries without generating such an upheaval. And these dramatic events occurred only after the tsar fell. By themselves they do not explain why the old regime collapsed.

ABSOLUTE MONARCHY. Holding this enormous and divided country together was the Russian state, headed by the tsar, justified by the Orthodox Church, and supported by a burgeoning bureaucracy and a huge military establishment. Far more than in the constitutional monarchies of western Europe, the Russian state dominated the society it governed. Neither the church nor the nobility, nor a small merchant and professional class, and certainly not the peasantry had much independent power. To a remarkable extent, the state had "swallowed society." Even at the dawn of the twentieth century, the tsar had complete and unchecked authority. He felt answerable only to God, and no representative bodies or parliaments limited his prerogatives. Here, too, was a potential source of revolutionary action as other groups in society sought access to political power.

REFORM AND REVOLUTION

The more immediate stimulus to revolution was not so much old Russian society as the changes that the nineteenth century brought to that society. Most of these changes had been initiated by the Russian state in an effort to maintain its role as a great power in the endlessly competitive politics of the European state system. The British and French victory over Russia in the Crimean War (1854–1856) demonstrated the apparent hollowness of Russia's claim to real "great power" status. In an age of industry, the vast majority of Russia's population lived in rural areas, and most still derived their living from a very inefficient agriculture. In an age of democracy and capitalism, the Russia state still dominated virtually every aspect of social life but was unable to tap the energies of its people. A growing awareness of this widening gulf between Europe and Russia stimulated a series of major reforms during the second half of the nineteenth century, but, far from creating a new stability, these reforms generated pressures that contributed much to revolution in the early years of the twentieth century.

ENDING SERFDOM.   Among the most far reaching of these reforms was the abolition of serfdom in 1861. But while this action granted legal freedom to the former serfs and gave them a substantial part of the nobles' land, it also saddled them with "redemption payments" for the land they received. The land remaining in the hands of the nobility also irritated the peasants, especially as their rapidly growing numbers only aggravated the shortage of land. Nor did abolition do much to modernize Russian agriculture as inefficient strip farming, and the authority of conservative village communes remained intact.

INDUSTRIALIZATION.   The Russian state also acted vigorously to promote industrialization, now so necessary for "great power" status. In the 1890s, Russia experienced a remarkable spurt of industrial growth, especially in heavy industries such as steel, coal, oil, and railroads. But this, too, had disturbing implications as new social groups appeared quite suddenly in Russian life. A substantial urban working class, numbering several million by 1900 and drawn mostly from rural villages, was concentrated in Moscow, St. Petersburg, and a few other cities. Employed in large factories or mines where they worked under grim conditions, this Russian proletariat became quite militant, often engaging in large-scale strikes. At the same time, a growing middle class of businessmen and professionals took shape. As modern and educated people, many of them objected to the conservatism of the tsarist policies and wished for a greater role in political life. But they were often dependent on the state for contracts and jobs and for suppressing the growing radicalism of the workers, which they greatly feared.

MAKING THE EMPIRE RUSSIAN.   Seeking to strengthen the unity of a diverse population, the tsarist regime also launched a program of Russification, which, like industrialization and the abolition of serfdom, also backfired. Pushing the use of Russian while restricting that of other languages especially offended educated Polish and Ukrainian people. Further legal restrictions on the country's Jewish population and official support for violent anti-Semitic pogroms pushed many Jews into revolutionary groups. As the monarchy increasingly defined itself as a Russian rather than a Romanov dynasty, urban intellectuals in many non-Russian regions responded by creating their own national identities—Ukrainian, Georgian, Polish, Lithuanian, and others—each complete with its own language, history, and culture, and each demanding greater autonomy from and protection against the dominant Russians.

REFUSING DEMOCRATIC REFORM.   While these social and economic reforms proved unsettling rather than stabilizing, the absence of real political reforms made the situation worse. In 1864, Tsar Alexander II had created a series of local elected bodies, called *zemstva,* with responsibility for elementary education, roads, bridges, prisons, and other matters, but when members of these councils, largely from the upper classes, demanded representation at the national level, the tsars absolutely refused, believing that they were responsible to God alone for ruling the country. Thus Russia, alone among the great powers of Europe, entered the twentieth century with no national parliament. The various and growing discontents of Russian society, deriving from peasants, workers, the middle class, and non-Russian nationalities, had no legal outlet.

1905 REVOLUTION.   In 1904, Russia's imperial ambitions in East Asia came into conflict with those of imperial Japan, leading to yet another humiliating military defeat for the tsar in the Russo-Japanese war. That defeat also triggered a vast and spontaneous insurrection throughout Russia. Workers in Moscow and St. Petersburg went on strike and created their own representative councils, or "soviets." Peasant uprisings, student demonstrations, revolts of non-Russian nationalities, and mutinies in the military all contributed to the upheaval. This 1905 revolution, though brutally suppressed, forced the regime to make more substantial reforms than it had ever contemplated. It granted in effect a constitution, legalized both trade unions and political parties, and finally permitted the election of a national legislative body, called the Duma. But Tsar Nicholas II dissolved the first two Dumas when they failed to agree with his programs, and he changed the electoral laws to favor the landed nobility. Thus, Russia still lacked a political system in which the people, even the middle class, had an effective voice. The representatives of even the privileged classes had become so alienated by the government's intransigence that many felt revolution was inevitable.

REVOLUTIONARIES BEFORE THE REVOLUTION

Yet a further source of upheaval lay in the activities of a sizable group of revolutionaries that had crystallized by the end of the nineteenth century. They derived from a uniquely Russian social group know as the *intelligentsia.* Its members were well-educated individuals, often drawn from the nobility or emerging professional groups, who felt strongly alienated from official Russia and were committed to "serving the people" by changing Russian life fundamentally. Because the government allowed no legal outlet for political expression, many had committed themselves to revolution by the mid-nineteenth century.

LIBERALS AND SOCIALISTS.   But they were a diverse group, and they argued passionately over the direction that Russia should take and how, exactly, the revolution might come to pass. Some favored Western-style liberalism, with its emphasis on private property, constitutional govern-ment, and some form of democracy. Most, however, looked to some variant of socialism as the solution for Russia's problems. Among these were the Socialist Revolutionaries (SRs), organized as an underground party in 1901, with a special interest in building socialism on the basis of peasant communal traditions. Others, noticing Russia's rapid indus-trial development and the growth of a militant working class, became attracted to Marxism with its focus on a proletarian revolution. They, too, formed an underground party called the Social Democrats in 1898. But even the Marxists soon split into separate factions growing out of the difficulties of applying Marx's theories, developed in Europe's most advanced industrial societies, to the conditions of a relatively backward country.

The Marxist theory of history generally taught that all human soci-eties moved in stages from feudalism through capitalism to socialism. Because Russia was, in this scheme of things, still in the feudal stage, Marxist Socialists should first work to establish a fully capitalist society by supporting a bourgeois rather than a proletarian revolution. One faction of the Social Democrats, known as the Mensheviks, or "the minority," was willing to accept this uncomfortable role: to build a large, broadly based socialist movement; to ally with the bourgeoisie to over-throw the tsar; and to create a liberal-democratic-capitalist regime. Only later, when Russian industrialization had been completed under capital-ist auspices, would the country be ready for a socialist takeover.

THE BOLSHEVIKS.   The other Marxist faction, called the Bolsheviks, or "the majority," was led by Vladimir Ilyich Ulyanov, better known as Lenin. Born into a solid middle-class family and a lawyer by training, Lenin had been a man of ferocious revolutionary will ever since his brother was executed for conspiring to assassinate the tsar. Tempera-mentally unwilling to wait for history to unfold, Lenin sought to force its pace, believing that Russia could largely skip the capitalist stage. He sought to seize the moment and to prepare actively and constantly for a socialist revolution. To this end, he advocated a small, highly disciplined party of dedicated professional revolutionaries who could act quickly, decisively, and ruthlessly. In part, this conception of the party was a response to existing conditions in Russia, where open political activity merely invited arrest. But it also reflected Lenin's distrust of the work-ing class, which, he feared, could be lured away from revolution and socialism by mere economic gain. The party thus claimed to act as a "vanguard" of the proletariat and in the workers' best interests as interpreted by the party's leadership. Nor would Lenin work with the bourgeoisie, for whom he had an active contempt and who were in any event a weak and timid force in tsarist Russia. Rather, he argued, Russia's small working class should find its allies among the peasantry, whose revolutionary potential he recognized. Thus, Lenin adapted Marxism to the unique conditions of Russia and so positioned the Bolsheviks to ride the revolutionary wave in 1917.

These various revolutionary groups published pamphlets and newspapers, organized trade unions, and spread their messages among workers and peasants. In the somewhat freer political atmosphere after 1905, they could work more openly and even participate in the limited elections to the Duma. Particularly in the cities, these revolutionary parties had an impact. They provided a language through which workers could express their grievances; they created links among workers from different factories; and they furnished leaders able to act when the revolutionary moment arrived.

WAR

That moment arrived in the midst of World War I in which autocratic Russia was allied with democratic France and Britain against Germany, the Austro-Hungarian Empire, and the Ottoman Empire. The war proved to be the final link in a long chain of causes that led to the Russian Revolution of 1917. By the beginning of that year, the war was going badly for the Russians, with casualties numbering in the millions. Additional millions fled their homes in the face of German incursions. Furthermore, the war brought the Russian economy close to collapse. Inflation raised the cost of living, and food was in short supply. All of this dramatically undermined popular support for the government and for the tsar personally. The royal family's association with the disreputable "holy man" Rasputin further diminished its sinking prestige. Even conservative members of the Duma were outraged at the incompetence of the authorities and the tsar's refusal, even then, to appoint a more popular and representative government. Practically the whole of Russian society had turned its back on the tsarist system.

THE FEBRUARY REVOLUTION.   In late February of 1917, the capital city of St. Petersburg erupted in spontaneous upheaval. Women, workers, students, and soldiers took to the streets. Military units sent to suppress them refused to fire and instead joined the revolutionaries. The news from the capital stimulated similar movements in other major cities. Politicians from the various political parties took part in the insurrection, but they had not created this revolution, nor did they control it. For a brief and exciting moment, all of Russia seemed united against a despised and hated system and shared a vague vision of a better, freer, and more just future. It was in light of this overwhelming opposition that Tsar Nicholas reluctantly abdicated the throne. An old way of life had passed into history.

THE COLLAPSE OF OLD REGIMES: CHINA

Five years before the collapse of the Russian monarchy, Chinese court officials announced the abdication of five-year-old emperor Puyi, thus bringing to an end 268 years of Qing dynasty rule and more than 2,000 years of Chinese imperial history. Like the abdication of Tsar Nicholas, Puyi's departure from the "dragon throne" of China marked the end of a unique way of life that had evolved over many centuries in eastern Asia. It, too, was rooted in a long historical process, and it likewise opened the door to a complex struggle that brought communist rule to this ancient land.

OLD CHINA

But the setting was distinctive. While Russia operated culturally on the margins of a broader European and Christian civilization, China was the core of its own civilization, which had greatly influenced its immediate neighbors, such as Japan, Korea, Manchuia, and Vietnam. That civilization found expression in a rich philosophical tradition known as Confucianism and in elaborate artistic and literary achievements. China had also experienced a degree of political unity and continuity unique in world history. While various ruling dynasties rose and fell, interrupted on occasion by nomadic invasions from the north, the Chinese emperor had long provided a central focus for the Chinese state and was supported by a bureaucratic system that recruited its members through a comparatively open process of civil-service examinations. Unlike the Russian Empire, which encompassed a vast diversity of culturally different peoples, the Chinese state was populated overwhelmingly by ethnic Han Chinese, whose written language could be understood by all who were literate.

SOCIAL TENSIONS IN OLD CHINA.   The major social division in old China, as in Russia, was that between a small landlord class and the vast majority of peasants. In China, however, the landlords, often referred to as the gentry, had far smaller landholdings—rarely more than 50 acres, compared to the huge estates of some of the Russian nobility. Nonetheless they were in a stronger position and had greater independent power than their counterparts in Russia, who were thoroughly dominated by the tsarist state. Many Chinese landlords had the immense prestige that came from passing even the lowest level of the examinations. Those with more advanced degrees were appointed to bureaucratic positions, but many who could not be accommodated in the bureaucracy served as informal agents of the Chinese state at the local level, where they enriched themselves by charging fees for their various services as well as rent from their peasant tenants. Most Chinese peasants owned some land, but many had to rent additional land or hire out their labor to survive. They lived out their lives in market communities, consisting of a dozen or more villages, but with little of the collective organization or autonomy that village communes provided for Russian peasants. Within these market communities, individual peasant families managed agricultural production, and local gentry dominated the clan, religious, and welfare organizations that sustained peasant life. Thus, Chinese peasant rebellions were more often directed against agents of the state, such as tax collectors and local officials, than against the landlords, as was the case in Russia. These differences help to explain why peasant upheaval in Russia occurred immediately following the collapse of the monarchy, whereas in China it took decades of military struggle and communist party leadership to nurture a peasant revolution.

CHINA AND THE WEST

In both Russia and China, humiliation and defeat at the hands of western powers, and later Japan, undermined the legitimacy of their old regimes, for the chief purpose of any government is protection from foreign threats, and those unable to achieve it easily lose credibility. Russia had been part of a highly competitive European state system for centuries. Its many military defeats within that system had prompted repeated reforms as it attempted to catch up with more powerful rivals. China, on the other hand, had long been the center of an east Asian international system that recognized no equal states. China's conception of itself was as the "middle kingdom," infinitely superior to all surrounding peoples. Its relationships with them were governed by the "tribute system" in which the non-Chinese participants ritually acknowledged the superiority of China and their own dependent status by sending tribute to the Emperor and "kowtowing" or prostrating themselves before him. In return they received lavish gifts and much-desired trading opportunities within China. For some 300 years (1500–1830s), these principles shaped the activities of small numbers of European merchants and missionaries who had operated in China in sharply limited ways and almost entirely on Chinese terms.

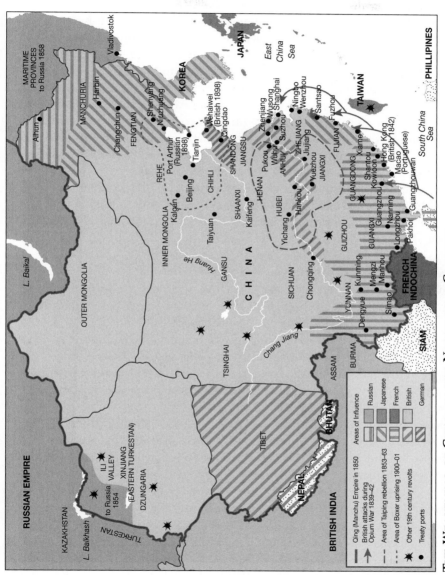

The Weakening of China in the Nineteenth Century:

Western and Japanese imperialism combined with major internal rebellions to seriously weaken China in the 19th century.

OPIUM WARS. But then, quite abruptly it seemed to the Chinese, the balance of power shifted. Europe's Industrial Revolution gave it unsurpassed military power and new economic reasons for seeking unrestricted access to China. Matters came to a head over the issue of opium, which English merchants had been exporting to China in growing quantities at great profit to themselves though in violation of Chinese law. When Chinese authorities took drastic action to end the opium trade, which had caused a massive addiction problem, the British sent in their gunboats. Military defeat in the Opium Wars (1839–42 and 1856–58) required China to sign a series of "unequal treaties" that seriously compromised Chinese sovereignty. Numerous coastal ports were opened to foreign trade, and Europeans living in them were no longer subject to Chinese law. Foreign vessels and gunboats gained access to China's inland waterways, the country was opened to missionary penetration, and the Chinese government was required to protect them. China's ability to levy tariffs on imported goods was sharply limited, and it had to compensate European powers for their wartime expenses by paying large indemnities.

IMPERIALISM IN CHINA. Nor was this all. Further military defeats at the hands of the French in the 1880s and a rapidly modernizing Japan in 1894–95 resulted in the loss of Vietnam and Korea, which had been Chinese tributary states, and the island province of Taiwan as well. And by the late 1890s, a scramble for concessions carved China into "spheres of influence" in which the various European powers received the right to establish military bases, extract raw materials, and build railroads in particular parts of the country. By the end of the century, China had become a semi-colony of the great powers. This was a quite different experience from that of Russia, which, despite defeats in the Crimean War of 1854–56 and in the Russo-Japanese War of 1905, maintained its sovereignty intact and continued to function as one of the great powers of Europe.

Thoughtful and educated Chinese wondered if their country could survive. It was, many believed, being "sliced like a melon" and threatened with partition into colonies, as was happening in Africa at the same time. Increasingly, Chinese were forced to think of themselves not as the center of the civilized world but as just one of many nations in a world of nation-states, and an oppressed and beleaguered one at that. It would be hard to imagine a more profound humiliation for the ruling class of the "middle kingdom." These perceptions stimulated the growth of anti-imperialist and nationalist ideas. But they also reminded people that the Qing or Manchu dynasty was itself of foreign origin from Manchuria.

Despite several centuries of accommodating themselves to Chinese culture and ways of governing, Qing rulers remained distinctive. Their evident failure to protect China from the barbarian Europeans and even from the "dwarf bandits" of Japan set many people to thinking that something had to change if China were to persist as a nation. Some began to question if perhaps the Qing dynasty should be removed from power or even the entire imperial structure dismantled in favor of a republic. Thus China's experience with imperialism clearly weakened support for the old regime and contributed to various currents of revolutionary thought.

THE CRISIS WITHIN

China's increasingly desperate confrontation with Western and Japanese imperialism coincided with severe internal problems that further weakened the Qing dynasty. Chief among these was a rapidly growing population that nearly doubled between 1750 and 1850, but without the kind of technological breakthroughs that Europe's Industrial Revolution provided for its increasing number of people. China's previously impressive economy was reaching the limits of its ability to provide for its growing numbers. This meant smaller farms for peasants and more misery, famine, and disease. It also meant a growing number of failed examination candidates whose frustration fueled unrest. Western economic penetration generated further disruption and contributed to a growing problem of opium addiction. China seemed to be experiencing the symptoms traditionally associated with the end of a dynastic cycle—official corruption, weakening military strength, decaying irrigation facilities, and most ominous of all, peasant rebellion.

PEASANT REBELLION.   Such rebellions punctuated Chinese history in the nineteenth century and were especially widespread between 1850 and the early 1870s. They revealed deep hostility among ordinary people with Qing rule. The most serious of them, the Taiping Rebellion, came close to toppling the Qing dynasty and had, in fact, drawn up plans for a revolutionary reorganization of Chinese society, including the elimination of Confucianism, gender inequality, private property, and the gentry class. The devastation caused by these rebellions and their suppression seriously disrupted and weakened China's economy. Vast expanses of the Yangzi River Valley became virtual wastelands, as travelers reported walking for days in previously densely populated regions without seeing a living person. Some 20 to 30 million people died. But the most important consequence of these rebellions lay in the way they were defeated. Western military forces aided the beleaguered

Qing dynasty, which identified the Chinese rulers even more clearly as collaborators with imperialism. And as the shaken imperial military forces proved incapable of subduing the Taipings, provincial gentry leaders came forward to mobilize their own local armies, which in the end destroyed the revolutionary rebels. Thus the Qing court and the central government lost power to regional gentry leaders who commanded their own armies, collected their own revenues, and dispensed their own justice. It was yet another source of weakness for an increasingly beleaguered dynasty.

REFORM AND REVOLUTION

SELF-STRENGTHENING.   Official Chinese response to the staggering problems of foreign imperialism and domestic rebellion was known generally as the "self-strengthening movement." Lasting from the 1860s to 1890s, it sought to rejuvenate a sagging dynasty and a failing society by vigorous application of traditional Confucian principles, such as finding honorable men for official positions, combined with very limited and cautious borrowing from the West. But China undertook nothing comparable to Russia's centrally directed industrialization drive, for its conservative and powerful gentry class feared the social unrest that urban, industrial, and commercial development might generate. Chinese officials, however, were impressed with western military technology and established a few modern industries, arsenals, shipyards, foreign language schools, and telegraph and railroad lines. But these were largely under the control of local gentry and regional military leaders and so served to strengthen provincial centers of power more than the Chinese state as a whole. The humiliating defeat by Japan in 1895, the scramble for concessions that followed, and the occupation of Beijing by foreign troops in 1900 clearly demonstrated the failure of this very limited approach to reform. China was still in danger!

OPPOSITION TO THE QING DYNASTY.   Thus, while pressures for fundamental change in Russia derived from the economic successes of an ambitious program of industrial development, those in China occurred as a consequence of a very limited and reluctant reform efforts that showed few signs of rescuing the country from its many difficulties. But despite the limits of Qing reforms, western ideas increasingly penetrated Chinese intellectual life, and growing numbers of educated Chinese, including many in official elite positions, became highly disillusioned with the ineffective policies and corrupt practices of the Qing dynasty. By the late 1890s, they were organizing a variety of clubs, study groups, and newspapers to examine China's desperate situation and explore alternative paths—the National Rejuvenation Study Society, Society to Protect the Nation, and Understand the National Shame Society. They admired not only western science and technology but also western political practices that limited the authority of the ruler and permitted wider circles of people to take part in public life. They believed that only a truly unified nation in which rulers and ruled were closely related could save China from dismemberment at the hands of foreign imperialists. Some among the intellectuals, such as the highly influential Kang Youwei, rationalized their demands for serious reform by interpreting Confucius as a radical reformer rather than a conservative authority. As in Russia, substantial parts of the official elite had largely deserted the system that had nurtured them.

THE CONSEQUENCES OF REFORM.   These pressures finally roused the Qing dynasty in the first decade of the new century to more serious reform, but these efforts, like those of Russia at the same time, generally backfired and fueled the demand for even greater change. New schools, many open to women for the first time, offered a western curriculum, and thousands of students were sent to study abroad in Europe, America, or Japan, where they picked up a variety of new and unsettling ideas—constitutionalism, democracy, socialism, and much more. In 1905 the ancient examination system was abolished, which ended the gentry's traditional access to the state bureaucracy and opened up new opportunities for men of wealth, modern education, and local prestige. Military academies provided training for a New Army and generated modern-minded and highly patriotic officers. Chambers of Commerce in major cities provided an outlet for a growing merchant and business class that accompanied a measure of modern economic development. And impressed with the great success of Japan's constitutional monarchy, Qing authorities permitted highly restricted elections for Provincial Assemblies in 1909 and a National Assembly in 1910 with the promise of an actual parliament in 1917. These assemblies became a platform for local gentry who favored a more modern but decentralized China in which their own interests could prevail, rather than seeking to strengthen the central state and its foreign Qing dynasty.

Thus by 1910 a variety of new groups with new aspirations and ideas had emerged to challenge the old China of the Qing dynasty—disaffected degree holders, students, merchants, army officers, urban workers, and a newly politicized provincial gentry. What they increasingly shared was a growing nationalism directed against both foreign imperialists and a Qing dynasty, itself of foreign origins, which seemed unable to respond effectively to China's dire situation. A popular pamphlet written in 1903 by a student studying in Japan expressed this sentiment in passionate terms:

> Scholars: put down your brushes. Farmers: lay down your rakes. Traders: abandon your business. Artisans: put down your tools. Every-one, sharpen your knives, supply yourself with bullets, swear an oath, and cry out . . . If the Manchus help the foreigners kill us, then first kill all the Manchus. If those corrupt officials help the foreigners kill us, then first kill all the corrupt officials.[2]

Even some peasants made this connection between imperialism and China's ruling dynasty. "Sweep away the Qing; destroy the foreigners" was the slogan of an early-twentieth-century peasant movement in north China protesting the payment of indemnities to missionaries who had lost property in an earlier peasant rebellion.[3] Thus, while Russia's revolutionary movement was driven largely by class conflict, that of China was nurtured by a growing nationalism and anti-imperialism. At this stage, it was less social justice than national survival that propelled the opposition to Qing rule.

DIVISIONS.   If growing numbers of Chinese agreed on the problem, they were sharply divided on the solution. Many of the "new people"—students, merchants, and military officers—were thoroughly progressive in their outlook, whereas peasant-based secret societies were frequently hostile to modern innovations such as schools and railroads and the taxes necessary to build them. Some sought a strong central state that could effectively combat imperialists, but provincial gentry, though anti-imperialist, favored greater regional autonomy. Impoverished peasants and wealthy landlords certainly did not view the world in the same way. And some intellectuals favored gradual reform toward a constitutional monarchy, while others believed that only a revolutionary overthrow of the Qing dynasty and its replacement by a republic could save China. A few people had discovered the writings of Karl Marx and other European socialists, although, unlike Russia, no socialist parties had been organized before the collapse of the old regime.

THE REVOLUTION OF 1911.   As it happened, the revolutionaries triggered, but certainly did not cause, the final collapse of the Qing dynasty. In 1905 several groups of active revolutionaries came together in the Revolutionary Alliance, led by a western-educated Chinese doctor, Sun Yat-sen, and financed in large part by Chinese living abroad. By 1911, they numbered perhaps 10,000. Many had been students in Japan; some were members of the new provincial assemblies, and others were soldiers or officers in various New Army units. A substantial number were women who sought new roles for themselves in a new China. Sun also had strong connections with traditional secret societies that were also strongly anti-Qing. Lacking a disciplined organization and clear leadership, these revolutionaries had staged a number of abortive uprisings after 1905. Then in October 1911, revolutionaries in Wuhan accidently detonated one of the bombs they were making, thus forcing them to make yet another attempt at seizing power in the region. This time, the Qing governor-general panicked and fled, and local units of the New Army sided with the revolutionaries. Within weeks, numerous other provinces fell under the control of local gentry and military leaders, who likewise declared their regions independent of the capital. By this time, virtually all sectors of Chinese society had deserted the Qing dynasty and, as in Russia by 1917, the monarchy stood alone. In these circumstances, the Qing court negotiated the abdication of the boy emperor in February 1912. Chinese history had turned an uncertain corner.

Organized revolutionaries played even less of a role in the collapse of old China than they had in Russia. The Qing dynasty had alienated every major group in China from the most traditional gentry, scholar-officials, and peasants to the most modern students, businessmen, military officers, and urban workers. In Russia it took a devastating war to push the country into revolution, whereas China's old regime collapsed in peacetime with only a modest nudge from revolutionaries.

NINE MONTHS: THE BOLSHEVIKS AND THE RUSSIAN REVOLUTION

When tsarist Russia and imperial China collapsed, hardly anyone imagined that those old regimes would be replaced by revolutionary communists. Few Chinese had even heard of Karl Marx, and no communist or socialist organization existed in China in 1911. Socialists of various kinds had been active in Russia for several decades prior to the 1917 revolution, but the Bolshevik faction was hardly a serious candidate for the country's leadership. Its numbers were modest; its radical views put the party on the fringe of mainstream socialist thinking; and its leader, Lenin, who lived abroad, was vitriolic in his arguments and unwilling to cooperate even with fellow socialists. How then can we explain the unlikely seizure of power by revolutionary communists in both of these enormous countries? And how did that process differ in the two cases?

THE PROVISIONAL GOVERNMENT

When the Russian monarchy fell in February of 1917, power was assumed by the Provisional Government, which shortly became a coalition of leading middle-class liberals from the old Duma, or parliament, and representatives of the mainstream Socialist parties, the Mensheviks and Socialist Revolutionaries. These leaders recognized themselves as only a temporary government and promised a democratically elected Constituent Assembly to draw up a new constitution for the shattered country. Almost everyone expected that this would result in a European-style democratic state controlled by a coalition of the major parties, both Socialist and non-Socialist. In the meantime, the Provisional Government proceeded to dismantle the old system and lay the foundation for a liberal order. All citizens received equality before the law; personal free-doms, including those of speech, assembly, religion, and the right to strike, became real for the first time in Russian history. Local government was made more democratic, the eight-hour workday was declared for some workers, and ethnic minorities were promised autonomy. With broad international and domestic support, the Provisional Government seemed to be taking Russia on the road to a Western-style regime. But the Provisional Government proved unable to stabilize the country, and in less than a year the possibility of a democratic and capitalist society in Russia had been swept away, replaced by a one-party system domi-nated by the Bolsheviks and committed to creating a socialist society. What had happened?

SOCIAL REVOLUTION IN THE MAKING

The fall of the old regime had unleashed a massive torrent of social upheaval, an elemental popular demand for radical change, with which the Provisional Government proved unable to cope. In the face of this spontaneous upsurge of revolutionary fervor, the generally moderate and well-educated leaders of the Provisional Government hesitated, acted indecisively, and by October were swept aside. The Bolsheviks who replaced them had certainly not created this mass convulsion, but they alone proved able to ride the tidal wave to power.

A DEMAND FOR PEACE.   One dimension of this revolutionary upheaval occurred in the armed forces, which had suffered appalling casualties numbering in the millions. A growing desire for peace took shape both in the army and in society generally, especially after the disastrous fail-ure of a Russian offensive in June of 1917. Furthermore, the deepening class hatreds of Russian society were replicated in the army, in which officers were largely from the educated and wealthy classes while the ordinary soldiers were mostly peasants. "Between us and them," wrote one officer in his diary, "it is an impassible gulf . . . In their eyes what has occurred is not a political but a social revolution, which in their opinion they have won and we have lost . . . We can find no common language."[4]

But in the face of overwhelming demands for peace and increasing rates of desertion from the military, the Provisional Government determined to continue the war and defend the homeland. This action radicalized many of the soldiers and made them ever more attentive to those political leaders who promised peace.

SEIZING THE LAND. In the countryside, peasants, acting spontaneously through their village communes in the summer and fall of 1917, seized landlords' estates, burned their manor houses, and redistributed their lands according to traditional communal principles, with the poor and landless peasants receiving the greater share. Peasants who had previously left the commune to become individual small farmers were brought back into the traditional framework of Russian rural life. Within a few months, the old nobility simply ceased to exist as a viable social group. A few were killed; others fled; those who stayed were allocated a small plot of land. Thus, the peasants in Russia made their own revolution, largely apart from urban-based political parties and acting on the basis of their old organizations and values. But as peasants began to seize the estates of the landlords, the Provisional Government again temporized, urging them to wait until the Constituent Assembly could arrange for an orderly transfer of land. But the peasants would tolerate no delay, and the government's inability to move boldly on the land question cost it the support of many in the countryside.

THE RISE OF "SOVIETS." The popular mood in major industrial cities was equally revolutionary. Rising prices, declining incomes, widespread shortages, and factory closures all drove the demand for government regulation of the economy or, in some cases, for workers themselves to control their factories. When the Provisional Government, sharply divided between its socialist and non-socialist members, proved unable to take decisive action, many workers turned to an alternative source of possible action—the soviets. These grass-roots organizations of workers and soldiers had sprung up in the 1905 revolution and reemerged in 1917. In the capital, the Petrograd Soviet, a body of about 1,500 deputies elected from the factories and military units of the city, regarded itself as a watchdog of the revolution and frequently countermanded or undermined the actions of the Provisional Government. The popularity of the soviets, in which Bolsheviks became increasingly prominent, increased as the Provisional Government seemed unwilling or unable to address popular demands. Outside of the capital, local "soviets" appeared all over the country in an explosion of grass-roots organizing. New trade unions also sprang up to defend workers, and at the plant level, "factory committees" began to exercise worker control in what were still privately owned

FIGURE 2-1 COMMUNISM IN THE SOVIET UNION:
Lenin (on the left) was the architect of the communist victory in the Russian Revolution, while Stalin led the USSR in the building of the first socialist society.

businesses. Increasingly, workers and soldiers viewed the Provisional Government as the illegitimate and ineffective agent of the wealthy classes and the soviets as speaking for the exploited laboring masses and as a potential alternative government for the country. The conflict between the two bodies reflected the deepening class antagonisms of Russian society.

EXITING THE EMPIRE. If the revolution brought Russia's class conflicts to the boiling point, it also fragmented the country along national lines. Weakening central authority and greater freedom of expression allowed nationalists in non-Russian areas of the country to assert varying degrees of cultural or political autonomy or even independence. In Ukraine, Poland, the Baltic region, Muslim areas in Central Asia, and elsewhere, urban intellectuals led movements that threatened to shatter the Russian Empire. The Provisional Government was slow to recognize the depth and seriousness of these national tensions and felt committed to maintaining the territorial integrity of the Russian state. Thus, the agitation of nationalist movements combined with the bitter class struggles of 1917 to generate a widespread sense of chaos and uncertainty.

BOLSHEVIK TAKEOVER

In this atmosphere of growing radicalism, the Provisional Government was unable to respond effectively to popular demands. The alliance between its liberal and socialist members was increasingly strained. It faced threats from conservative forces eager to crush the radicals and from street crowds in St. Petersburg equally eager for drastic revolutionary action. Despite growing calls for the Petrograd Soviet to take power, its leaders from the moderate socialist parties were reluctant to do so, believing that Russia was not yet ready for socialism.

These conditions gave the Bolsheviks their opening. As the only major socialist party that had not affiliated with the Provisional Government, it alone was untainted by the failures of that government. Thus, the Bolsheviks grew rapidly in popularity and in numbers of party members, especially in the large cities and among workers and soldiers. Their program, drawn up by Lenin, was far closer to the mood of the masses than that of the Provisional Government. It called for immediate peace, confiscation of landowners' estates, workers' control in the factories, and self-determination for non-Russian nationalities. In its slogan, "all power to the Soviets," the Bolsheviks called for the overthrow of the Provisional Government and the beginning of class warfare. On that basis, Lenin insisted that the Bolsheviks seize formal state power from the increasingly unpopular Provisional Government. On the night of October 24–25, Bolshevik-led armed forces took control of major centers in the capital, but they did so in the name of the All-Russian Congress of Soviets, which was then assembling in the city. Thus, the Bolsheviks presented their takeover as a defense of the revolution and as a way of bringing a government of the soviets to power. So unpopular had the Provisional Government become that there was little initial resistance to what the Bolsheviks called the October Revolution. And over the next several months, Bolshevik-led soviets in many other cities also seized power and joined the revolution, sometimes peacefully and at other times with considerable fighting.

HOLDING ON: THE RUSSIAN CIVIL WAR, 1918–1921

Seizing power was one thing; holding it was quite another. By the middle of 1918, the Bolsheviks found themselves in a civil war against many enemies. Some of them were supporters of the tsarist regime—army officers, aristocrats, and landowners. Others had supported the February Revolution but bitterly opposed a Bolshevik or "soviet" takeover in October. Many socialists were offended when, in January 1918, the Bolshevik government cavalierly disbanded the long awaited multiparty Constituent Assembly, which had been elected to draw up a constitution. This action signaled the Bolshevik's intention to create a one-party state rather than majority rule involving several political parties. And various groups objected to the signing of a humiliating peace treaty with Germany, which took Russia out of the war but with large territorial losses. Soon the Bolsheviks' many enemies, generally known as the Whites, began largely uncoordinated military actions against the Communist government.

For three years the Bolsheviks, now known as Communists, battled their various foes and by 1921 they had staggered to victory in a bitter conflict which decisively marked the new regime. That victory was in part the product of the divisions and reactionary reputation of their White opponents, some of whom clearly wanted to restore lost properties to the landlords. The Bolsheviks' identification with the popular soviets and their willingness to endorse peasant seizure of land clearly gave them an edge in competing for popular support. Their ability to integrate a number of lower-class men into the newly formed Red Army and into new institutions of local government provided a measure of social mobility for many. Because a number of capitalist powers, including Britain, France, the United States, and Japan briefly entered the conflict on the side of the Whites, the Communists could present themselves as patriotic defenders against foreign intervention. In the decades to come, they often used this threat of "capitalist encirclement" to justify harsh internal policies. And as the Bolsheviks triumphed over their "White" opponents, they also brought back into the Soviet Union most of the non-Russian regions that had pulled away from the Russian Empire after 1917.

The experience of civil war made a heavy military imprint on what had been a largely civilian party and thus added to its already authoritarian character, its inclination to use force, and its willingness to rule by decree. The revival of a secret police and its use as an organ of terror, summary justice, and political control was regarded by the Communists as a temporary expedient, but it was an ominous sign of things to come. By the early 1920s, the Communist government had outlawed all other political parties. The Soviet Union was a one-party state!

The practical demands of the civil war and the ideological desire to move quickly to a communist society combined to produce a highly centralized economic system called "war communism." It involved nationalization of large-scale industry, the abolition of free trade, and the forced requisition of grain from the peasants. But the system far outran the government's limited administrative capacity. Furthermore, the civil war devastated the country's economy, sent industrial production plummeting to 20% of its 1913 level, scattered half of the urban working class to the villages, and created widespread famine. Active opposition from some of the Bolshevik's most ardent supporters—peasants, workers, and soldiers—soon prompted the victorious but beleaguered Communists to moderate their policies in the early 1920s. By this time, however, the Communist Party was in firm control of the country, and the effort to construct a socialist society was about to begin.

THIRTY-EIGHT YEARS: THE MAKING OF THE CHINESE REVOLUTION

Chinese communists came to power, following the collapse of the imperial system in 1911, in a process quite different from that of their Russian counterparts. Most obviously, it took far longer. Whereas the Bolsheviks seized power only nine months after the end of tsarist Russia and consolidated their power after a three-year civil war, Chinese communists did not even emerge as a political grouping for a full decade after 1911, and then they struggled for another 28 years before finally achieving power in 1949. Whereas the Russian civil war occurred after the communist seizure of power, in China civil war preceded the communist takeover.

Furthermore, in China, no spontaneous revolutionary upheaval followed the abdication of the last emperor, for the gentry had far more substantial local roots and independent power than did the Russian nobility, and Chinese peasants had less autonomy and capacity for independent action than did their Russian counterparts. The Bolsheviks in Russia came to power on the back of a revolutionary upheaval that they had done little to create, but the Chinese Communist Party (CCP) had to spend decades nurturing a revolution, persuading an often reluctant and fearful population that a different life was possible and carving out various "liberated areas" throughout the country only with great difficulty. Furthermore, the primary focus of Chinese revolutionary efforts took place in widely scattered and largely rural settings with peasants as the major actors, whereas the Bolsheviks were an urban-based party that championed industrial workers in a few major cities, especially St. Petersburg. And China, despite its ethnic homogeneity, disintegrated more completely and for a much longer time than did the more culturally diverse Russian Empire, which had been reconstituted as the Soviet Union by 1922. Finally, the role of war was very different in the two

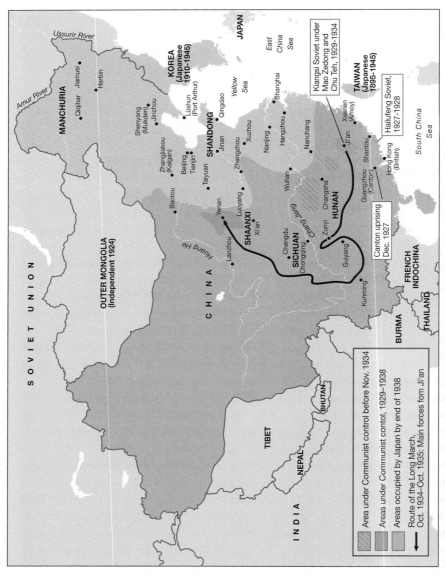

The Rise of Communism in China:

The Long March and the Japanese invasion of China were crucial events in the rise of communism.

countries. In Russia, Bolshevik opposition to participation in World War I gained them many supporters, while in China, the CCP's vigorous prosecution of World War II against the Japanese invaders contributed much to the party's success.

COMMUNIST BEGINNINGS IN CHINA

The 1911 Revolution in China, and the republic to which it gave birth, soon proved a bitter disappointment to its most ardent supporters. Intended to create a unified and modern nation-state that could effectively confront both foreign imperialism and the country's immense social problems, it in fact did little more than remove an exhausted Qing dynasty from the historical stage. What followed 1911 was the almost complete disintegration of central authority as power flowed out to local gentry in the countryside and to regional military strongmen known as warlords. Frequently at war with one another, many of these warlords also squeezed the peasants without pity, imposing dozens of new taxes and further inhibiting the economic growth of the country. Furthermore, an impotent central government was altogether unable to deal with the problem of imperialism, which grew even worse. Japan placed increasingly harsh demands on China and brought Manchuria in particular under its economic domination. And despite China's participation on the winning side in World War I, the victorious allies awarded German territory in China to Japan rather than returning it to Chinese control. It was a shattering blow for those who had put their faith in the principle of "self-determination," proclaimed by the allies, and who had expected the end, finally, of the unequal treaties.

THE MAY FOURTH MOVEMENT.   These disappointments provoked among young educated Chinese a profound change in outlook—indeed, a cultural revolution, widely known as the May Fourth movement after a major anti-imperialist demonstration that took place on that day in 1919. In hundreds of newspapers, magazines, study groups, and literary societies, these young students and their teachers undertook a searching examination of China's venerated traditional culture and explored alternative future paths. Their most fundamental concern was the survival of China as a nation-state. What could be done to rescue the once proud "middle kingdom" from its present sorry condition—divided into rival warlord regimes, lacking any effective central government, and humiliated for the past 75 years by foreign imperialists? Clearly the simple elimination of the monarchy and its Qing dynasty was not enough. And so the passionate young people of the May Fourth generation demanded a deepening of the revolution to include a rejection of almost all of China's old culture. Confucianism, classical education, arranged marriages, sexual inequality, reverence for age—all these were regarded as sources of the country's weakness and had to be destroyed if China were to save itself as a nation. To replace all of this they advocated a thorough westernization. Western writers of all kinds were translated into Chinese and their works eagerly devoured. Science, democracy, socialism, humanitarianism, Darwinism, anarchism, Christianity and the social gospel, feminism—all of these had their advocates as the young and educated sought to find the secret of western power and to use it for China's resurrection.

THE ATTRACTIONS OF MARXISM.   In this context, growing numbers of young Chinese intellectuals turned their attention to Marxism. Earlier, mainstream European socialism, with its emphasis on the urban working class as the agent of socialist revolution, had seemed irrelevant to the needs of an overwhelmingly agrarian Chinese society with a tiny industrial proletariat. But the dramatic success in 1917 of the Bolsheviks in Russia, likewise a backward country compared to western Europe and the United States, prompted many to take a second look at Marxism, particularly in its Leninist version. Lenin had introduced the idea of a vanguard party, which would give intellectuals a significant role to play in a socialist revolution. And Lenin had developed a theory of imperialism that attributed the weakness and poverty of nations such as China to imperialist exploitation and domination. Such ideas justified China's emerging nationalism and its anti-imperialist movement. Thus Marxism/ Leninism was a thoroughly modern and western body of ideas, and yet it attacked offensive features of western life, such as capitalism and imperialism. Furthermore, the new Soviet government, unlike western states, seemed willing to relinquish the rights that the tsarist regime had acquired under the unequal treaties. And so, in 1921, a mere handful of recent converts to Marxism, with the encouragement of Soviet representatives in China, met in Shanghai and formally established the Chinese Communist Party. At the time it had only about 60 members. One of them was Mao Zedong, a 26-year-old school teacher and librarian and the son of a reasonably well-to-do peasant family. From these small and almost unnoticed beginnings emerged the Chinese Communist Party, which 28 years later came to govern the most heavily populated nation in the world. How can we explain such an unlikely outcome?

CONFRONTING THE GUOMINDANG

The victory of the CCP was all the more surprising because it faced a formidable foe, far more robust and resourceful than the Provisional Government over which the Bolsheviks had triumphed in Russia. That foe was another political party, the Guomindang (GMD) or the Nationalist Party, established in 1922, about the same time as the CCP. For over a quarter of a century, these two political parties engaged in an epic struggle for control of China.

THE NORTHERN EXPEDITION. For much of this time, all of the advantages seemed to lie with the GMD. Led initially by the venerable and widely respected revolutionary Sun Yat-sen and focused on the southern city of Canton, the Guomindang was an outgrowth of those groups that had overthrown the Qing dynasty in 1911. It, too, sought a strong, modern, and unified China, although without the clear socialist commitments of the CCP. A major source of its support came from the well-to-do of Chinese society—modern urban businessmen and larger landlords in the countryside. But like the CCP, it also looked to the Soviet Union for advice, training, and support. That advice required the young Communist Party to subordinate its revolutionary goals and to join the larger and more broadly supported GMD in a military campaign to defeat the warlords and unify the country. Known as the Northern Expedition, that campaign began in 1926 and had largely succeeded by 1928. Warlords had been defeated, bribed, or absorbed into a newly unified country, controlled by the GMD, which was now led by a military man, Chiang Kai-shek, following the death of Sun Yat-sen in 1924.

THE SLAUGHTER OF THE COMMUNISTS. But in the course of the Northern Expedition, Communist Party organizers, operating within the GMD, had tapped into a vein of intense social discontent. Huge strikes among urban workers, peasant movements demanding rent reductions, and women seeking greater equality—all of this greeted the victorious armies of the Northern Expedition. These upheavals encouraged communists to think that perhaps a social revolution was at hand, but they frightened the more conservative GMD, many of whose wealthy and privileged supporters felt deeply threatened. Thus, in 1927 Chiang Kai-shek turned decisively against his communist allies and unleashed a wave of terror against them that cost the lives of many thousands of Communists, labor leaders, workers, and peasant organizers. Decimated and disorganized, the Communist Party was driven out of China's cities, its few remaining leaders fleeing to remote and inaccessible regions in the countryside. By the late 1920s, the fledgling Chinese Communist Party seemed all but destroyed, and the GMD, led by Chiang Kai-shek, seemed poised to consolidate its control in a newly unified Chinese state.

TURNING TO THE PEASANTS

In these dire circumstances, some communists began to grope their way toward a new strategy—mobilizing peasants for revolution—which over the next 20 years played a critical role in their eventual victory. But it was no easy sell. The party leadership, under Soviet influence, continued to give priority to urban revolution and to the country's tiny factory working class. Marx and his followers had always been suspicious of peasants, believing that their traditional values, their narrow and provincial outlooks, and their desire to own small plots of private property made them inevitably conservative. It was only slowly and with much controversy that the Chinese Communist Party worked its way out of the urban mentality of orthodox Marxism to adopt a peasant orientation that became its distinctive hallmark.

ORGANIZING PEASANTS.   Furthermore, peasants themselves proved enormously difficult to organize. Unlike their Russian counterparts, they had no organizations to enable collective action. Many were apathetic, unable to imagine an alternative way of life or belonging to a group larger than the market community. Others had personal ties to their landlords or feared retaliation from them. Nor did rural Chinese villagers constitute a single group. Millions with no land at all worked as carters, haulers, or agricultural laborers, were unable to marry, and usually died young. "Poor peasants" had farms too small to sustain their families and had to work for others and even, in hard times, sold their own children. "Middle peasants" could usually support themselves, and "rich peasants" could afford to hire others to work their land. The mix of misery and prosperity varied greatly from place to place, but in the 1930s a combination of devastating floods, Japanese aggression, the worldwide depression, and callous landlords combined to reduce growing numbers to mere subsistence or even less. These conditions provided the raw material for a peasant-based revolution, but it did not erupt spontaneously. It was the Chinese Communist Party that slowly and with many setbacks gave purpose, direction, and outlet for the suffering of rural China.

MAO ZEDONG.   Although a few communist leaders had, with some success, tried to organize peasants in the early and mid-1920s, it was not until Chiang Kai-shek had chased the battered communists out of the cities that some in the party turned their attention seriously to China's vast peasant population. In more than a dozen "base areas," most in remote locations in the countryside, communists experimented with various ways of mobilizing China's rural misery for a communist revolution. The largest and best known of these efforts occurred in Jiangxi province in southern China, where Mao Zedong emerged as the local leader. His fundamental idea was to create rural base areas under communist control as the jumping-off place for a long-term struggle. The heart of Mao's approach centered on peasant support. This required the creation of a Red or Communist Army from a ragtag collection of soldiers who had deserted, bandits, and poor peasants, for local people could hardly be expected to take part in a revolution unless they felt reasonably secure from retribution.

Furthermore, Mao directly addressed the chief cause of peasant poverty—landlessness. He conducted meticulous studies of local social conditions and experimented with various approaches to confiscating land from the wealthy and redistributing it to the poor. In doing so, he learned the importance of involving peasants themselves in revolutionary struggle rather than having the Communist Party or the Red Army do it for them. To recruit women for the revolution, Mao drew on the CCP's commitment to women's liberation and established a Marriage Law that outlawed arranged or "purchased" marriages, made divorce easier, and gave women the right to vote and own property. But Mao was also willing to compromise communist principles of equal distribution of land to avoid offending better-off peasants, and to keep the loyalty of his soldiers, he did not permit women to seek divorce from men on active military duty.

THE LONG MARCH.   From 1928 through 1934, the Red Army, using techniques of guerilla warfare rather than fighting frontal battles, was able to protect this Jiangxi "liberated" region from Chiang Kai-shek's encircling armies. Then, however, Chiang's numerically superior and better-equipped forces finally drove the Communists out of Jiangxi and forced them into an enormous trek, known as the Long March, across virtually the entire country. During a single year (1934–1935), the Communist forces marched 6,000 miles from Jiangxi to a new base in the northwest province of Shaanxi. Of the 100,000 men and 35 women who began the march, only 8,000 survived to see the city of Yanan, where the new government was established. Crossing several major mountain ranges, forging scores of rivers, and fighting a full-dress battle on average every two days, the survivors emerged with an intense sense of mission, comradeship, and even invincibility. Moreover, by the time the Communists reached their new base in Yanan, the party had become fully committed to a peasant-based revolution, and Mao Zedong had gained control of the CCP in defiance of Stalin's wishes. From then on, the CCP was independent of the Soviet Union. And with a new base area in Yanan, Mao set out to re-create the successes of Jiangxi in a new location.

THE WAR WITH JAPAN

Again, however, the prospects for Communist success seemed dismal. The Long March had decimated and exhausted their ranks and landed them in a region even more remote and impoverished than Jiangxi. Their chances of surviving a widely expected attack by Chiang Kai-shek's forces were grim. What gave the communists a new lease on life was the increasingly ferocious assault on China by Japan, a conflict that soon merged into the larger struggles of World War II. Growing pressure throughout the 1930s turned into a full-scale invasion in 1937, and within a year Japan had occupied eastern China—including most of the major industrial centers and the country's most fertile land—in a brutal and rapacious campaign. The Japanese invasion destroyed Guomindang control over much of the country and forced it to retreat to a new capital at Chongqing, a thousand miles up the Yangzi River. There the GMD lost touch with its urban sources of support and found itself even more dependent on conservative landlords. And Japanese aggression forced the reluctant GMD into a "united front" with the Communist Party to ensure a unified national defense. Although frequently violated, the "united front" eased the pressure on the beleaguered CCP.

The war years (1937–1945) witnessed a spectacular reversal of CCP fortunes. By the end of the war in 1945, the party had grown from a mere 40,000 members in 1937 to 1.2 million, while the People's Liberation Army or the Red Army had mushroomed to 900,000 men, supported by an additional 2 million militia troops. Communists controlled much of northern China, with a population of some 90 million people, and stood ready to confront the GMD on more nearly equal terms. How had such a dramatic transformation of the party's position occurred?

COMMUNISTS AS NATIONALISTS.   One answer to this question involves the vigor with which communist military forces waged the struggle against the Japanese invaders. Using guerilla warfare techniques pioneered in Jiangxi, the Red Army established itself behind enemy lines and, despite periodic setbacks, offered a measure of protection and security to many Chinese faced with Japanese atrocities. CCP aggressiveness in confronting the invaders gained the communists a reputation as ardent defenders of the nation as well as social reformers. In this way, the CCP attracted support not only from peasants but from many others—intellectuals, middle-class urban dwellers, even some businessmen—who regarded themselves as Chinese nationalists. Furthermore, the Red Army, unlike most other military forces in Chinese history, treated civilians decently, generally paying for supplies rather than seizing them, behaving respectfully toward women, and even helping out in the fields.

MOBILIZING PEASANTS.   During the war, the CCP moderated but did not abandon its efforts to address peasant grievances. For a time, the party stopped outright confiscation of landlord property and limited itself to reducing rents, taxes, and interest charges for the peasants in order to minimize class conflict and attract as many people as possible to the struggle against Japan. Elections permitted all adult villagers to vote for delegates to local and regional councils, thus involving ordinary people in political life. And in areas controlled by the CCP, mass campaigns aimed at increasing production, teaching literacy to adults, and mobilizing women for the struggle brought large numbers of people into a wider world than they had known before. Even these "moderate" policies were revolutionary, for they brought both a nationalist and a socialist consciousness to many Chinese peasants. And they marked a distinct break with the intense localism of the past and with older patterns of economic and political domination by the gentry.

As the war drew to a close, the party returned to more radical action. Teams of communist operatives called *cadres* encouraged poor peasants to "speak bitterness" in public meetings, to "struggle" with their landlords, and to "settle accounts" with them. In the process, men and women who had long been passive and inarticulate in the face of landlord oppression became politically conscious and active, and many landlords lost their property and often their lives. Thus the CCP addressed directly the twin problems of modern Chinese history—foreign imperialism and social injustice.

The war years also enabled the CCP to vastly strengthen itself as an organization and to deepen its connections with rural life. A distinctly Chinese communist ideology, centered on the writings of Mao, was hammered into the rapidly growing number of party members and cadres in endless meetings and study sessions in which people were expected to publicly criticize themselves and others for various failings. Intellectuals and party cadre were sent "to the villages" where they worked directly with peasants in an effort to overcome their elitist tendencies and cultural snobbery. The creation of mass organizations for young people, women, and workers was yet another way of bringing the party's message directly to ordinary people. And in what was called the "mass line," Mao required communist officials to listen carefully to peasant demands and then to reformulate these demands in terms of the party's socialist goals. Thus the CCP rooted itself deeply among rural villagers in a way that the Bolsheviks in Russia were never in a position even to attempt.

THE FAILURE OF THE GUOMINDANG

But did the CCP win the struggle for China or did the Guomindang lose it? At virtually every stage in their 27-year rivalry, the GMD seemed to possess greater resources and decisive advantages. They largely destroyed the CCP's urban bases in 1927 and then chased them out of Jiangxi in 1934. For almost a decade (1928–1937) the GMD governed a largely unified China, far longer than the Provisional Government had ruled Russia. And the regime did have some achievements to its credit. Roads, railroads, light industry, a banking system, medical facilities, universities, electric grids, and airline, telegraph, and telephone service— all of these indicators of modernity grew substantially under GMD rule. But they were largely limited to major urban areas and had little effect in the vast regions of rural China. Shanghai in particular became a huge, cosmopolitan, and westernized city with cinemas, shopping complexes, and sexually aggressive advertising.

DEPENDING ON THE WEALTHY.   The GMD, however, was unable or unwilling to address frontally China's central domestic problem—massive peasant poverty. A land law passed in 1930 to limit rents to 37% of the harvest went almost wholly unenforced. This reluctance to tackle the problem of land reform derived from the class basis of GMD support. The party's center of gravity was urban, and its rural support came largely from the gentry landlords who felt deeply threatened by efforts to improve peasant life. Furthermore, many warlords had been absorbed into the GMD rather than thoroughly destroyed. Their remaining power in the countryside limited the ability of the central government to act effectively or even to collect adequate taxes. Fear of communism likewise inhibited effective action because those advocating reform risked being identified as communists. Chiang Kai-shek, it seemed, was more interested in destroying the CCP militarily than in addressing the social and economic conditions that generated the communists' support.

During the war against Japan, Chiang's forces fought vigorously, but largely in defensive actions. Isolated in the interior of China, Chiang and his commanders were reluctant to take the offensive against the Japanese, saving their strength for an expected showdown with the communists. Thus, the CCP, far more aggressive in the struggle against the invaders, emerged as the primary champion of Chinese nationalism. Massive corruption among GMD officials, incompetent military leadership, and terrible mistreatment of both civilians and their own troops further eroded GMD support and contrasted sharply with the performance of the CCP.

CIVIL WAR.   These weaknesses came into play as outright civil war between the GMD and CCP resumed following the Japanese defeat in 1945. Even then, however, the initial advantage seemed to lie with the Guomindang. Their forces outnumbered those of the CCP by four or five to one, and the communists had no air force and few heavy guns. Furthermore, the GMD had received a great deal of international, especially American, support throughout much of the 1940s. But the GMD regime was by that time increasingly a hollow shell, and within a few years communist forces swept to victory and Chiang Kai-shek retreated to Taiwan in defeat. The communists' revolutionary program of "land to the tiller" and cancellation of all debts clearly appealed to many peasants. And their standing as ardent nationalists and anti-imperialists, coupled with a reputation for honest and effective government, won them considerable support among intellectuals and urban dwellers from various classes. These achievements made it possible for Mao Zedong, in October 1949, to enter Beijing in triumph, where he proclaimed the communist victory and the founding of the People's Republic of China by declaring that "the Chinese people have stood up."

CONCLUSION: UNEXPECTEDNESS AND CONJUNCTURE

Because historians know the outcomes of the stories they tell, it is easy to assume in retrospect that those outcomes were always "in the cards." But few people in early 1917 Russia, and not many in China between 1911 and the early 1940s, could have imagined their countries in communist hands. Despite the poverty, oppression, class conflict, and foreign imperialism that they endured, other outcomes seemed far more likely. The communist victories urge us to ponder the role of accidents or unexpected events in the historical process. Had World War I not intervened, might the tsarist system have preserved itself? After all, the tsarist government had initiated modest political reforms and quite serious economic and social changes. Even Lenin feared that those actions might undermine the possibility of revolution. Or if the Provisional Government had taken Russia out of the war immediately, could the Bolshevik takeover have been avoided? If the Japanese invasion of China occurred a few years later, might Chiang Kai-shek have eliminated the beleaguered communist forces? What would have happened had Mao Zedong died on the Long March or had Lenin been arrested in 1917? Without the Bolshevik victory in Russia, could the Chinese revolution have ended in a communist triumph? Although we cannot rerun the tape of history, such questions remind us about the surprising and unexpected character of much of human history.

They also remind us about the importance of what historians call "conjuncture"—the more or less simultaneous occurrence of various events and processes. Clearly no one "cause" explains the Russian or Chinese revolutions. Understanding how things came together at roughly the same time is a more useful way of grasping these complex revolutions. For example, it was the coinciding of foreign imperialism, rural misery, the Bolshevik example, the Japanese invasion, and GMD weaknesses that led to the communist victory in China. Remove any one of these elements and the outcome would likely have been different.

However we explain the Russian and Chinese upheavals, their revolutionary significance is clear. But the collapse of the old imperial states and the subsequent communist victories represented only the start of a much longer and more fundamental transformation as the new revolutionary regimes now began to construct for the first time in world history modern socialist societies.

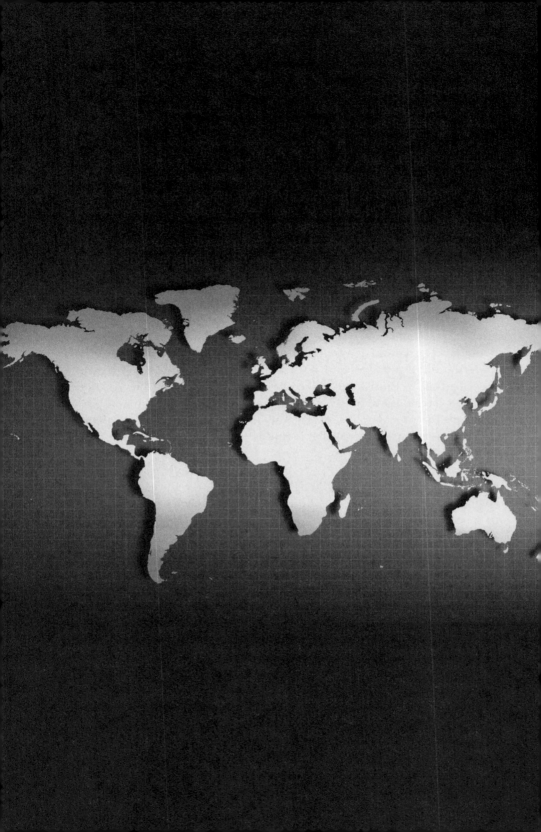

BUILDING SOCIALISM ALONE: STALINISM AND THE SOVIET EXPERIMENT

> **GETTING STARTED ON CHAPTER THREE:** As the world's first large-scale socialist society, the Soviet Union raises many questions for historians. What did it mean, in practice, to "build socialism"? In what ways did Soviet society resemble modernizing western societies and in what ways was it distinctive? What held this socialist order together? And perhaps most important, why did this experiment in building socialism, conceived as a more humane alternative to capitalism, become such a repressive, violent, and brutal regime?

Once firmly established in power, the Communist Parties of the Soviet Union and China faced enormous tasks. The first was reconstruction from the devastation of years, or even decades, of foreign aggression, civil war, and revolutionary violence. And beyond reconstruction lay the multiple tasks of modernization, of catching up in technology and production to the more developed capitalist countries. Communists, of course, were firm believers in modernity and progress, and so they sought to stimulate economic growth, to promote industrial development, and to foster scientific and technological education. They also needed to defend their countries—and their hard-won revolutions—from external capitalist threats by modernizing their military forces. In these ways, communist regimes had goals similar to those of other "developing countries" during the twentieth century.

But communist countries sought a uniquely *socialist* modernity, quite distinct from the modernization programs of other "developing countries" such as Turkey, India, Indonesia, or Nigeria. In their own understanding, this commitment to socialism put their countries in the vanguard of human progress, far ahead of the exploitative and imperialist nations of the West. Building socialism meant a frontal attack on long-standing inequalities of class and gender, the prevention of new inequalities as the process of modern development unfolded, and the promotion of cultural values of selflessness and collectivism which could support a socialist society. In creating new societies, these communist regimes hoped to mold new men and women, weaning or wrenching them away from the passivity, localism, and religious superstitions of their old societies (what the communists called "feudalism") as well as from the competitiveness, individualism, and materialism of an emerging capitalism.

Such efforts to radically transform both human society and human consciousness on a massive scale mark the Soviet and Chinese regimes as a distinctive element of twentieth-century world history. They posed an alternative vision of modern society that fundamentally challenged the prevailing capitalist/democratic values of the West. They paved the way for enormously powerful, oppressive, and intrusive states and for human suffering of epic proportions. And they generated great conflicts within both Communist Parties as their leaders hammered out policies to modernize their societies and to create socialism at the same time.

THE FIRST SOCIALIST SOCIETY

Karl Marx would have been horrified! He had imagined that socialist societies would be constructed only where industrial capitalism had already generated great wealth. And he envisaged an international socialist revolution all across the developed capitalist world. Contrary to all of this, the leaders of the Soviet Union in the early 1920s were proposing to create the world's first socialist society in a still very backward country that had only begun to industrialize. Worse yet, World War I, and the revolutionary violence that followed, had largely destroyed what little modernity Russia had achieved as its factories closed, its skilled working class scattered to country villages, and its educated elite fled abroad or perished in the revolution. Despite Lenin's fervent hopes, no socialist revolutions took hold in western Europe to rescue and assist the battered Soviet Union. A solitary socialist island in a sea of hostile capitalist countries, the Soviet Union was condemned to build socialism alone.

If this were not enough, the Communist Party's brutality and oppression had already alienated many of its strongest supporters. By 1920, scattered groups of peasants, workers, and soldiers were in virtual insurrection against the fledgling communist state. In 1921, a disastrous famine struck parts of the country, killing almost 5 million people. Furthermore, the revolution's charismatic leader, Lenin, suffered a series of strokes, became increasingly incapacitated, and died in early 1924. This triggered a behind-the-scenes struggle for power among the Communist Party's leading figures. This leadership crisis coincided with a bitter internal debate on how, precisely, socialism should be constructed. Neither Marx nor Lenin had left a blueprint, and the task itself was unprecedented in world history. It would be hard to imagine worse circumstances in which to undertake the socialist transformation of the world's largest country.

STARTING SLOW: THE NEW ECONOMIC POLICY

No wonder then that Lenin and the Communist Party leadership chose caution for much of the 1920s. Called the New Economic Policy, or NEP, this cautious approach recognized, reluctantly, that the country was not ready for serious socialism and that a battered economy badly needed a chance to revive. Thus, the forced requisition of grain from peasants, which had driven many to the point of revolt, was replaced by a fixed tax, and farmers, owning their land as private property, could now sell their surplus on the open market. Private traders and small businesses were allowed to operate freely. Even foreign investors—the much hated capitalists—were permitted to enter the country, although few chose to do so. The state controlled the "commanding heights" of the economy, such as banks and large industries; however, much of the country's economy was free to operate on market, or capitalist, principles. Under these moderate policies, the Soviet Union gradually recovered from the ravages of the recent past as both agricultural and industrial production revived to prewar levels by 1925. But free market opportunities generated a small and very visible class of traders and businessmen whose growing wealth and conspicuous consumption of fancy clothing, good restaurants, and prostitutes deeply offended dedicated communists. They had not made a revolution for this!

A DECADE OF COMMUNIST FEMINISM

Among the most revolutionary actions of the Soviet state during its first decade in power was an unprecedented effort to address the oppression of women. Soon after the Revolution of 1917, the new Soviet government issued a series of laws and decrees that gave women legal equality and the right to vote; made marriage a civil, rather than religious, procedure; allowed wives to keep their own family names; made divorce easy to obtain by either party; legalized abortion; and ended legal discrimination against illegitimate children. Marriage was now to be "a free union of equal citizens." It was the world's first state-directed program aimed at the emancipation of women.

ZHENOTDEL. Beyond these legal measures, the Communist Party created a Women's Department, called *Zhenotdel*, which worked to further empower women and to mobilize their support for the new regime. Women by the tens of thousands attended Zhenotdel conferences, where they learned to organize day-care centers, laundries, and clinics. Zhenotdel publications encouraged women to aspire beyond traditional roles. "Can a Woman Be a Metal Worker?" was the title of one article. The answer was yes! Zhedotdel speakers fanned out to schools, factories, and villages, bringing the message of women's emancipation to millions. In Muslim regions of Central Asia, Zhenotdel activists pushed women to remove their veils. Zhenotdel expressed the widespread belief among communists that the revolution had opened the door to the making of a whole new world.

The legacy of this state-directed feminism was mixed. Certainly millions of women were introduced to a wider world than they had known before. Basic literacy and technical education were now available to millions. Employment opportunities on farms and in factories beckoned to many as the Soviet regime came to depend on women workers for its crash program of modernization. A minority entered professions such as law, science, medicine, and teaching. But work remained sexually segregated with women in the lowest-paid positions. Furthermore, little changed in terms of household responsibilities so that most women experienced the "double burden" of housework and paid labor. Likewise in the political arena, women received legal equality and many joined the Party and its affiliated organizations, but few made it into major leadership positions. Men continued to dominate the Party, the government, and the management levels of industrial enterprises.

BACKLASH. Furthermore, Zhenotdel had stirred considerable opposition. Many male communist officials felt threatened and argued that a separate women's movement divided the workers and peasants. Peasant women themselves, after a decade of upheaval, sought the reassurance of traditional family life and resented this intrusion. Outraged Muslim men killed hundreds of Zhenotdel workers and local women who had removed their veils. This opposition contributed to the Party's decision to end Zhenotdel in 1930, declaring that the "women's question" had been solved. Thereafter, the state offered rather less direct support to women and withdrew some of the earlier assistance by forbidding legal abortion and making divorce more difficult. From the viewpoint of Josef Stalin, now the country's undisputed leader, the Soviet Union needed to focus its undivided attention on the massive effort of "socialist construction," undistracted by divisive gender issues.

STALINIST SOCIALISM

THE RISE OF STALIN

As the 1920s drew to a close, many in the Party began to question the NEP approach. At the same time, Josef Stalin emerged from the leadership struggle that followed Lenin's death as the undisputed "first among equals" in the Communist Party. Stalin was not a Russian, but a Georgian, born into an impoverished and brutal family; he had joined the Bolsheviks as a young man and gradually rose within its ranks. Though he played only a modest role in the Revolution of 1917, he emerged as one of the central figures in the Party's leadership with special responsibility in the administrative side of party life and was known as "Comrade Index File." At the end of his life, Lenin became disillusioned with Stalin's crudity and brutality and recommended his removal from a leadership position. But with Lenin's death, Stalin maneuvered skillfully among the various factions and claimed, with some success, to be Lenin's most faithful follower.

CHANGING DIRECTIONS.   Although he had earlier supported the moderate policies of NEP, Stalin, by the late 1920s, became a spokesman for a major change in direction for the party and the country. It was now time, he argued, to abandon the cautious policies of NEP and to get on with the revolutionary task of building real socialism in the Soviet Union. This meant ending private ownership of land and collectivizing agriculture; it meant rapid industrialization under state control; and it meant an end to the toleration of those noncommunists who had grown wealthy or prominent during the 1920s. These ideas were increasingly popular with many in the Party who were disgusted with the slow pace of change and feared that capitalism was making a comeback. By 1929, Stalin had achieved clear dominance within the Communist Party and enjoyed considerable support among its rank-and-file members.

It was largely under Stalin's leadership from 1929 until his death in 1953 that Soviet socialism was constructed—so much so that the term "Stalinism" is often used to refer to the kind of society that emerged. The process of "building socialism" in the Soviet Union generated enormous social upheavals, brutality and oppression on a gigantic scale, and victims numbering in the tens of millions. It also provided new opportunities for other millions and strengthened the country militarily, allowing it to defeat Nazi Germany in World War II and to emerge as a global superpower in the postwar world.

RAISING QUESTIONS.   For historians, the contradictions of Stalinism raise any number of questions. Some are descriptive. How should we describe Stalinist society? Was it, as the regime claimed, socialism in the making? Was it simply another variant of "modernization"? Or does the term "totalitarian" better capture the unique features of this society? Other questions are explanatory. Why did a revolution dedicated to creating a humane socialism of equality and abundance turn into such a brutal and oppressive system? What held this society together for so long? Was it simply fear and force or did Stalinism attract some real support as well? Still other questions seek to evaluate the Soviet system. How can we grasp both the crimes and the achievements of the Soviet system? Does Soviet socialism mark a radical break with the Russian past, or did it perpetuate in new forms major themes of Russia's history? These are some of the issues we will confront as we consider the making of Soviet socialism.

SOCIALISM IN THE COUNTRYSIDE: THE COLLECTIVIZATION OF AGRICULTURE

THE CASE FOR COLLECTIVE AGRICULTURE.   The early Soviet Union was still an overwhelmingly rural and agricultural country. If socialism was to be a reality, it had to embrace the countryside. But the revolution of 1917 had given peasants the land as private property and had, ironically, strengthened the traditional village commune, or *mir*, with its individual and widely scattered strips of private farmland. Communists had always viewed this arrangement as inefficient, backward, and temporary. Sooner or later it must give way to large-scale, mechanized agriculture on collective farms where private property would be a distant memory. Almost everyone assumed that rural socialism would occur gradually and voluntarily as the Party persuaded peasants to give up their individual plots and join larger collective farms equipped with tractors and other modern machinery.

GRAIN CRISIS.   By the late 1920s, however, the government was increasingly unable to secure the grain it needed from individual peasant farms to feed the cities and the soldiers and to sell abroad in return for machinery. With few consumer goods available, peasants had little incentive to sell their grain for cash. But in Stalin's view, this grain crisis was a direct challenge to Soviet power, for it held back the country's industrialization efforts. Responsibility for this crisis, Stalin declared, lay with the rich peasants, or *kulaks,* who deliberately withheld their grain and insisted on higher prices. To Stalin it meant class war against an incipient capitalist enemy in rural areas. How could the Party crush this enemy and seize control of the countryside where real communists were vanishingly rare? His answer was rapid collectivization—by force if necessary—and the total elimination of the *kulaks.* The moderate policies of NEP were over. The Revolution had resumed and "Socialist construction" had begun in earnest!

ENDING PRIVATE AGRICULTURE.   Between 1929 and 1932, collectivization unfolded explosively all across the Soviet Union as a centuries-old way of life was destroyed. Rural party officials, aided by thousands of urban party activists, fanned out in teams to Soviet villages, using a combination of promises and threats to "persuade" peasants to sign documents enrolling themselves in a collective farm. By doing so, they gave up their private strips of land, their livestock, their machinery, and their stores of grain. For many of its young organizers, collectivization was part of a grand effort to build a new society. One young woman wrote to a friend:

> I am off in villages with a group of other brigadiers organizing *kolhozy* [collective farms]. It is a tremendous job, but we are making amazing progress . . . [O]ur *muzhik* [peasant] is yielding to persuasion. He is join- ing the *kolhozy* and I am confident that in time not a peasant will remain on his own land. We shall yet smash the last vestiges of capital- ism and forever rid ourselves of exploitation . . . The very air here is afire with a new spirit and a new energy."[1]

For peasants, it was a very different story. Millions of slightly better- off peasants, branded as *kulaks,* lost everything and were shipped off to distant labor camps or industrial sites, or in some cases were arrested and shot. Those who remained, often fearing being labeled a *kulak,* reluc- tantly joined the collective farm. An American observer reported a conversation with one such peasant:

> We are not learned; we are not wise. But a little self-respect we have and we like the feeling of independence. Today we feel like working, and we work. Tomorrow we feel like lying down, and we lie down . . . We do as we please. But in the *kolhoz,* brother, it is do-as-you- are-told, like a horse . . . or you'll get it hard, a stroke or two of the whip on bare flesh . . . We'll wither away on the socialist farm, like grass torn out by the roots.[2]

RESISTANCE.   Widely viewed as a return to serfdom, collectivization took place against enormous resistance. Often led by village women, groups of peasants confronted party organizers, sometimes killed them, and at least for a time refused to join the *kolhoz.* They slaughtered and ate huge numbers of their cattle, pigs, sheep, and chickens rather than turn them over to the collective farm. Once inside the collective, resistance continued in the form of legal appeals and petitions to authorities and widespread indifference to their work responsibilities. One organizer in 1930 wrote that "the people were so repulsed by the forced collectivization of farms that they were consumed by apathy."[3] Although this scattered and uncoordinated resistance could not prevent collectivization, it forced the communist government to make some minor concessions. Peasants were allowed to keep cows, pigs, and chickens as private property, to farm a small plot of land for their own use, and to sell their produce in nearby "farmers' markets." For many, these private plots were essential for survival, as the collective farms did not produce enough surplus, beyond their obligations to the state, to keep their members alive.

FAMINE.   The immediate outcome of the collectivization effort was grim indeed. Famine on a massive scale hit the country's breadbasket in the early 1930s, as state authorities demanded amounts of grain beyond what peasants were able or willing to supply. Some 5 million people died. One peasant described the situation in her village to a party official:

> I will not tell you about the dead. I'm sure you know. The half-dead, the nearly dead are even worse. There are hundreds of people in Petrovo bloated with hunger. I don't know how many die every day. Many are so weak that they no longer come out of their houses. A wagon goes around now and then to pick up the corpses. We've eaten everything we could lay our hands on—cats, dogs, field mice, birds . . . The trees have been stripped of their bark, for that too has been eaten. And the horse manure has been eaten. Yes, the horse manure. We fight over it. Sometimes there are whole grains in it.[4]

Over the long term, collectivization enabled the state to capture the grain supplies it needed for industrialization, but the price was high—a perpetually inefficient agriculture as a demoralized and resentful peasantry had little incentive to work hard. In 1971 an observer described the results:

> The collective farm "serf" discharges his labor obligation to the "master" carelessly, grudgingly. He refuses to concern himself with the fertility of the "collective" land. It is not his. He does not see the public weeds, nor the rust on the collective machine, nor the private cow that grazes just inside the collective cornfield. He steals from the collective or habitually turns a blind eye when his fellows do so.[5]

FIGURE 3-1 INDUSTRIALIZATION AND WOMEN:
The tractor came to symbolize Soviet industrial success and the woman driver represented the communist liberation of women.

How unique was the Soviet experience of collectivization, considered in world historical terms? After all, modernization has everywhere involved the destruction of traditional peasant societies as industries and cities siphoned off millions from the countryside. And small-scale farming with horses and scythes has often given way to much larger, more efficient farms using fertilizers, tractors, and combines. In these ways, Soviet collectivization paralleled global trends. But in the Soviet Union, what was elsewhere an extended process measured in decades or centuries was compressed into a few years. Furthermore, it was brutally imposed by state authorities, and it resulted in an ineffective state-run collective farming system rather than private commercial agriculture. The creation of rural socialism in the USSR was in these respects a distinctive and tragic process.

INDUSTRIALIZATION SOVIET STYLE

Collectivization represented one element in the "Great Turn" toward socialism that the Soviet Union took in the late 1920s. A second was industrial development. Marx had assumed that capitalism would have already done that job, but Russian backwardness required Communists themselves to undertake this massive task. During the next dozen years (1928–1940), the Soviet Union charted a course toward industrialization that differed sharply from earlier capitalist patterns and that decisively marked the character of Soviet socialism.

A DISTINCTIVE INDUSTRIALIZATION.   What distinguished Soviet efforts most clearly from European or American industrialization was the role of the state and planning. The entire industrial enterprise in the USSR was owned by the state, and every worker was a state employee. Furthermore, state planning agencies, centered in Moscow, determined every last detail of the process in a series of Five Year Plans—where factories and mines would be located, what they would produce and in what quantities, where they would find their supplies, to whom they would sell their products, and at what price. All of those thousands of decisions made by many private owners and managers in capitalist countries were determined in the Soviet Union broadly by Communist Party leaders and in detail by planning agency bureaucrats. The great advantage of centralized planning was the ability to establish clear priorities and allocate resources to those projects. In Stalin's thinking the priority was clear—heavy industry such as coal, iron, steel, and machinery at the expense of light or consumer industries such as housing or clothing.

"WE REFUSE TO BE BEATEN."   The international situation lent great urgency to such thinking. The Soviet Union was almost entirely alone in the world. Hostile capitalist powers had intervened in the Civil War in 1919–21 on the side of the Party's enemies, and a "war scare" in 1927 suggested to Stalin that another attack was imminent. The rise of the Nazis in Germany and militarism in Japan by the early 1930s meant serious threats to both the east and west. Stalin summed up the case for crash industrialization in this way:

> To slacken the tempo would mean falling behind. And those who fall
> behind will get beaten . . . No, we refuse to be beaten. One feature of
> the history of old Russia was the continual beating she suffered
> because of her backwardness. She was beaten by the Mongol
> Khans . . . by the Turkish Beys . . . by the Swedish feudal lords . . . by
> British and French capitalists . . . by Japanese barons . . . That is why we
> must no longer lag behind . . . We are fifty to a hundred years behind
> the advanced countries. We must make good this distance in ten years.
> Either we shall do it, or we shall go under.[6]

With Stalin insisting on rapid industrialization, planners and party officials competed to announce ever higher targets for industrial production. To fulfill or exceed production quotas became the expectation for managers. Failure often meant accusations of "sabotage" or "wrecking" with fearful consequences. The Five Year Plan, ran one slogan, must be completed in four!

SUCCESS?   This emphasis on speedy completion of huge projects meant that careful and rational planning, at least early in the process, was out the window. Waste and confusion were everywhere, little care was taken to protect either the environment or the workers, and the most extreme goals were never met. Nonetheless, the planning process succeeded after a fashion. During the 1930s, the Soviet Union experienced remarkable rates of economic growth; whole new cities and industrial complexes such as Magnitogorsk emerged in remote areas of the country. Huge hydroelectric dams crossed the country's rivers. Millions made their way from rural villages to urban factories, and a rapidly expanding system of technical and scientific education gave many of them the opportunity to move up in the new Soviet society. A process of industrialization that had taken the Americans and west Europeans 50 years or more to achieve, the Soviet Union had accomplished in 10!

But the clearest evidence of success occurred during World War II. In that epic conflict, the Soviet Union's new factories actually out-produced Germany. They provided the economic foundations for the country's victory over Hitler and for its emergence as one of the world's superpowers after the war. That victory, although purchased at the price of some 27 million deaths, remained for decades among the chief supports of the Soviet system. "The fact is," wrote one such supporter, "that in 30 years under Stalin's guidance . . ., we covered the road from the wooden plow to the atomic reactor. The fact is that we overcame all industrial backwardness, and if that had not been done, the last war would not have been won."[7]

SOCIALIST WORKERS

What kind of society emerged from these gigantic upheavals of collectivization and industrial development? How might we compare Soviet society to that of western industrial countries? And how did Soviet society measure up to the socialist ideals of Marx and Lenin?

A GROWING PROLETARIAT. Like industrializing countries everywhere, the Soviet Union experienced rapid urbanization and the growth of a factory working class. But because this occurred in the 1930s, it meant that while when millions of American and European workers lost their jobs in the Great Depression, the Soviet Union was moving toward full employment. But the Soviet working class differed in many ways from its western counterpart. A part of its labor force was distinctly unfree. Prisoners in the network of labor camps strung all across the country provided cheap labor for mining, canal and road building, and the timber industry in the most remote and difficult parts of the country. Furthermore, the Soviet working class was far more heavily female—women made up about 39% of the nonagricultural labor force by 1939. And the working class was celebrated by the regime. After all, a socialist Soviet Union claimed to be a workers' state with the proletariat as its "leading class." Whereas wealthy industrialists were folk heroes of industrial America, in the Soviet Union, workers in their steel mills and peasants astride their tractors were held up as models in heroic statues, media stories, awards, and honors. At least in the rhetoric of the regime, individual workers were making a contribution to a world-changing process—the building of socialism—rather than simply making a living for themselves and their families.

URBAN HARDSHIPS.   But the reality of workers' lives often contradicted such appealing images. Work was often dangerous. Most workers were peasants who only just arrived from their rural villages and were unaccustomed to city life and industrial regimentation. Housing was in very short supply. Many workers in remote sites lived in barracks, or even tents for a time. Those fortunate enough to find apartments usually had to share kitchen and bathroom facilities with other families. Furthermore, wages were low and consumer goods scarce as the state diverted available resources to heavy industry. As a result, people constantly left their workplaces as workers scrambled to find slightly better jobs.

THE ABSENCE OF PROTEST.   But these conditions did not stimulate much active worker protest. While western workers organized unions, went on strike, engaged in sometimes violent protest, and joined socialist parties, their Soviet counterparts were largely quiet. In theory, of course, the workers controlled the state, and so protest by workers against their own state was defined as illegitimate. As a practical matter, the pervasive presence of the Communist Party and various police agencies made active protest dangerous in the extreme. Some, however—no doubt a declining number as time went on—were genuinely devoted to building socialism. An American engineer in the Soviet Union during the 1930s commented: "Tens of thousands of people were enduring the most intense hardships in order to build blast furnaces, and many of them did it willingly, with boundless enthusiasm . . ."[8] Others found advantages in the new cities—education, advancement, vacations, pensions, cultural opportunities. If nothing else, it was better than life in the countryside. One recent migrant to the city wrote in 1933: "Here on the collective farm I am living the life of a badly fed animal. I have been robbed of my grain and all my reserves. My cattle have been taken . . . Life is impossible. I go to town, get a job as a workman, and there will be fed."[9] Finally, Communist Party control of cultural expression made it possible to define a way of thinking to which there were few real alternatives. Work was constantly celebrated as the primary form of social identity, and various means of rewarding good work and shaming poor performance reinforced this identity. Capitalism—widely despised and bogged down in depression—had little appeal.

A SOCIALIST ELITE

Alongside a distinctly Soviet working class emerged an equally distinctive Soviet elite—high-ranking party officials; administrators and bureaucrats within the many government agencies that ran the country; and managers and technical specialists, mostly engineers, who staffed the rapidly proliferating industrial enterprises. Largely male and with a narrow technical education, these were people who had moved up within the Soviet system and clearly had benefited from it. This "new class" was privileged in many ways—they had access to special stores, hospitals, schools, and apartments; they took luxurious vacations and had access to weekend cottages in the countryside. They had servants and chauffeurs and enjoyed high social status. But these privileges derived from their positions in the Soviet establishment, not from their own wealth or ownership of property, as in capitalist societies. And those positions were highly insecure. People could be, and frequently were, purged from the Party, arrested, sent off to the labor camps, or even executed.

SOVIET CONSERVATISM.   This combination of privilege and insecurity generated a surprising conservatism among the elite of a supposedly revolutionary country. They imitated the manners and fashions of the formerly despised bourgeois and aristocratic classes; they honored and sought to acquire the culture associated with prerevolutionary figures in art, music, literature, and dance. Much later, a high Soviet official described what was required of the elite: "Sit tight, do your work, and take advantage of the privileges and benefits offered to you. Don't try to yank the fishhook out of your mouth or it will be certain death."[10]

In fact, by the mid-1930s, the Stalinist regime as a whole emphasized order and tradition in many spheres. In education this meant a prescribed curriculum, school uniforms, and heroic historical figures in place of the more experimental policies of the 1920s. In family policy it meant tightening up the requirements for divorce, forbidding abortion, and emphasizing traditional gender roles in sharp contrast to the more "feminist" agenda of the post-1917 decade. In the economic realm it meant abandoning socialist equality and promoting wage differentials as an incentive for hard work. Workers who produced well above the established norms received both material rewards and high status.

SOVIET INEQUALITIES.   But was this the communism of which Marx had dreamed? Stalin argued that the country was not yet ready for full communist equality. Production was the priority, and toward that end, various kinds of inequality could be tolerated and even encouraged. Some scholars have suggested that a kind of implicit bargain had been struck. The elite could enjoy its privileges so long as its members rendered absolute loyalty to the regime and the party line. Furthermore, industrial society of any kind—capitalist or socialist—perhaps requires an elite of technical specialists and managers to operate an enormously complex economic system. However we might explain it, a new social and political hierarchy emerged that reminded many of the inequalities of the old tsarist society. In 1934 a worker expressed this widespread feeling:

> How can we liquidate classes, if new classes have developed, with the only difference being that they are not called classes? Now there are the same parasites who live at the expense of others . . . There is a huge apparat of factory administrators where idlers sit. There are many administrative workers who travel about in cars and get three to four times more than the worker. These people live in the best conditions and live at the expense of the labor of the working class.[11]

To this worker, and many like him, the socialist vision had been betrayed.

THE SOVIET STATE

A new inequality was not the only deviation from communist ideals. Marx had argued that individual freedom under socialism would grow and that the coercive power of the state would "wither away." Nothing of the kind occurred. Instead, there emerged a new kind of political authority—the party-state—which deeply penetrated and largely dominated Soviet society. Its claim to virtually total authority is reflected in the label so often attached to it—totalitarian.

This unique political system had two major elements—the state itself and the party. The legislative branch of the state derived those grassroots councils, or "soviets," which had sprung up during the revolution. Within a few years, however, these lively, popular, and revolutionary bodies had lost their insurgent spirit and their independence to become the largely powerless legislative branch of the new Union of Soviet Socialist Republics, and they remained so until the late 1980s.

Soviets were organized on every level—villages, towns and cities, regions, provinces, republics and the union—some 50,000 in all. The hierarchy of soviets culminated in the Supreme Soviet of the USSR, the country's national parliament. Elected periodically from a single list of unopposed party-prescribed candidates, their members' formal function was legislative; in fact, they generally passed in rubber stamp unanimity the laws and the Five-Year Plans developed by the party leadership.

The executive or administrative branch of the Soviet state was embodied in a huge and hugely complex bureaucracy. This is perhaps not surprising because the Soviet state, from the late 1920s on, abolished private property in favor of state ownership, undertook the enormous task of industrializing the country, and was the effective employer of virtually everyone. Thus, ministries and "state committees" proliferated. Some were responsible for ordinary functions of government (health, education, defense, justice), but the majority served to manage the economy. Some were involved with planning, and dozens managed some branch of the economy: electronics, oil, automobiles, light industry, construction, chemicals. They composed an immense bureaucratic machine with hundreds of thousands of employees. Their task was nothing less than running the entire country.

THE COMMUNIST PARTY

But the Soviet state was itself controlled by the Communist Party, which took responsibility for establishing policy, appointing people to important state positions, checking up on the implementation of policy, and generally leading the march to socialism. It claimed to be "the leading and guiding force in Soviet society." But over the course of several decades under Stalin's leadership, what had once been a revolutionary party that encouraged debate and provided real leadership became an obedient agent of a tyrannical regime. It was another huge bureaucratic machine, paralleling and penetrating state institutions and focusing primarily on preserving the careers and privileges of its elite leaders.

In early 1917, that party had about 24,000 members, and it peaked in the late 1980s with some 20 million, almost 10% of the adult population. Recruited with considerable care and subject to a rigorous screening process, party members were to be the country's best and brightest. Personally upright, well schooled in Marxist-Leninist ideology, model workers, and active in public life, party members were to be the disciplined exemplars of socialist society in the making. In return they acquired, in varying degrees, elite status in that society. It generally meant public respect, a measure of visibility, and important contacts. At its higher levels it provided preferential access to housing, scarce goods, better schools, travel opportunities, and certain jobs.

Clearly, not all party members were equal. The vast majority were quite ordinary people who lived and worked much like their nonparty neighbors. But they paid party dues, attended and organized endless meetings, discussion groups, and lectures, got out the vote at election time, and otherwise took part in the routines of party life. The real party elite, known as the *apparat*, were those actually employed by the party itself in its top positions.

The party penetrated Soviet society through an elaborate hierarchical organization. At its base were Primary Party Organizations (PPOs), party cells organized at virtually every workplace in the country—factories, collective farms, shops, restaurants, schools, and offices. Members of these cells exercised the party's "right of control," monitoring the operation of their respective enterprises, keeping alert for problems, inefficiencies, and violations of party policy. They represented the local eyes and ears of the ever-present party.

Above the PPOs rose a series of party committees at each level of administrative organization—district, region, republic, and all-union. The whole system culminated at the national level in Moscow. There the leading figures hammered out the main lines of policy, and the *apparat* supervised and coordinated state agencies and managed the party's internal affairs. Within the Party, an almost military style of discipline prevailed, with lower organs absolutely subordinate to higher ones.

IDEOLOGY

MARXISM-LENINISM.   Underpinning this entire system was a single official ideology. Although all societies generate legitimating ideas and values, the Soviet Union was remarkable for the extent to which such an ideology was elaborated, made explicit, and propagated through the educational system and state-controlled media. This set of ideas, known as Marxism-Leninism, explained the origins of the Soviet Union in an inevitable and heroic revolution led by the Bolsheviks, described the present as a period of hard work to build a socialist society, and projected a utopian future of communist prosperity and equality. In the global struggle against capitalism and imperialism, the Soviet Union had a mission of world historical significance. Here was an attempt to create a new mythology, worldview, or even a substitute religion. It provided "correct" and "scientific" answers in virtually every area of life. Art, literature, music, film, and history—all of these cultural expressions had to hew closely to the party line. Deviation from it meant arrest and often execution.

OFFICIAL ATHEISM.   Accompanying the propagation of this new ideology was an assault on the old ideology—religion. Many churches were closed or converted into "museums of atheism"; priests were arrested; church property was seized; atheistic propaganda was pushed by a public organization called the League of the Godless. Local "clubs" or the

FIGURE 3-2   THE STRUGGLE AGAINST RELIGION:
Combating organized religion was a part of building socialism in the Soviet Union.
In this propaganda poster, entitled "Religion is Poison: Safeguard the Children," a
child reaches toward a school while the grandmother attempts to pull her toward a
crumbling church.

Communist Party itself provided organizational alternatives to the
church. "Red weddings" and "Revolutionary funerals" could substitute
for Christian life-cycle rituals. An elaborate "cult of Lenin" established
his writings as the new scriptures, his tomb as a shrine, and his picture
or statue as new icons. New holidays such as the anniversary of the revolution, Red Army Day, and International Women's Day replaced the
many religious holidays of the Russian Orthodox Church.

A TOTALITARIAN SOCIETY?

That the Soviet political system claimed total authority and attempted
total control of society is fairly clear. But did it succeed? Historians in
recent decades have begun to question whether the term "totalitarianism" effectively describes the Soviet system. Their research has found a
great deal of bureaucratic infighting and policy debates that are at odds
with the notion of Stalin as an absolute and unquestioned dictator. Furthermore, the central leadership of the Party in Moscow had only tenuous control over its branches in the rest of the country and often had
great difficulty getting its decisions carried out. Nor did the Party rely
entirely on fear and terror in controlling Soviet society. Sometimes it

made concessions to various social groups, such as allowing collective farmers a small private plot and permitting the elite a range of quite unsocialist privileges. During World War II, the regime eased its restrictions on the church in order to gain support of religious citizens for the war effort. And the Party benefited as well from a measure of real voluntary support. Many thousands of young people volunteered for construction projects or political work in remote and difficult areas, full of enthusiasm for building socialism. And many others gained new skills, educational opportunities, and a chance to move up in society. They were grateful. One such person explained his gratitude in this way:

> I am a Tatar . . . Before October, in old tsarist Russia we couldn't even dream about education or getting a job in a state enterprise. And now I'm a citizen of the USSR. Two years ago . . . I was the first person to enter the kolkhoz and then I led the collectivization campaign . . . In 1931 I came to Magnitogorsk. From a common laborer I have turned into a skilled worker. I was elected a member of the city soviet . . . I live in a country where one feels like living and learning. And if the enemy should attack this country, I will sacrifice my life in order to destroy the enemy and save my country.[12]

But if the image of Stalin's USSR as an efficient totalitarian dictatorship based only on fear needs to be modified, the Soviet Union was clearly different from other industrialized states in Europe or the United States. There private property, competitive politics, a broad range of personal freedoms, many voluntary organizations, and the absence of an official ideology gave rise to societies quite distinct from that of a socialist Soviet Union. Perhaps the biggest difference, however, lay in the growing role that terror and violence came to play in Stalin's USSR.

THE SEARCH FOR ENEMIES: A SOVIET HOLOCAUST

To the leaders of the Communist Party, their revolution faced serious threats, not only from hostile external powers, but also from within the country. They had fought a bitter civil war with anti-communist opponents between 1918 and 1921. In the early 1920s, other socialist parties, now regarded also as enemies, were forbidden to operate and their members often arrested. Later in the decade, a trial of some 53 "bourgeois engineers" on charges of sabotage highlighted the growing suspicion with which non-communist specialists were regarded. The *kulaks* were another such enemy, and Stalin insisted that they be "liquidated as a class." As socialism approached, Stalin argued, the class struggle against internal enemies only increased.

But increasingly, the search for enemies occurred within the Party itself. Periodic "purges" expelled from the Party many thousands who were viewed as incompetent, lazy, immoral, or otherwise unworthy of party membership. More significant, perhaps, were those Communist leaders who had opposed Stalin during his rise to power. What awaited these various "enemies" included expulsion from the Party, arrest, deportation to the gulag, or labor camps, and sometimes execution. The use of force, state power, and violence was deeply embedded in Soviet life.

THE TERROR

But all of this was dwarfed by the spasm of violence—known simply as "the Terror"—that engulfed the country in the late 1930s. The public face of the Terror lay in a series of fantastic "show trials" where prominent party officials confessed to a variety of horrendous and altogether unlikely crimes—spying for foreign countries, plotting against Stalin, seeking to overturn the revolution. Virtually all of the "old Bolsheviks" associated with Lenin were caught up in this part of the Terror and eliminated. So, too, were the leading officers of the Soviet military. Far more widespread was the secret Terror. Based on suspicious associations in the past, denunciations by former colleagues, or simply bad luck, millions were arrested, usually in the dead of night, then tried and sentenced either to death or to long years in the gulag. Although high-ranking Communist officials were most vulnerable, many others were likewise swept up in the carnage—members of the intelligentsia, people with foreign connections or relatives living abroad, former kulaks and criminals, and not a few ordinary people who had uttered unguarded remarks or made the wrong enemies.

VICTIMS AND VICTIMIZERS. The number of victims is still being debated. But we know that close to a million people were executed between 1936 and 1941. Perhaps 4 or 5 million more were sent to the gulag, where they were forced to work in horrendous conditions and died in appalling numbers. Victimizers, too, were numerous as the Terror consumed the energies of a huge corps of officials, investigators, interrogators, informers, guards, and executioners.

LIVING THROUGH THE TERROR

ARREST AND INTERROGATION. What was it like to actually experience the Soviet terror? Here is the story of one woman, Irina Kakhovskaya, who was an ardent revolutionary, though not a party member. Like hundreds of thousands of others, she was caught up in the mass arrests of 1937–38 and served 17 years in prison or a labor camp. Freed in 1954, she wrote this account of her arrest and interrogation:[13]

> Early on the morning of February 8, 1937, a large group of men appeared at the door of our quiet apartment in Ufa. We were shown a search warrant and warrants for our arrest. The search was carried out in violent, pogrom-like fashion and lasted all day. Books went pouring down from the shelves; letters and papers, out of boxes. They tapped

the walls and, when they encountered hollow spots, removed the bricks. Everything was covered with dust and pieces of brick . . .

At the prison everything was aimed at breaking prisoners' spirits immediately, intimidating and stupefying them, making them feel that they were no longer human, but "enemies of the people," against whom everything was permitted. All elementary human needs were disregarded (light, air, food, rest, medical care, warmth, toilet facilities) . . .

In the tiny, damp, cold, half-lit cell were a bunk and a half bunk. The bunk was for the prisoner under investigation and on the half bunk, their legs drawn up, the voluntary victims, the informers from among the common criminals, huddled together. Their duty was never to let their neighbor out of their sight, never to let the politicals communicate with one another . . . and above all to prevent the politicals from committing suicide . . . The air was fouled by the huge wooden latrine bucket . . . No books were allowed and . . . prisoners had to sit on the bunk facing the guard's peephole so that authorities could be sure the "enemies of the people" never slumbered or dozed.

The interrogation began on the very first night . . . Using threats, endearments, promises and enigmatic hints, they tried to confuse, wear down, frighten, and break the will of each individual, who was kept totally isolated from his or her comrades . . . Later stools were removed and the victim had to simply stand for hours on end . . .

At first it seemed that the whole thing was a tremendous and terrible misunderstanding, that it was our duty to clear it up . . . But it soon became apparent that what was involved was deliberate ill will and the most cynical possible approach to the truth . . .

In the interrogation sessions, I now had several investigators in a row, and the "conveyor belt" questioning would go on for six days and nights on end . . . Exhaustion reached the ultimate limit. The brain, inadequately supplied with blood, began to misfunction . . . "Sign! We won't bother you any more. We'll give you a quiet cell and a pillow and you can sleep . . . " That was how the investigator would try to bribe a person who was completely debilitated and stupefied from lack of sleep.

Each of us fought alone to keep an honest name and save the honor of our friends, although it would have been far easier to die than to endure this hell month after month. Nevertheless the accused remained strong in spirit and, apart from the unfortunate Mayorov, not one real revolutionary did they manage to break.

IN THE CAMPS.   Following arrest and interrogation was either immediate execution, usually a single bullet in the back of the head, or long terms in the gulag, where prisoners were worked—often to death— building roads and canals, cutting timber, mining gold, and other arduous tasks. Here is one description of life in the gulag at a camp in the remote and frigid far-eastern corner of the Soviet Union called Kolyma:

The work to which I was assigned . . . went by the imposing name of "land improvement." We set out before dawn and marched in ranks of five for about three miles, to the accompaniment of shouts from the guards and bad language from the common criminals who were included in our party as a punishment for some misdeed or other. In time we reached a bleak, open field where our leader, another common criminal called Senka—a disgusting type who preyed on the other prisoners and made no bones about offering a pair of warm breeches in return for an hour's "fun and games"—handed out picks and iron spades with which we attacked the frozen soil of Kolyma until one in the afternoon. I cannot remember, and perhaps I never knew, the rational purpose this "improvement" was supposed to serve. I only remember the ferocious wind, the forty degree frost, the appalling weight of the pick, and the wild, irregular thumping of one's heart. At one o'clock we were marched back for dinner. More stumbling in and out of snowdrifts, more shouts and threats from the guards whenever we fell out of line. Back in the camp we received our longed-for piece of bread and soup and were allowed half an hour in which to huddle around the stove in the hope of absorbing enough warmth to last us halfway back to the field. After we had toiled again with our picks and spades till late in the evening, Senka would come and survey what we had done and abuse us for not doing more. How could the assignment ever be completed if we spoiled women fulfilled only thirty percent of the norm? . . . Finally a night's rest, full of nightmares, and the dreaded banging of a hammer on an iron rail which was the signal for a new day to begin.[14]

LEFT BEHIND AND WAITING.   Those who were left behind—most often wives, mothers, and children numbering in the many millions—also suffered terribly. Frequently they did not know where their loved ones were, or even if they were still alive. Sending mail or parcels to prisoners became a virtual occupation for many, requiring endlessly standing in long lines and appearing before uncaring bureaucrats to receive the necessary permissions. Anna Akhmatova, perhaps Russia's greatest modern poet, wrote eloquently about those left behind based on her own experience as the mother of an imprisoned son. In a famous introduction to her poem "Requiem," she evoked those terrible years:

> In the awful years of [the Terror], I spent seventeen months standing in line in front of various prisons in Leningrad. One day someone "recognized" me. Then a woman with blue lips, who was standing behind me . . . came out of the stupor which typified all of us and whispered into my ear (everyone there spoke only in whispers): "Can you describe this?" And I said, "I can." Then something like a fleeting smile passed over what once had been her face.[15]

The poem itself described the impact of such experiences:

> I have learned how faces fall to bone,
> how under the eyelids terror lurks
> how suffering inscribes on cheeks
> the hard lines of its cuneiform text,
> how glossy black or ash-fair locks

turn overnight to tarnished silver,
how smiles fade on submissive lips,
and fear quivers in a dry titter.
And I pray not for myself alone
but for all who stood outside the jail
in bitter cold or summer's blaze
with me under that blind red wall.[16]

EXPLAINING THE UNIMAGINABLE

Like the Nazi holocaust, the Soviet Terror has presented historians with a terrible problem of explanation. How could a socialist revolution have generated such grotesque brutality? How could the Party have turned on so many of its own clearly committed followers? Stalin and the Party leadership were clearly central in the process. They seemed to have sincerely believed that enemies abounded and that many of them had contacts with foreign power, also hostile to the Soviet Union. Stalin was convinced that his long-time party rival Leon Trotsky, now in exile, was orchestrating a vast conspiracy from abroad. In his mind, all this was a continuation of class war that threatened both the revolution and Stalin's own power and justified using ruthless methods, even if innocent people were damaged in the process. After all, it was war, and nothing less than the revolution and socialism were at stake! Furthermore, notions of conspiracy were widely accepted in the Soviet Union. Many arrested people believed that although their case was a "mistake," others were no doubt guilty as charged. Stalin's own actions had indeed created much dissatisfaction and many potential enemies, but any organized conspiracy or real threat to his power was largely a fantasy.

Beyond Stalin's fears—real or imagined—other factors provided the Terror with additional momentum. Acting from patriotism, jealousy, or fear, large numbers of people participated in "denunciations," providing authorities with information leading to further arrests. Lower-ranking party elites benefited as their seniors were denounced and eliminated. The secret police had "quotas" of arrests and often asked for permission to go beyond them as a means of demonstrating their vigilance to their superiors. Anti-elite feelings by workers and peasants, angered at the brutality and oppression of local "bosses," provided fodder for still more denunciations and accusations. Real economic problems and a widespread belief in conspiracies to wreck the fragile Soviet economy further fostered a search for scapegoats.

LEGACIES OF THE TERROR

The terror peaked in 1937–38 and then was gradually brought under control, although arbitrary arrest and execution at lower levels continued to play a role in Soviet society for years to come. The legacy of those terrible events has shaped, and haunted, Soviet society ever since. One outcome, of course, was simple fear, most prominent among high-level officials and party members. That fear became a major prop of the Soviet regime and lasted long after the overt terror had diminished. It contributed to the passivity and the reluctance to take initiative, which so many observers have noticed in Soviet life from the Politburo to the factory floor. Institutionally, Stalin's terror enhanced the role of the secret police and diminished that of the party. It also greatly increased the population of the gulag, which held some 5 million prisoners by the early 1950s. This slave labor force provided the manpower for any number of Soviet economic development projects in the most remote and inhospitable regions where free laborers were difficult to attract.

Famine, deportations, purges, arrests, executions, slave labor camps, victims numbering in the many millions—suffering on such an epic scale, and created by the regime itself, was extraordinarily difficult to square with any conception of socialism, and much of it was therefore repressed and not officially acknowledged. It produced, in the judgment of one scholar, "a nation traumatized by its own past."[17] The need to reckon with that past, to come to terms with the crimes of the Stalin era, echoed repeatedly in the decades that followed. It was among the major legacies which that era bore to the later years of the Soviet Union.

WORLD WAR II AND BEYOND: STALIN'S FINAL YEARS

DESTRUCTION UNBOUNDED.   The Second World War had a strange impact on the Soviet Union. On the one hand, it bled the country white. Some 27 million people were killed, and another 25 million were made homeless; 1,700 towns and 70,000 villages were destroyed along with some 31,000 industrial enterprises. The city of Leningrad, now St. Petersburg, lived through a siege of 900 days by German forces amid immense hardship. Many areas faced starvation as the war ended in 1945. Virtually no one remained untouched by the destruction of that epic conflict.

THE CULT OF THE WAR.   And yet, the Soviet Union had won the war! That victory, despite casualties and physical devastation almost beyond imagination, became a source of enormous pride for many people from all social classes and seemed to demonstrate the validity and necessity of Stalin's harsh measures in the 1930s. After all, the question went, would we have won the war without those measures? Furthermore, the war added a traditionalist patriotic element to Soviet identity, as Stalin invoked ancient warriors, tsarist generals, and "mother Russia" to sustain his people in that great struggle. In the decades that followed, Soviet leadership nurtured a virtual cult of the war. Memorials were everywhere. Wedding parties made pilgrimages to them and brides left their bouquets behind. May 9, Victory Day, saw elaborately orchestrated cel-ebrations. Veterans were honored and granted modest privileges. Both victim and victor, the Soviet Union had achieved its finest hour through the wise leadership of Stalin, the dedication of the party, and the heroic action of a united people and its armed forces. That was the message of the Great Patriotic War cult. For decades, those perceptions served as a major prop for the Soviet regime and a source of legitimacy for Soviet communism.

NO FRESH START.   It also meant that no fundamental changes in the Soviet system were required, and so the process of rebuilding the Soviet Union took place along the same Stalinist lines as before: a centralized command economy, priority given to the defense industry, suspicious isolation from the West, party domination of society, and a continuing search for enemies within. Many Soviet citizens had anticipated some relaxation of state and party controls after the war, but Stalin soon made it clear that no such thing was in the cards. The demands of reconstruc-tion and the new challenge of the Cold War with the United States per-suaded Stalin that yet more sacrifice, discipline, and internal vigilance were necessary. Campaigns to root out nationalism and western influ-ences in the arts and sciences imposed sharp ideological restrictions on Soviet intellectuals, particularly those of Jewish origins. Many scholars believe that Stalin was planning yet another major purge of the Party, interrupted only by his death in 1953. Thus while Germany and Japan, defeated in war, received a fresh start and substantial western aid, the Soviet Union followed its victory in war by a return to the practices of Stalinism, developed in the 1930s. The legacies of the Stalin years, there-fore, persisted well beyond the dictator's death.

CONCLUSION: EXPLAINING STALINISM

RUSSIAN ROOTS?   For historians, the problem has been how to explain the Stalinist phenomenon and the many tragedies that accompanied it. Some have sought to locate the oppressive and brutal features of Stalin-ism deep in the Russian past. The despotic authoritarianism of the tsars, along with their desperate efforts to "catch up" with the more advanced western countries, seemed to be replicated in the Stalinist era. A widely told story had Stalin's aging and infirm mother asking her son what kind of work he did. "Well, Mother," Stalin allegedly replied, "do you remem-ber the tsar? Now I'm the tsar." Furthermore the backwardness of old Russia—its wretched poverty and a superstitious peasantry only a few decades removed from serfdom—as well as it enormous size and cul-tural diversity, meant that any effort to haul it into the modern world would require a powerful state willing to force a transition that many of its uneducated people were reluctant to undertake.

THE SOCIALIST IDEA?   Other scholars, especially those ideologically opposed to communism, found the roots of Stalinism in the socialist idea itself and in the Soviet Union's revolutionary origins. The end of private property, favored by socialists of all kinds, arguably provided a foundation for a highly oppressive system by eliminating the economic independence of ordinary people. If the state employs everyone and owns everything, how can individual people oppose the state? In addition, communist dreams of perfect equality and collectivist culture are so utopian, so far from human reality, as to require great force to even approach them. And yet, they are such compelling visions that revolutionaries may feel justified in using any means—even the most brutal—to achieve them. Lenin certainly did. In this view, Lenin's fanaticism, his use of violence, his intolerance for competing ideas, and his insistence on absolute Communist Party dominance laid the foundation for Stalin's totalitarianism.

ALTERNATIVES.   But was Stalinism the only possible outcome of the Bolshevik Revolution? Lenin, after all, favored the more gradual and moderate approach of the New Economic Policy and by the end of his life had come to distrust Stalin and sought his removal from the Party's leadership. Might another leader following different policies have avoided the horrors of Stalinism? Such a viewpoint finds the roots of Stalinism in Stalin—his personality, his drive for absolute power, his inclination to see "enemies" everywhere.

STALINISM AND THE TWENTIETH CENTURY.   A final explanation for Stalinism focuses on the international context of the early twentieth century. It was a time of unparalleled violence and political ruthlessness that found expression in two world wars, in German Nazism and the holocaust, and in Japanese militarism and expansion in Asia. Many countries were altogether willing to spend their citizens' blood in the pursuit of some grand ambition. The socialist vision set out to change all this. But if the Soviet Union, as sole outpost of socialism, was to survive in such a hostile environment, perhaps dictatorial and ruthless methods were necessary, at least temporarily, as the leadership mobilized its backward and uncomprehending people to protect the fragile possibility of a socialist world. "Such an evaluation," writes one historian, "reveals that far from being the monsters they are often portrayed as, Soviet leaders such as Vladimir Lenin and Josef Stalin followed the only practical course of action to ensure the survival of their country."[18]

The debate about Stalinism continues!

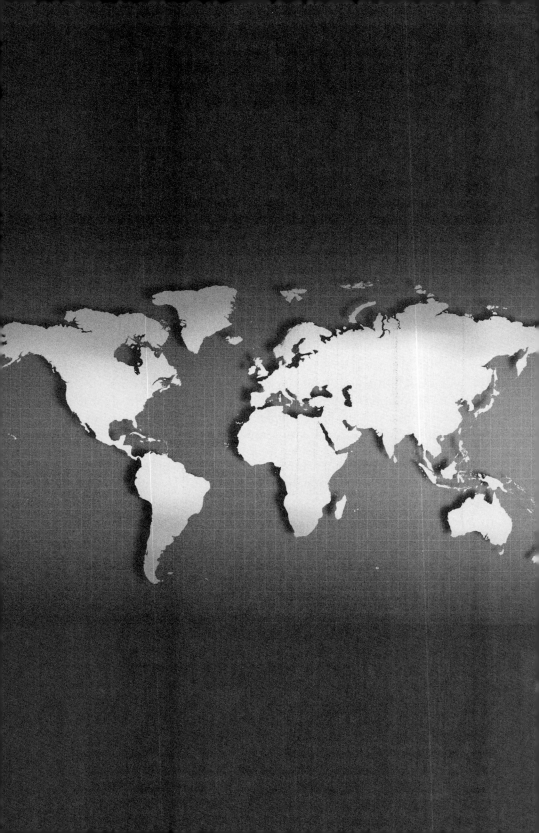

CHAPTER FOUR

MAO'S PATH: BUILDING SOCIALISM IN CHINA

GETTING STARTED ON CHAPTER FOUR: The central issue in this chapter is comparative. In what ways did Chinese efforts to construct socialism resemble those of the Soviet Union? Did the very effort to construct socialist societies impose broad similarities on the two countries? How did the Chinese process unfold differently? To what extent were the differences the product of conscious choice—a deliberate Chinese effort to avoid the mistakes of the Soviet Union? Or did the unique features of Chinese socialism reflect different cultural and historical patterns?

Some 30 years after the Bolsheviks launched the Soviet Union on the path to socialism, the Chinese Communist Party (CCP) was poised to do the same in the world's most populous country. It was 1949 and the Chinese communists, under the leadership of Mao Zedong, had triumphed in their long struggle with the Guomindang. But an even greater struggle lay ahead as the CCP made plans to transform this ancient and conflicted civilization into a modern and socialist nation.

STARTING POINTS: COMPARING CHINA AND THE SOVIET UNION

CHINESE ADVANTAGES. In some ways, China was better prepared for this enormous task than the Soviet Union had been in 1917. China's decades-long civil war was over, and the country's leadership could look to the future without fearing internal military opposition. A communist Russia, by contrast, had to survive a bitter and debilitating three year civil war before it could begin to plan seriously for building socialism.

In addition, Chinese communists came to power on the heels of victory over the Japanese in World War II, whereas the Russian communists had withdrawn their country from World War I and signed a humiliating treaty with the Germans, surrendering large chunks of territory. Many saw the Bolsheviks as traitors, but the CCP was widely praised for successfully defending the nation.

Furthermore, China faced a more hospitable international environment. In 1917, the Soviet Union, as the world's first communist country, had confronted near universal hostility from the established powers and faced the future alone. But in 1949, one of the world's superpowers—the Soviet Union—was a communist state, an ally, and a potential source of aid and experience for China. Communism seemed on the march in the late 1940s and early 1950s as Eastern Europe and North Korea also joined the communist bloc of nations, while communist parties asserted themselves in France, Italy, Vietnam, Indonesia and elsewhere.

Beyond these advantages, Chinese communists had accumulated decades of experience in governing large groups of people. By the early 1940s, they already ruled an area with 100 million inhabitants. The Bolsheviks, by contrast, had come to power almost overnight and had governed nothing larger than their own small party. As an urban-based party, they also had almost no presence in the countryside, whereas the CCP seized power with the support of the rural masses who constituted the vast majority of China's population. Even in the cities, where communists had few roots, many educated, professional, and business people, weary beyond measure of war and chaos, looked favorably on the party as more honest, patriotic, and effective than the Guomindang had been. Thus the CCP came to power with a much broader base of support than its Russian counterpart.

Finally, the CCP had perhaps fewer illusions about the difficulties that lay ahead than Russian communists had in 1917. Lenin and the Bolshevik leadership fully expected that the advanced European countries were on the edge of revolution and that a socialist Europe would come to the aid of a battered and backward Soviet Union. Nothing of the kind occurred, of course, and Mao Zedong had no such expectations. "Our past work is only the first step in a long march of ten thousand *li*," Mao wrote.[1]

CHINESE DISADVANTAGES. But China's economic backwardness was even more pronounced than that of the Soviet Union. China's manufacturing sector was half the size of prerevolutionary Russia's, while its total population was four times larger. Furthermore, its agricultural production on a per capita basis was only 20% of Russia's. Literacy and modern education were likewise far less developed in China, as was its transportation network.[2] And Chinese society had been battered for decades by conflict among regional warlords, civil war between the communists and the Guomindang, and by ferocious Japanese aggression. Even more than the Soviets, Chinese communists had to build a modern society from the ground up.

FIRST STEPS

The first priority for the CCP was not socialism but the consolidation of its power and the reconstruction of the economy. In these efforts, it made remarkable progress in the first several years of its rule (1949–1953). It was a phase of Chinese history similar to the Soviet Union's New Economic Policy in the 1920s.

CREATING A STRONG STATE

A NEW POLITICAL SYSTEM. Since the middle of the nineteenth century, China had been without a strong and effective state. The Communist Party now proceeded to create one. Like the Soviet Union, it was a party-dominated state in which the Communist Party created the state bureaucracy, defined its agenda, and supervised its operation. Mao Zedong was the acknowledged and formal leader of both the party and the government.

ENDING THE LEGACY OF IMPERIALISM. This new political system gained great credibility and legitimacy by bringing an end to the foreign domination that had divided and humiliated China for a century. Communist authorities quickly reunited the territory of China, including outlying areas of Xinjiang, Tibet, and inner Mongolia. The continuing exclusion of Hong Kong, under British control until 1997, and especially Taiwan, the offshore island to which Chiang Kai-shek and the remnants of his Guomindang forces had fled, were painful reminders of unfinished tasks. The new Chinese government also expelled the remaining foreigners, demonstrating symbolically that a century of imperialist domination of China had finally and decisively ended. These actions were very popular, even among people who had little sympathy for communists.

PENETRATING THE SOCIETY. China's new political structure sought to unify the country by providing opportunity for cooperative non-communist political groups to take part in the government, though under the clear control of the CCP. But those defined as "counter-revolutionaries"—Guomindang supporters, collaborators with Japan, active opponents of CCP rule—were treated harshly and tens of thousands were executed. The rapid growth of the Party (from about

FIGURE 4-1   REVOLUTION AND LAND REFORM:
The confrontation of Chinese villagers with their landlords was a defining feature of the Chinese Revolution.

4.4 million in 1949 to 12 million by 1957) allowed the new state to penetrate Chinese society more deeply than ever before in Chinese history. Mass organizations for students, women, workers, and various professional groups enabled the party to mobilize and indoctrinate millions. "Urban resident committees" of 100 to 500 households provided yet another means of control at the level of city neighborhoods.

CLEANING UP THE CITIES.   This kind of control enabled the CCP to end the chaos that had beset the country for decades. Inflation was brought under control. Essential city services were restored and the streets became safe again. Pervasive urban vices such as opium addiction, prostitution, and gambling were attacked with a combination of harsh penalties (including execution), rehabilitation programs, and massive public education. In just three years, these vices were virtually eliminated. With public order restored, the economy also revived, and by 1952 the output of industry and agriculture had returned to prewar levels and was growing. So was education. Enrollment in primary and secondary schools more than doubled in the four years after the CCP seized power.

COMPLETING LAND REFORM

CONFRONTING THE LANDLORDS. By far the most important task for the CCP in its first few years in power was to finish the process of land reform. It had begun in north China during the 1940s, but only about 20% of China's villages had been affected by 1949. Now hastily trained land-reform teams were dispatched to the newly liberated areas of China, where they mobilized the poorer peasants in thousands of separate villages to confront and humiliate the landlords, seizing their land, animals, tools, houses, and money for redistribution to the poorer members of the village. The most difficult task was breaking the age-old deference that peasants had traditionally rendered to their social superiors. One young woman activist described the meetings intended to break this ancient pattern:

> "Speak bitterness meetings," as they were called, would help [the peasants] to understand how things really had been in the old days, to realize that their lives were not blindly ordained by fate, that poor peasants had a community of interests, having suffered similar disasters and misery in the past—and that far from owing anything to the feudal landlords, it was the feudal landlords who owed them a debt of suffering beyond all reckoning.[3]

It was, as Mao put it, "not a dinner party." Estimates range that between 1 and 2 million landlords were killed in the process, which was largely over by 1952.

The great significance of land reform lay in the destruction of this ancient class that had dominated rural China for centuries, that had stifled earlier efforts at modernization, and that posed the primary obstacle to communist rule. More than the seizure of power in Beijing, it was land reform that wrote the last chapter in the history of old landlord-dominated China. That process also contributed much to the making of the new China as it politicized millions of peasants, planted the authority of the Communist Party solidly in the villages of this vast country, and witnessed the emergence of a new, younger, and mostly male leadership in the countryside, drawn largely from the middle and poor peasants. CCP officials argued that land reform was historically necessary, not only as a matter of social justice, but also to expand agricultural production and lay the foundation for the country's industrialization.

WHO GAINED? WHO LOST? Land reform was profoundly revolutionary, but it was not particularly socialist. Peasants received their new allotments of land as private property, complete with title deeds, and they were free to buy, sell, or rent their lands. Nor did land reform result in a completely equal redistribution of property. The old landlord class obviously lost the most. If they survived the process, landlords were allocated a piece of land equivalent to that of a poor peasant. Millions of previously landless peasants or those with tiny plots gained an acre or two of precious land, which provided at least a possibility of realizing the ancient peasant dream of an independent family farm. The so-called rich and middle peasants were less affected by the redistribution and generally wound up with larger-than-average farms. Some were able to rent out pieces of land to tenants or to employ hired workers for wages. The whole process leveled Chinese society considerably, with about 60% of the population gaining some land, and led to a system of small privately owned farms throughout China.

LIBERATING WOMEN

MARRIAGE LAW OF 1950.   Like the Soviet Union, communist China also launched an early effort to address the oppression of women, who were frequently abused and clearly subordinated within traditional Chinese society. Dating back to the 1920s, women's liberation had been a major concern of the CCP and of Mao personally. Thus, in June of 1950 in one of its first acts, the new government proclaimed a new Marriage Law. Its purpose was to end the "feudal marriage system" of forced, compulsory marriages and to lay the framework for "a new democratic marriage system . . . based on the free choice of partners, on monogamy, on equal rights for both sexes, and on the protection of the lawful interests of women and children." The law abolished "bigamy, concubinage, child betrothal, interference in the remarriage of widows, and the exaction of money or gifts in connection with marriages," and, among other things, extended to women the rights to own property and to divorce. The most immediate effect of the law was upon the tens of thousands of women who used divorce to end unhappy or abusive marriages.[4]

Initially, the CCP was reluctant to push the Marriage Law, fearing it would distract attention from the more fundamental task of land reform. But by 1953, as land reform was being successfully completed, the party undertook a mass campaign to inform the entire population of the content of the Marriage Law and of the new rights of women. Unlike the land reform effort, the campaign to study the Marriage Law used educational, not confrontational, tactics.

The CCP also launched a Women's Federation, a mass organization enrolling millions of women. Its leadership, however, was far less radical than that of the Bolshevik feminists who led *Zhenotdel* in the 1920s. In China there was little talk about "free love" or the "withering away of the family," as there had been in Russia. But it did encourage women to get involved in economic production and sponsored literacy classes and other programs aimed at uplifting the condition of Chinese women.

GAINS.   In the long run, the Marriage Law did change China's marriage patterns and did reform the family structure. Divorce was more readily available, and many of the abuses of the Confucian family system, such as forced marriages, child marriages, and concubinage, were largely eliminated. Women gained a higher, though certainly not an equal, status within the family and society. The return of stability and security, coupled with land reform, enabled millions of Chinese to establish stable nuclear families, something that had been out of reach for so many during the economic and social chaos of the previous half-century.

LIMITATIONS.   But within these families, peasant male prerogatives were left largely intact. The Marriage Law did not touch the custom of "patrilocal marriage," in which young women moved to their husbands' households, a practice that limited the independence of young brides and provided little incentive for the education of girls. Titles to the new family farms were vested in the household, most often headed by a man. Nor did the party make much effort to change the existing division of labor within the home, leaving Chinese women with the "double burden" of both domestic chores and paid labor. So Chinese patriarchy was reformed and "democratized," but not fundamentally challenged.[5] Although the liberation of women was a concern of the CCP, it took second place to fostering production. Furthermore, the party sought to avoid alienating Chinese peasant men, who provided the main support for communist rule, as well as those women who saw marriage reform as a threat to family life rather than an opportunity.

RESISTING AMERICA

THE KOREAN WAR.   The early years of communist rule in China were shadowed by a major military confrontation with the United States. It was similar to early Soviet history, which witnessed western military intervention in Russia's civil war. But in China's case, the conflict occurred outside of China proper. The issue was Korea. That country had been a Japanese colony and, following the defeat of Japan in World War II, was divided between a Communist North and an American-installed regime in the South. When North Korean forces invaded the South in 1950, the United States, acting under the auspices of the United Nations, sent troops to South Korea. As U.S. forces advanced north toward the Chinese border, the new Communist leadership, fearing that the Americans were seeking to overthrow their revolution, sent their army to assist the North Koreans. Chinese forces drove the Americans back to the original dividing line, and a cease-fire in 1953 left North and South Korea in roughly their prewar positions.

REPRESSION. The consequences of this conflict for the fledgling communist country were profound. It raised the possibility of foreign invasion of China itself and seemed to strengthen domestic enemies of the regime such as landlords and supporters of the Guomindang. Some of them dared to hope that the hated communist regime might be overthrown. As a consequence, CCP policies toward these groups hardened and became markedly more repressive as a wave of terror swept through the country in 1951, seeking to identify and punish counterrevolutionaries.

PRIDE. But the war also benefited the communist regime by stimulating enormous pride in China's military achievement. Chinese forces had fought heroically while suffering close to a million casualties, including Mao's own son Anying. A country that had been repeatedly defeated by western states for a century now battled the United States, the world's greatest military power, to a stalemate. In doing so, China prevented the establishment of a hostile American-backed state on its Manchurian border. Mass rallies under the slogan "Resist America and Aid Korea" tapped into a wellspring of patriotism, and countless books, films, plays, and tales of heroic soldiers celebrated the sacrifices that the nation had made to preserve its revolution and its independence.

ISOLATION. The war also had international implications for China. Plans to invade Taiwan were put on hold indefinitely as the United States signaled its military and political commitment to Chiang Kai-shek's regime. American hostility to communist China, now deeply cemented, kept the country out of the United Nations for two decades and sharply limited its interaction with the world economy in terms of trade and investment. This enforced isolation pushed China even more strongly toward the Soviet Union as its only major ally in a threatening world.

TOWARD SOCIALISM: FOLLOWING THE SOVIET MODEL

By 1953 the Chinese Communist Party had consolidated its authority, completed land reform, stood up to American military might, and begun to address the oppression of women. It had also constructed a political system much like that of the Soviet Union—a single, mass party claiming a Marxist ideology, deeply penetrating Chinese society, controlling the official state structures, and led by a dominant figure. Now as the Party leadership turned its attention to the task of building socialism, it was natural—almost instinctive—to imitate major features of the Soviet experience. Chinese leaders shared a basic outlook with the Soviet Union and badly needed the experience and the assistance that might be gained from the "elder socialist brother." Its isolation from the larger international community of capitalist countries left it little alternative. Thus, both in bringing socialism to the rural areas and in pursuing industrialization, China began by following the Soviet model.

A SECOND RURAL REVOLUTION: COLLECTIVIZATION IN THE COUNTRYSIDE

WHY COLLECTIVIZE?　The outcome of land reform in China was similar to that of the Soviet Union. In both countries, centuries of landlord domination (what communists called "feudalism") had ended, replaced by millions of small, privately owned family farms. Although this was an almost ideal situation for peasants, who had long dreamed of owning their own farms, it was hardly socialism as CCP leaders understood it. Small-scale fragmented agriculture was unsuited for modern mechanized farming and was unlikely to produce the surpluses that could support China's industrialization. Furthermore, Mao and others saw signs that classes, inequality, and even the hated capitalism were beginning to develop again in the countryside. "During the past few years," Mao wrote in 1955, "new rich peasants have emerged everywhere, and many prosperous middle peasants are exerting efforts to turn themselves into rich peasants. Many poor peasants . . . still remain in poverty, some of them having contracted debts; others are selling their land or renting out their land . . ."[6] As in the Soviet Union, both economic and social motives encouraged the CCP leadership to move beyond land reform and to bring socialism to the countryside.

THE MEANING OF COLLECTIVIZATION.　Doing so was a profoundly revolutionary process. The ideal of private ownership of land was even more deeply rooted in China than in the Russia, where the village commune provided some cultural basis for cooperative agriculture. Now Chinese peasants were being asked to give up land held in their families for generations, or in some cases, to surrender a few precious acres recently acquired during land reform. Turning over animals, often considered "half of the family," to the collective farm was perhaps the most difficult step. One peasant described what collectivization meant at an emotional level:

> Some people found it hard to get used to. For some months after we turned the land over to the coop, we never called it "our land" and the same was true of animals and implements. We used to say, "I am going out to Hung-er's land," "I'm going to load Wang's cart," "Harness up Tien-hsi's mule." That's the way we used to speak. I can't really remember when the word "our" took over. But it must have been at least a year, perhaps more.[7]

THE CHINESE DIFFERENCE.   As in the Soviet Union, this "second rural revolution" occurred quite quickly. Originally planned to take a decade or more, it was essentially complete by the end of 1956. But collectivization in China occurred far more smoothly than in the Soviet Union, with little of the violence, active resistance, economic chaos, and famine that beset the USSR in the late 1920s and early 1930s. How might we explain this remarkable contrast?

COLLECTIVIZATION IN STAGES.   One answer lies in the gradualism of the Chinese approach, unlike the Soviet policy of pushing peasants almost overnight into fully collectivized farms. The Chinese began during the land-reform process to encourage peasants to join Mutual Aid Teams of six or more households that would help one another work their privately owned farms. The next stage, semisocialist cooperatives, brought together larger groups of 30 to 50 households, which pooled their land and tools and agreed to farm cooperatively as a single unit. But inequalities remained as they shared the harvest or the profit from the farm in part according to how much land each family had contributed. The final stage of fully socialist collective farms involved even larger groups—often an entire village or more of 100 to 300 families—and rewarded individuals according to their labor, calculated in terms of "work points" assigned to various tasks. Between 1952 and 1956, about 100 million Chinese households moved through these stages, with virtually the entire countryside enrolled in some 485,000 fully collective farms by the end of 1956.

POOR AND RICH PEASANTS.   A further difference between the Chinese and Soviet cases lay in the makeup of the peasantry. Far more Chinese peasants—some 60% or more—were officially classified as "poor" and thus most likely to benefit and least likely to lose from joining a collective farm. Furthermore the "rich peasants" were not excluded from the collective farms as the Russian *kulaks* had been. Although they were certainly not enthusiastic about the prospect, better-off Chinese peasants ultimately gave in to overwhelming social pressures to join the collective farms. Thus, China experienced nothing remotely like the violent "dekulakization" that so disrupted and disfigured Soviet collectivization.

RURAL COMMUNISTS.   An even more important difference was the massive presence of the Communist Party in the rural areas of China, where some 90% of the villages had party branches by the end of 1955. This was the legacy of a revolution that had taken shape in the Chinese countryside and of a Communist Party that had aligned itself with the peasantry since the mid-1930s. Thus, the leadership for the collectivization process came from local party activists, or *cadre*, in these villages, many of whom were themselves poor peasants and genuinely enthusiastic about socialism. In the Soviet Union, by contrast, the revolution had been based in the cities, and the Communist Party had hardly any rural presence and little real knowledge about conditions in the countryside. There collectivization was seen as something imposed from outside, and it resulted in an extended struggle—almost a civil war—between urban-based activists and village folk.

FEARS AND RESISTANCE.   Still, collectivization in China was no cakewalk. Rich peasants and those who hoped to become rich peasants were decidedly reluctant. But government controlled access to credit, supplies, and marketing opportunities allowed state authorities to apply pressure and to force them into collective farms. Others wondered where collectivization would end. Would everyone be required to eat from one big pot? A four-line verse expressed some of the fears:

> Pooling private property,
> Pooling land thrives.
> Next pool children,
> Then pool wives?[8]

LEADERSHIP CONFLICTS.   Collectivization also prompted considerable conflict within the party leadership over the pace of bringing socialism to the countryside. Many felt the process should be delayed until the country had produced more modern agricultural machinery; they feared that a rapid movement toward collectivization would disrupt production and alienate the peasantry as it had in the Soviet Union. But in mid-1955, Mao decisively intervened in this debate, using his enormous prestige to push a more rapid movement toward full collectivization. The people, Mao argued, "are full of immense enthusiasm for socialism," while some in the Communist Party are "tottering like a woman with bound feet." When collectivization was completed far more quickly than even Mao had predicted, he felt confirmed in his boundless faith in the revolutionary potential of the masses. Here was the beginning of what became a deep division in the CCP leadership and generated no end of trouble in the years to come.

ACHIEVEMENTS.   What did collectivization accomplish? Primarily, of course, China had brought socialism to the countryside both quickly and relatively peacefully. That process enabled peasants to eat better than they had in the early 1950s, and the vegetables, chickens, ducks, and pigs that peasants raised on their small private plots enriched urban diets as well. But the chief function of collectivized agriculture, as in the Soviet Union, was to support the drive toward industrialization. It enabled the state to transfer resources out of the countryside and into industrial development. So much so, in fact, that peasant standards of living grew little, if at all, over the next 20 years. It is one of the great ironies of the Chinese revolution that although Mao and the CCP presented themselves as champions of the peasants, their policies, like those of the Soviet Union, gave priority to urban industrial development and left the rural areas behind.

CREATING A MODERN ECONOMY: CHINESE INDUSTRIALIZATION

CHINA'S HISTORIC TASK.   For almost a century, Chinese nationalists and patriots had sought to build a modern industrial economy in their country. How else, they argued, could China escape foreign domination, end the poverty of its enormous population, and reclaim its rightful place in the world? This desire had long been frustrated by the incompetence of weak governments, the opposition of the landlord class, the interference of western imperialists, and the disruption of Japanese aggression and civil war. By 1953, these conditions had been largely overcome, and the CCP set about this great task.

WHY FOLLOW THE SOVIET MODEL?   In undertaking the industrialization of their country, the CCP chose to follow the Soviet example even more closely than in collectivizing agriculture. In large measure this was because the two countries faced a common dilemma: what was a Marxist socialist party to do when it came to power in an economically backward country? Karl Marx had assumed that socialist revolutions would occur in advanced, economically developed countries, where the task of socialists would be to end the inequalities of the old order with the wealth from an already existing industrialized economy. But Russian and then Chinese revolutionaries found themselves in a quite different situation. Their task was to create the wealth, to industrialize their impoverished countries for the first time—in short, to undertake the task that their capitalists had failed to accomplish. The Soviet Union under Stalin's leadership had shown the way to resolving this dilemma through a massive state-planned industrialization drive. Rapid economic growth and victory in World War II demonstrated the success of this effort, which the Chinese now proceeded to imitate. And beyond the Soviet example lay the possibility of Soviet aid. After the Korean War, China could expect no assistance from the West, and the Soviet Union agreed to provide modest financial aid as well as 156 industrial plants, some 12,000 engineers and technicians from the Soviet bloc countries, and training for thousands of Chinese students and workers. Thus, both the apparent success of the Soviet example and the prospect of Soviet help tied China to the Soviet model of industrialization.

IMPLEMENTING THE SOVIET MODEL.   Following the Soviet path meant that those enterprises remaining in private hands were now nationalized as the entire economy came under state control. An elaborate state apparatus for planning and operating the economy was established. A State Planning Commission began work in 1952 and dozens of ministries, committees, and other agencies soon followed in an explosion of bureaucracy. An initial Five-Year Plan set ambitious goals for the 1953–1957 period. As in the Soviet Union, that plan gave priority to heavy industry such as steel, machine tools, electric power, and basic chemicals. Light industry producing consumer goods as well as agriculture got far less of the scarce investment funds that were available to state planners. This meant that the agricultural sector of the economy subsidized the industrialization drive, as peasants were required to sell about 25% of their grain to the state at low fixed prices, whereas agriculture received only 7.6% of state investment funds.

OUTCOMES.   The economic results were impressive. Industrial production grew at the amazing rate of about 18% per year, even more rapidly than Soviet industry had grown during its first Five-Year Plan. The output of rolled steel, cement, coal, and electric power doubled or more in five years. China began to produce trucks, tractors, merchant ships, and airplanes. Agriculture, on the other hand, grew much more slowly, about 3% per year, just a little faster than the rate of population growth at 2.2% annually.

Like all industrializing societies, China experienced substantial urbanization, with 13 cities populated by more than 1 million people in 1957, compared to only 5 in 1949. Within these cities, the industrial working class grew rapidly from about 6 million in 1952 to 10 million in 1957. So, too, did elite groups necessary for operating a complex industrial economy. A bureaucratic elite of planners and managers and a technical elite of scientists and engineers—all of them specialized experts in some field—gained status within urban China and enjoyed its comforts and opportunities. Managers within the factories, following the Soviet example, imposed increasingly strict labor discipline on workers as they sought ever higher levels of productivity. Even Communist Party cadres were divided into 26 distinct ranks, with corresponding differences in their salaries, depending on their role in the industrializing process.

All of this was "normal." Similar patterns of inequality, bureaucracy, expertise, and discipline had been part of capitalist industrialization in the nineteenth century, and they characterized the Soviet experience in the 1930s as well. But was it socialism? That was the question that increasingly haunted parts of the CCP leadership and Mao Zedong in particular.

TOWARD SOCIALISM: FINDING A CHINESE PATH

Until the mid-1950s, China's path toward socialism largely followed the example of the Soviet Union. After that, it increasingly diverged from the Soviet model. This new path reflected the distinctive features of China's culture, history, and revolutionary experience, but it also reflected the powerful impact of one man's ideas, those of Mao Zedong. The victory of the CCP in 1949 and the early success of the Party in unifying China, in fighting the Americans, in collectivizing its agriculture, and in beginning its industrial development had given Mao, the party's undisputed leader, enormous stature and influence. In the two decades that followed 1956, he repeatedly used his unique position to push the party and the country onto an increasingly radical path, quite different from that of the Soviet Union. In doing so, Mao provoked a decisive split within the communist leadership in China, unleashed enormous social upheavals, and brought the country to the brink of civil war. Here was a situation in which a single powerful leader decisively shaped the country's trajectory. No wonder that China's approach to building socialism has often been referred to as "Maoism."

DEFINING THE CHINESE DIFFERENCE

What then was distinctive about the Chinese path to socialism? At its heart it was Mao's growing insistence that the social and cultural transformation of China must occur together with its economic development. This was contrary to orthodox Marxist thinking that a socialist society and socialist values could come about only *after* industrial development had created the economic base for socialism. And it was contrary to Soviet practice, which permitted, and even encouraged, many inequalities to develop, believing that economic growth, not immediate socialism, was the first priority. Mao, however, refused to wait. A socialist mentality and forms of society, he argued, would actually enable economic development to take place more rapidly. They were a prerequisite for growth, not a result of it. In practice, this meant mobilizing China's huge labor force for the enormous task of modern economic growth rather than relying on technology, which was in short supply in China. "Men are more important than machines," ran one of the slogans that summed up this different approach. In economic terms, it was a labor intensive, rather than a capital intensive, path to development.

SOCIALIST ENTHUSIASM.   And what would motivate Chinese people to undertake this huge project? Certainly not profits nor material rewards! That was capitalist thinking. Rather, it was their own socialist consciousness, nurtured by the Communist Party. Mao's faith in the revolutionary spirit of the masses, born during the long struggle for power in rural China, was now applied to the tasks of economic development. He expressed this faith in a famous passage:

> Throughout the country, the communist spirit is urging forward. The political consciousness of the masses is rapidly rising . . . In view of this, our country may not need as much time as previously thought to catch up with the big capitalist countries in industrial and agricultural development. The decisive factor, apart from leadership by the Party, is our 600 million people . . . They are first of all, poor, and second, blank. That may seem like a bad thing, but it is really a good thing. Poor people want change, want to do things, want revolution. A clean sheet of paper has no blotches, and so the newest and most beautiful pictures can be written on it.[9]

"ENGINEERING THE SOUL."   Thus the key to both economic development and building socialism was "the remolding of people." It would be a revolution that "would touch men's very souls." In this process, "thought reform" was an important ingredient. By studying Marxist-Leninist-Maoist literature, by openly criticizing one's own ideas and behavior, by accepting such criticism from others, by working with ordinary people, individuals could acquire a "socialist consciousness," even before a socialist economy had emerged.

All this required a major commitment to equality, overcoming the ancient divisions between city and countryside, between intellectuals and working people, between rulers and the people. Mao had long distrusted city life in general and intellectuals in particular. His experience as a revolutionary had been largely with peasants in the rural areas where all shared hardships equally and everyone grew their own food. Now he sought to recapture this spirit of revolutionary equality and apply it to the tasks of modern development. He especially feared the emergence of new elites—party and state officials more concerned with their careers and their personal lives than with building socialism. Millions of such people were "sent down" to the countryside where they lived and worked in peasant villages and experienced the harsh realities of rural life while "learning from the masses." It was one way of confronting the potential inequalities of the new China. Another was the constant study of Mao's writings and a willingness to criticize oneself and others on the basis of those values. Yet another was administrative decentralization, as Mao cut the central bureaucracy drastically while urging China's provinces and local regions to act autonomously. China's mobilized masses, motivated by Mao's thoughts and led by local party officials, could "move mountains." They would lead the way to modern development, not relying on privileged urban elites and state or party bureaucrats.

CONTINUOUS REVOLUTION.   For Mao, the seizure of power by the CCP was by no means the end of the revolution, and the future of socialism remained in doubt. Continuous struggle was therefore necessary to avoid reproducing the values and outlook of capitalism and to keep the spirit of the revolution alive and fresh. "Never forget the class struggle" was one of his often quoted sayings.

CRITICIZING THE SOVIET MODEL.   All of this represented a sharp criticism of Soviet practice and reflected Mao's growing disenchantment with the Soviet approach to building socialism. In the Chinese view, the Soviet Union had neglected and even exploited its peasantry, while focusing almost exclusive attention on urban industries. China, Mao urged, must "walk on two legs," pursuing agricultural and industrial policies, urban and rural development, in a more balanced fashion. Furthermore, Mao implied, the Soviet Union had permitted sharp new inequalities to emerge and had sought to motivate its people with material incentives such as differential pay rates and bonuses. It had created a huge bureaucracy of privileged people, largely cut off from, and looking down upon, those they were supposed to serve. And that bureaucracy was highly centralized in Moscow, allowing little opportunity for initiative in the rest of the country. The Soviet Union, in this view, had clearly deviated from the socialist path, raising questions as to whether it was a socialist country at all. Mao's pointed criticism of the Soviet path to socialism was one of the factors that led to a sharp deterioration in the relationship between the two communist countries during the 1960s. The surprising breakdown of this communist alliance marked the emergence of a distinctly Chinese, or Maoist, approach to socialism.

CAMPAIGNS.   What did Maoism mean to the people who lived through it? Most fundamentally, perhaps, it meant frequent mass campaigns, directed by the party and intended to change public thinking and behavior. Involving huge rallies, massive propaganda, and endless small group study and criticism meetings, these campaigns were aimed sometimes at party officials and at other times at particular groups in society. In the early 1950s, a campaign to "Resist America and Aid Korea" encouraged people to identify alleged spies or enemy agents and resulted in the removal of most foreigners from China. It was followed by a campaign against domestic "counterrevolutionaries"—people who harbored sympathies for the now outlawed Guomindang Party. This campaign turned violent and brutal, with hundreds of thousands of executions. Other campaigns in the early 1950s targeted waste, corruption, and the abuses of bureaucracy and led to the humiliation of many senior officials and the virtual elimination of a private business sector in the country.

A HUNDRED FLOWERS AND THE
ANTI-RIGHTIST CAMPAIGN

Among the groups most difficult for the Communist Party to deal with were intellectuals—writers, artists, teachers, students, scientists, and technical experts of all kinds. Their skills and knowledge were necessary for the drive toward modernization, but they were inclined to be critical and independent, resistant to Party authority. By 1957, Mao had come to believe that the Party was strong enough and the country sufficiently unified to invite criticism from the masses and in particular from intellectuals. Such criticism would allow the Party to keep in touch with the people and overcome any difficulties between them. This was the origin of the call to "let a hundred flowers bloom and a hundred schools of thought contend."

"BLOOMING AND CONTENDING."   What emerged was far more than the Party and Mao had imagined, as an enormous outpouring of grievances, complaints, suggestions, and alternatives poured forth. Intellectuals severely criticized the Party for not living up to the country's constitution or to its socialist values. "Who are the people who enjoy a higher standard of living?" asked one outraged critic. "They are Party members and cadre who wore worn-out shoes in the past, but travel in saloon cars and put on woolen uniforms now."[10] Scientists decried Party control of their research agendas, and artists protested Party limitations on their freedom of expression. Students established a "democracy wall" at Beijing University, where they put up posters demanding a limitation of Party influence in university life and greater democracy in the country generally. There were even a few calls for the overthrow of the Party itself.

"POISONOUS WEEDS."   After only about a month of relative freedom, the Party leadership cracked down hard on its intellectual critics in what was called the "anti-rightist" campaign of 1957. Cultivating flowers ended; digging up "poisonous weeds" began with a vengeance. Party officials were ordered to identify arbitrary quotas of "rightists," as allegedly anti-communist intellectuals were called. More than 500,000 people received this feared label, which effectively ruined their lives. Few such people were executed, as they had been in the Soviet Union in the 1930s. Rather, they were jailed, packed off to labor camps for "reeducation," or "sent down" to rural areas for hard physical work. Many had to endure repeated "rectification meetings" where they were required to confess their political and ideological mistakes and beg forgiveness. "The whole nation is demanding a stern punishment for me, a rightist," wrote one such individual. "I am prepared to accept it. I hate my wickedness. I want to kill the old reactionary self . . . I will join the whole nation in the stern struggle against rightists, including myself."[11]

Denounced in the press and scorned by friends, "rightists" became a danger to their own families because being the child or spouse of a "rightist" contaminated the entire family. One young man described the agony his family experienced when his mother was declared a "rightist":

> Father believed in the Party with his whole heart, believed that the
> Party could never make a mistake or hand down a wrong verdict. It
> was a tortuous dilemma; Father's traditional Confucian sense of family
> obligation told him to support Mother, while his political allegiance
> told him to condemn her. In the end, his commitment to the Party won
> out and he denounced her. He believed that was the only course that
> could save the family from ruin.[12]

THE GREAT LEAP FORWARD

ON THE WRONG PATH?   Far more profound in its impact and far more decisive in defining a distinctly Chinese socialism was the Great Leap Forward, a massive effort in the late 1950s to speed up the country's economic development and to move rapidly toward full communism at the same time. Its origins lay in Mao's assessment of the consequences for China of following the Soviet model of development. Agricultural production had grown much less rapidly than urban-based industries, suggesting that the countryside was being exploited to benefit the cities. The central bureaucracy had grown enormously. New inequalities and privileged groups were emerging. Even within the Party, the spirit of service to the revolution seemed to be eroding, replaced by self-seeking careerism. Both economically and socially, the Chinese revolution was taking a decidedly wrong turn, in the view of Mao and his supporters.

PEOPLES' COMMUNES.   Mao found a solution to these problems in a new structure for rural life in China—the peoples' communes. These were gigantic institutions, created by combining dozens of collective farms into a single new commune, containing typically some 25,000 people, 10,000 acres, and 100,000 animals. Pushed by enthusiastic CCP officials in the countryside and greeted at least initially with widespread popular support, some 26,000 communes had been hastily established by late 1958. To Mao and his supporters, the communes would release the energies of the Chinese people and propel the country rapidly forward. The communes had the labor force to work large areas more efficiently and to undertake huge new projects such as dams and irrigation systems that could open up new farmland. For a time, many were genuinely enthusiastic. "Over a hundred thousand laborers worked on the dam at Hsiszuho," one participant recalled. "Red flags flew all over the place.

At night electric bulbs outnumbered the stars . . . All the cadre went down to work among the people and everybody worked with great determination."[13]

Communes were also large enough to undertake important industrial projects, such as workshops to repair farming equipment and small factories to produce fertilizer and process local crops. This effort at rural industrialization represented to Mao a way of overcoming the difference between city and countryside and a means of spreading modern technical skills into the rural areas. The most famous example of the process was the "backyard furnaces," intended to produce iron and steel. Peasant families were exhorted to donate their pots and pans, iron bed frames, and other metal objects to be smelted into useful metal. Many did so, but the metal produced by these efforts was generally of poor quality.

UTOPIA. Communes were also a vehicle for moving toward a more fully communist society, one in which an even greater degree of social equality and collective living prevailed. The desire to draw women into productive labor encouraged many communes to free women of traditional household chores by establishing communal dining halls and nurseries. Most private agricultural plots were eliminated and in the most radical communes, family pigs, chickens, furniture, pots, and pans were likewise turned over to the commune. The Party recommended that 70% of the surplus grain be distributed to families within the commune on the basis of need and 30% on the basis of labor. Educational experiments sought to combine classroom learning with practical work assignments as a way of overcoming the distinction between intellectuals and experts on the one hand and ordinary peasants on the other. The goal was for everyone to become both "red and expert"; that is, both communist-minded and technically skilled. During 1958, many millions of people in China were swept up in a wave of social utopianism, which seemed to promise both enormous economic gains and the creation of an ideal communist society.

One of the most utopian aspects of the Great Leap Forward was the suggestion that the communes would become a major unit of government and military organization, replacing many functions that had been performed by the central state and party bureaucracy. Popular militias at the commune level enrolled several hundred-million people, although only a fraction of them had access to real weapons. Here was a way of radically decentralizing power and Mao's answer to the persistent problem of "bureaucratism," which so troubled him. To some enthusiasts, Marx's prediction that under communism the state would "wither away" seemed to be coming true.

DISASTERS. Far from producing utopia, the Great Leap swept communist China into its most severe economic crisis. Industrial production dropped sharply, causing major shortages in manufactured goods. Even worse, a massive famine, dwarfing that of the Soviet Union in the early 1930s, brought death from starvation and malnutrition to an amazing 20 million or more people between 1959 and 1962. What had happened?

Fundamentally, the disasters were man-made, the product of the Great Leap itself. The speed with which communes were established created administrative chaos. Peasants were now working land they did not know intimately, and the longer hours expected of them were exhausting. CCP officials, with little local knowledge, insisted on policies that turned out to be disastrous, such as deep plowing and close planting. At one point the Party ordered peasants to kill millions of sparrows that were eating crops, only to find that without sparrows, insects ate even more.

Furthermore, wealthier collective farms resented being forced to join less prosperous ones, and peasant workers often resented the factory-style regimentation that now organized agricultural work. Rewarding workers according to need, rather than according to work, encouraged the less motivated to slack off. Local authorities exaggerated how much they produced; then higher-level officials used these inflated figures to calculate how much they owed to the state. The result was a shortage of grain for local consumption. Nor did the weather cooperate with Great Leap plans as droughts, floods, and typhoons brought added miseries to many areas. And the Soviet Union, increasingly disenchanted with Chinese radicalism, quite suddenly recalled its technical experts working in China during the summer of 1960.

As disasters accumulated, the Party backed off the most radical measures. Backyard furnaces and communal dining halls were abandoned, while private plots and local farmers' markets were restored. The regular state and party authorities assumed greater responsibility as the authority of the communes declined. Mao himself accepted some of the blame for the disaster and withdrew from day-to-day leadership of the country, giving up his position as head of state. The Great Leap Forward was over!

LEGACIES. The legacy of the Great Leap, however, echoed for years to come. The large-scale irrigation projects and exposure of many peasants to modern technology continued to benefit Chinese society in the years that followed. Millions of ordinary people, encouraged by the party, had begun to write poetry, long regarded as the exclusive preserve of scholars, and to collect folk tales and songs. In 1958, one peasant wrote his first poem:

> An illiterate like me takes pen to write poetry
> Joy fills my heart as water fills the river
> For a thousand years the tip of my pen never talked
> Now I have more to say than I can ever finish.[14]

But the scale of the Great Leap's failure, and the millions of deaths it occasioned, shattered the confidence of many peasants in the wisdom of the Party. Furthermore, the Great Leap and its disastrous outcomes had created very serious divisions within the Party leadership. Although his reputation had been damaged by the failures of the Great Leap, Mao retained enormous prestige in the country and the Party and continued to believe that mass mobilization and persistent struggle were necessary to achieve socialism. At one point, in fact, he threatened to lead a new revolution against the Party itself should the leadership reject his policies. The suspicions that Mao harbored against the more moderate Party leaders, by the early 1960s in control of day-to-day affairs, set the stage for an even more tumultuous upheaval that erupted in 1966.

THE CULTURAL REVOLUTION

Students by the hundreds of thousands clutching their "little red books" of quotations from Mao's writings while straining rapturously to see their elderly leader in Beijing's central square; veteran communists wearing pointed "dunce caps" paraded through the streets and jeered by the crowds; large character posters pasted on walls everywhere denouncing enemies and pledging allegiance to Mao and his "thought"—these are some of the lasting images of the Cultural Revolution that convulsed China in the late 1960s. It represented an almost fatal assault on the Chinese Communist Party and the system it had created since 1949. What made that upheaval unique was that it was set in motion by the regime itself and especially by its unquestioned leader, Mao Zedong. It was the largest, the most far-reaching, and the last of the great campaigns by which Mao had hoped to build socialism in China.

BACKGROUND.   The background to the Cultural Revolution lay in the more moderate leadership and policies that characterized China in the aftermath of the failure of the Great Leap Forward. With Mao on the sidelines, more temperate party leaders such as Liu Shaoqi and Deng Xiaoping sought to repair the damage, focusing on practical economic measures while discarding more radical efforts to achieve communism quickly. Industrial managers and technical experts saw their authority increase and with it the renewed widening of the gap between mental and manual labor. More workers were paid on a piece-rate basis and received bonuses, which increased inequality within the factory working class. Inequalities also surfaced in the countryside as private plots and rural markets expanded, while large-scale collective labor declined and the huge communes were divided into smaller units. Rural health care and educational projects, favored during the Great Leap, now enjoyed less support. In the more stable environment of the early 1960s, the Party itself, a huge organization of some 20 million members, became a means of social mobility for many. Its leaders at every level became at least as interested in preserving their positions and privileges as in leading the march to socialism.

THE RETURN OF CAPITALISM?   Mao viewed these processes with growing alarm. In part, he was concerned for his own power, complaining that party leaders were ignoring him, treating him like a "dead ancestor." He criticized educational policies that favored children of party leaders over those of peasants, health care policies that privileged urban hospitals over rural clinics, and agricultural policies that seemed to encourage private rather than collective farming. He warned that the Party was losing its socialist vision in its exclusive concern with economic development, stability, power, and privilege. Gradually, Mao came to a remarkable conclusion: China was on the verge of a return to capitalism and was being led in this direction by none other than the Communist Party itself! In his view, China was replicating the pattern of the Soviet Union, where a revolutionary commitment to socialism had badly degenerated, particularly in the years following Stalin's death. Beneath the rhetoric of socialism, Mao perceived the values of capitalism taking hold, even within the leadership ranks of the Party: personal interests prevailed rather than selfless dedication to the revolution; an emphasis on material rewards loomed larger than enthusiasm for socialism; private life took precedence over collective enterprise; stability seemed more important than struggle; power and privilege triumphed over service.

Mao's prescription was as bold (or bizarre) as his diagnosis: to mobilize the masses for a new revolution against those in the Party who were "taking the capitalist road." Such process, he believed, would test and renew the revolutionary commitment of the older generation of party members, while providing a genuine experience of revolution for the younger generation who had been born after the communist seizure of power.

Even more surprising than Mao's call for an assault on the party that he had spent a lifetime creating was the social response that this call generated. Various groups and millions of individuals rallied to the cause, with varying degrees of genuine enthusiasm, and in doing so, set in motion a three-year (1966–1969) upheaval in Chinese society which brought the country to the brink of anarchy and civil war.

MAO'S POWER BASE.   Among Mao's earliest allies in what became the Cultural Revolution were a group of radical intellectuals who had gathered around his wife, Jiang Qing. With Mao's blessing, they launched attacks on novelists, philosophers, historians, and writers who they believed had become infected with "bourgeois ideology" or who persisted in dealing with traditional or "feudal" themes. Jiang Qing was outraged that Chinese opera and theater still featured "emperors, princes, ministers, scholars, beauties . . . ghosts and monsters" rather than workers, peasants, and soldiers.[15] The most celebrated case involved the scholar Wu Han, who had written a play about a Ming Dynasty emperor who had unjustly dismissed a high official. The radicals charged that the play was an indirect criticism of Mao himself.

A further source of support for the unfolding Cultural Revolution came from the country's military forces, the People's Liberation Army (PLA). Its civilian leader, the Minister of Defense Lin Biao, was an ardent Maoist who had pushed political indoctrination within the army through the use of quotations from Mao's writings. He sought to revive the revolutionary spirit of the PLA by abolishing ranks and the uniforms and insignia that officers had worn. And he praised Mao to the sky, extolling him as surpassing even Marx and Lenin, "a great proletarian genius," "unparalleled in the present world." No wonder, then, that Mao urged the country "to learn from the PLA."

With this kind of support and making full use of his still massive prestige, Mao persuaded the Party's Central Committee to endorse his call for a Cultural Revolution in mid-1966. Its goal was nothing less than to "change the mental outlook of the whole of society" and to "struggle against and overthrow those persons in authority who are taking the capitalist road." The Party sought to set some limits to the Cultural Revolution by prohibiting the use of force and by insisting that it not interfere with economic production. Nonetheless, the country's highest authorities had given the green light for revolt.

RED GUARDS.   The most dramatic and disruptive group to respond to Mao's call for revolution were millions of high school and university students, mostly in major urban centers, who created a bewildering array of local Red Guard organizations, all supposedly dedicated to Maoist principles. Here were the shock troops of the Cultural Revolution. In late 1966, some 13 million of them traveled to Beijing where enormous and ecstatic rallies allowed them to catch a brief glimpse of their beloved leader. Free rail transportation encouraged them to travel all over the country "to exchange revolutionary experiences" and to visit, almost like a pilgrimage, the famous places of the Chinese revolution. Back home, they tried to implement the vague directives that they received from Beijing. Told to combat the "four olds"—old ideas, customs, culture, and habits—Red Guards prowled the streets, searching out examples of "bourgeois culture." They seized and shaved the heads of young people with long hair. Girls with tight slacks had to take the ink bottle test. If a bottle of ink could not slip easily through the slacks, the offending pants were slashed. Streets and stores with traditional names were replaced with more revolutionary titles. Number 26 Middle School near Beijing became the School of Mao Zedong's Doctrine. Some even insisted that traffic signals be changed so that "red" would mean "go" rather than "stop."

More seriously, many teachers, school administrators, and local party officials, now seen as "capitalist-roaders," were challenged, humiliated, beaten, and sometimes killed. Their homes were ransacked in a search for evidence of anti-Maoist thinking, and traditional Chinese writings and artifacts as well as western books, records, and art were seized and destroyed. The flavor of these encounters can be imagined from this description by one observer of a "struggle meeting" in a leading secondary school:

> On the athletic field and further inside, I saw rows of teachers, about 40 or 50 in all, with black ink poured over their heads and faces to show that they were now in reality a "black gang." Hanging on their necks were placards with words such as "reactionary academic authority so-and-so," "corrupt ring-leader so-and-so," "class enemy so-and-so," "capitalist roader so-and-so." . . . They all wore dunce caps painted with similar epithets and carried dirty brooms, shoes, and dusters on their backs.
>
> Hanging from their necks were pails filled with rocks . . . All were barefoot, hitting broken gongs or pots as they walked around the field crying out: "I am black gangster so-and-so." Finally they all knelt down, burned incense, and begged Mao Zedong to "pardon their crimes."[16]

Intense conflict among various Red Guard groups, each claiming to be more Maoist than the other, only increased the turmoil and often led to pitched battles. Local authorities, attempting to blunt the most radical groups, frequently promoted more conservative mass organizations.

By early 1967, the Cultural Revolution had spread beyond schools and universities to encompass factories and government offices throughout

FIGURE 4-2   THE CULTURAL REVOLUTION:
The humiliation of alleged "enemies"—those "taking the capitalist road"—occurred
repeatedly during the Cultural Revolution.

China as workers and lower-level officials organized to confront their
leaders. At the same time, a directive from Beijing urged these new mass
organizations to move beyond confrontation and criticism to actually
"seize power." Rebel organizations in Shanghai, for example, took over
factories, docks, newspapers, and the city government itself. Similar
events took place all across the country as "revolutionary committees"
replaced the regular state and party structures. Soon the centralized
authority of the Communist Party lay in shambles.

THE CULT OF MAO.   As the Cultural Revolution unfolded, the veneration
of Mao exploded extravagantly, even more so than the cult of Stalin had
in the Soviet Union. The whole country was reading his writings. Portraits,
statues, busts, and Mao badges proliferated everywhere. Many families
erected "tablets of loyalty" to Mao, much like those earlier devoted to
ancestors. People made pilgrimages to the "sacred shrines" associated
with key events in his life. Schoolchildren began the day by chanting "May
Chairman Mao live ten thousand times ten thousand years."

EXPLAINING THE CULTURAL REVOLUTION.   The emotional intensity and
fanaticism of the Cultural Revolution were both real and difficult to

explain. Certainly, the Cultural Revolution provided opportunity for the many tensions of Chinese communist society to find expression. At the top level, long-standing divisions within the Party between Maoists and more moderate leaders led to massive purges. Even Liu Shaoqi and Deng Xiaoping lost their positions and together with their families had to undergo mass criticism and humiliation. Many long-repressed young people found the call to abandon restraints and attack their elders appealing in the extreme. Strangely enough, the most radical students came from families of former capitalists, landlords, and intellectuals, for their opportunities for education and high position were distinctly limited in a system where class background counted for so much. Their resentments against the Party hierarchy fueled an intense devotion to Maoist radicalism. Likewise, temporary or contract workers in the cities envied the privileges of regular factory employees. And not a few ordinary people resented the corruption, high-handedness, and privileges of Party officials. Mao's radical rhetoric permitted and even encouraged the expression of these discontents and resentments.

TAMING THE CULTURAL REVOLUTION.   By the middle of 1967, China seemed on the edge of anarchy and even civil war. Party authority had largely disappeared at the national level and bitter conflict, often violent, among various mass organizations was rampant. Recognizing reluctantly that the Cultural Revolution had spun out of control, Mao turned increasingly to the army as the only way to restore order and prevent the complete meltdown of Chinese society. Red Guard and other mass organizations were ordered to turn in their weapons. Army authorities generally sided with the more moderate of these organizations and forcibly disbanded the most radical groups at the cost of many casualties. Large numbers of student rebels, who had embraced the Cultural Revolution, were now sent to the countryside for "reeducation" where they joined hundreds of thousands of party officials who had earlier resisted that upheaval. As the army restored order, the authority of the Communist Party was gradually reestablished. By 1969, the most disruptive and violent phase of the Cultural Revolution was over.

COUNTING THE COST.   The outcomes of the Cultural Revolution were both limited and profound. Confined largely to the major urban areas and their suburbs, the Cultural Revolution had little impact in the rural areas and not much lasting impact on the country's economy. But in the cities, practically everyone was touched by this massive upheaval. About a half-million people died as a result of the Cultural Revolution, most of them as the army repressed the radicalism of the Red Guards after 1967. Millions more were scarred for life by the humiliation, torture, and endless confrontations to which they were subjected. Families had been shattered as children denounced their parents or wives parted from their husbands for the good of the family. Intellectuals as a group were most severely targeted. Millions were arrested, packed off to labor camps, or "sent down" to do menial work in the villages. Party officials were purged from their positions in huge numbers—up to 70 or 80% at the regional and provincial level and 60–70% in the central Party bureaucracy. About 3 million were sent off to "cadre schools" in the countryside, where they combined hard labor and intense ideological study while developing "close ties" with nearby peasants. Some four million high school and university students, many of whom had been Red Guards, were likewise sent to the countryside, where their education ended and their career prospects floundered.[17]

MAOISM IN PRACTICE.   The Cultural Revolution left power firmly in the hands of the Maoists and of Mao himself, enabling them to implement favored egalitarian policies, some of which benefited the rural areas. Private plots and rural markets were once more subjected to sharp restrictions. A renewed emphasis on small-scale factories in the countryside laid the foundation for a remarkable flowering of township and village industry in the 1980s and beyond. Medical care now gave priority to modestly trained "barefoot doctors" who emphasized preventive medicine and the treatment of common ailments in the rural areas rather than elaborate high-tech hospitals in the cities.

EDUCATION AND CULTURE.   The Cultural Revolution had thoroughly disrupted the country's educational system. Universities closed for four years and high schools for shorter periods of time. Many students referred to themselves as a "lost generation." When classes resumed on a regular basis, the curriculum required heavy doses of political education and manual labor, entrance exams were abolished, and the criteria for admission gave priority to class background rather than academic achievement. This gave new opportunities to children of peasants and workers, but it lowered academic standards.

The country's cultural development was also deeply affected. Museums and libraries had been ransacked or closed. University research in the humanities and social sciences virtually stopped. Many artists, musicians, actors, and writers were forced out of their professions. Bookstores could no longer stock either traditional Chinese or foreign literature. On the other hand, writing and painting workshops in factories and communes, guided by professionals, enabled ordinary people to participate in creative work.

POLITICS.   The mass turmoil of the Cultural Revolution had largely ended by 1969, but sharp power struggles continued within the leadership ranks of the reestablished Communist Party throughout much of the 1970s. Conflict between military and civilian leaders led to the downfall in 1971 of Minister of Defense Lin Biao, accused of plotting a military coup and the assassination of Mao himself. Radical Maoists and more moderate party officials battled over policies dealing with agriculture, industry, and culture. Much of this was associated with the growing awareness that Mao was declining physically and would soon "go to meet Marx," as he put it. When he died in 1976, an intense two-year struggle ensued, which ended in a political victory for the moderates led by Deng Xiaoping, setting the stage for a dramatic repudiation of the Cultural Revolution and a sharp reversal of much that had characterized Chinese communism since 1949.

Even then, however, the memory of the Cultural Revolution continued to shape Chinese life. The enormity of the suffering caused by that upheaval gave rise to intense doubts and disillusionment about the Party and China's political system. One young Red Guard who was sent to the countryside described how his ideas changed as a result of this experience:

> [My time in the countryside] was another eye-opening experience. [The peasants] ceaselessly complained about their hard life. They said they had little food to eat . . . Times had been better, they felt, even under the Kuomintang, when a man could work, save some money, invest it, and improve himself. They also preferred Liu Shao-ch'i to Mao because they identified Liu with the private plots . . . I had thought that only capitalist-roaders and counterrevolutionaries had such thoughts. But I had heard them from the mouth of a revolutionary poor peasant who had worked for the Party for more than twenty years . . . My world outlook had been challenged by the reality of peasant life and attitudes.[18]

Furthermore, an intense fear of uncontrolled mass action gave the new leaders of post-Mao China additional reasons to shun any kind of "democracy" that might threaten Communist Party dominance.

CONCLUSION: SOCIALISM AND THE SEARCH FOR ENEMIES: COMPARING THE SOVIET UNION AND CHINA

Accompanying the building of socialism in both the Soviet Union and China was an intensifying search for enemies who would obstruct or subvert that process. In the Soviet Union, that search came to a climax in the wave of arrests, trials, and executions during the Stalinist terror of 1936–1939, whereas in China it was most dramatically expressed in the upheavals of the Cultural Revolution of 1966–1969.

DEFINING ENEMIES. Nor were these enemies wholly an illusion. Both communist regimes had come to power through violent revolutions, which left defeated groups hostile and antagonistic. It took little imagination to suppose that internal enemies might align themselves with the external foes of communism—Western capitalist powers that made no secret of their fear and hatred of communism. Those powers had intervened in Russia's civil war, and the United States actively supported Chiang Kai-shek's regime on Taiwan, which ardently sought the overthrow of communism in China.

Furthermore, both communist regimes made additional enemies by their own brutality and their insistence on retaining absolute power for themselves. A rigid Marxist ideology also fostered a perception of almost any opposition as an example of "class struggle" and a serious threat to socialism. It also justified virtually any action against perceived enemies as legitimate, for were they not threatening the bright future of socialism and the happiness of humankind for all time to come? Lenin, while stroking the heads of some children, once remarked to a friend: "Their lives will be better than ours: they'll be spared many of the things we have been forced to live through . . . Our generation will have carried out a task of great historical importance. The cruelty of our lives, imposed by circumstances, will be understood and pardoned. Everything will be understood, everything!"[19]

ENEMIES WITHIN THE PARTY. That communist regimes might perceive enemies in the larger society and abroad is not surprising. What is more remarkable is that in both the Soviet Union and China, the search for enemies came to focus within the Communist Party itself. During both the Terror and Cultural Revolution, those most vulnerable to attack were the highest-ranking party and state officials, as Stalin and Mao sought to eliminate any who might threaten their positions or their policies. But the scope of the search for enemies went far beyond the top leadership, giving rise to an immense social upheaval in both countries—killings, torture, deportations and "sending down," arrests, imprisonment, public humiliations, bizarre confessions, wrecked careers, broken families—all on an enormous scale. Still others benefited as they rose into positions vacated by displaced "enemies." In both countries, the Party was seriously damaged for a time. The search for enemies later discredited both Stalin and Mao, and for many people permanently tarnished the idea of socialism itself. It set the stage for subsequent reforms in both countries, and it has haunted the historical memories of their respective societies ever since.

DIFFERENCES. These broad similarities are balanced by significant differences in how the search for enemies unfolded in the two communist states. Perhaps the most prominent difference lay in the degree and kind of popular participation. In the Soviet Union, widespread denunciation of alleged enemies, called for by Stalin himself, delivered many hundreds of thousands into the hands of the police, and from there they were processed, tried, executed, or sent to the Gulag. Much of this occurred in secret and all of it under the control of established authorities. But in China, popular participation went much further as millions of Red Guards rallied in Beijing and then fanned out across the country where they attacked local party and government officials, teachers, intellectuals, factory managers, and others they defined as enemies. Rival revolutionary groups soon began fighting with each other, violence erupted throughout the country, and civil war threatened China. Finally, Mao called in the army to restore order. Nothing of the kind occurred in the Soviet Union, where the search for enemies remained largely within official channels, and little resistance to the process surfaced. Nonetheless, the death toll in the Soviet Union was far higher than in China, where no large-scale executions occurred. Most of the Chinese deaths apparently took place as the military suppressed the radical Red Guards and workers' organizations, whereas in the Soviet Union the country's leadership was able to bring the terror to an end by political rather than military means.

A further difference lay in the social radicalism of the Chinese experience. While Stalin claimed to be defending the "little people" of the Soviet Union against corrupt local "bosses," he largely accepted the urban focus of industrial development, the need for a scientific and technical elite, and a highly centralized and privileged party/state bureaucracy. Even in the 1930s, the outlines of a "conservative" society, which had discarded much of its revolutionary legacy, were apparent. Stalin himself endorsed Russian patriotism, traditional family values, individual competition, and substantial differences in wages to stimulate production as an earlier commitment to egalitarianism was substantially abandoned. His terror was directed against particular enemies, not against the inequalities of Soviet society generally.

The unique feature of Chinese history under Mao Zedong's leadership was a recurrent effort to combat these perhaps inevitable tendencies of any industrializing process, to revive and preserve the revolutionary spirit that had animated the Chinese Communist Party during its long struggle for power. By the mid-1950s, Mao and some of his followers had become persuaded that the Soviet model of industrialization was leading China away from socialism and toward new forms of inequality, toward individualistic and careerist values, and toward an urban bias that privileged the cities at the expense of the countryside. The Cultural

Revolution was Mao's final effort to correct these distortions, which he believed had penetrated even the highest ranks of the Communist Party. Unlike Stalin's Terror, the Cultural Revolution also involved new policies to bring health care and education to the countryside and to reinvigorate earlier efforts at rural industrialization under local rather than central control. In these ways, Mao struggled, though without great success, to overcome the inequalities associated with China's modern development and to create a model of socialist modernity quite distinct from that of the Soviet Union.

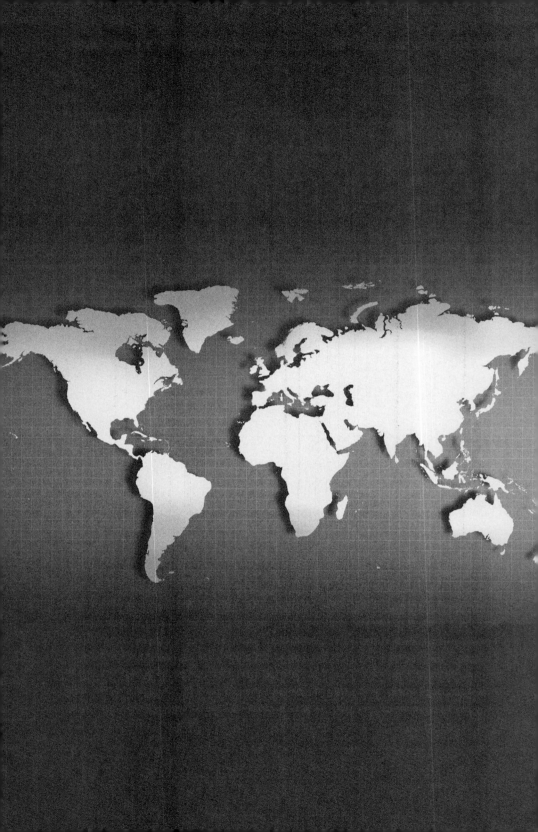

CHAPTER FIVE

COMMUNISM IN THE GLOBAL ARENA

GETTING STARTED ON CHAPTER FIVE: This chapter turns the focus from the making of socialist societies in the Soviet Union and China to the impact of communism in the larger world. In what ways did the communist world engage with the rest of the world? And what impact did communism have beyond the borders of the major communist societies themselves? How did a communist Soviet Union, standing alone in a hostile environment, choose to deal with the capitalist world? How was the cold war expressed? What sustained it for almost 50 years? And why did that bitter conflict never result in outright war between the major powers?

Revolutions in Russia and China and the creation of socialist societies in those two countries had profound reverberations throughout the world during the twentieth century as communism became a major global phenomenon. In the first place, communism spread well beyond these two giant countries and took root in Eastern Europe, Southeast Asia, North Korea, and Cuba. By the early 1970s, the communist-governed countries encompassed about a third of the world's population. Furthermore, the Russian and Chinese revolutions provided inspiration and models for liberation movements in Latin America, Asia, Africa, and the Middle East, some of which adopted a Marxist posture. Many western intellectuals likewise found in Marxism a tool with which to analyze and criticize their own societies. The rise of global communism thus created a new fault line in the world as a whole as it provoked a sharp anticommunist reaction, particularly in the major capitalist nations. This reaction began almost immediately after the Russian Revolution, but it became more pronounced after World War II in the form of the Cold War.

115

For almost a half century (1945–1991) the communist bloc, led by the Soviet Union, faced off against western democratic capitalist states, led by the United States, in a global struggle that brought the world to the brink of nuclear annihilation and elevated many local conflicts to a global stage. Sharp differences within the communist world, particularly between the Soviet Union and China, further complicated global politics in the twentieth century's second half. Finally, the communist phenomenon interacted with other global patterns—the rise of the Nazis, the end of European empires, the emergence of new "Third World" nations—to decisively shape the making of twentieth-century world history.

STANDING ALONE: THE SOVIET UNION AND THE WORLD, 1917–1945

For thirty years, the Soviet Union remained the world's sole outpost of communism. During those three decades, the Russian Revolution represented a beacon of hope to many oppressed and exploited people, living proof that alternatives to capitalism and imperialism were really possible. To most western governments and many of their citizens, however, the Soviet Union was a fearful threat to all that was civilized—democratic values, private property, personal freedom, national sovereignty—and a harbinger of a dark age to come. Within this context, the USSR's interaction with the larger world revolved around two issues: how to encourage the spread of communism beyond its borders and how to protect its own fledgling communist state against the almost universal hostility of the established powers.

COEXISTENCE AND REVOLUTION

THE FAILURE OF WORLD REVOLUTION.   The Russian Revolution of 1917 occurred amid extravagant expectations that world revolution, especially in the most industrialized countries, such as Germany, would soon follow. Lenin and others initially saw little need to develop systematic relations with other countries, for would these separate capitalist states not soon be replaced by a worldwide socialist federation? Short-lived uprisings or movements of radical groups in Germany, Hungary, Finland, and Poland briefly nurtured these unrealistic hopes. By the early 1920s, however, it was clear to all that no other revolutions were in the making. For the moment, it seemed to dismayed Soviet leaders that capitalism had stabilized, and the Soviet Union stood alone, a beleaguered socialist island in a sea of hostile capitalist states. World revolution would have to wait!

"PEACEFUL COEXISTENCE."   Such realities prompted the Soviet Union to begin behaving more like a normal state, maneuvering diplomatically among the country's many enemies in an effort to avoid a war which might well crush the infant revolution and seeking the economic benefits of trade with more developed countries. "Peaceful coexistence" with capitalist countries, at least temporarily, was Lenin's new approach to the world.

FEARING THE COMMUNISTS.   But implementing this new policy was not easy. The sheer reality of a large state dedicated to overthrowing the established order, along with Lenin's repeated denunciation of all things capitalist and his frequent calls for world revolution sent a shiver of fear throughout the capitalist world. In the United States, the end of World War I brought a wave of labor unrest, racial violence, and terrorist bombings that convinced some political leaders that "Bolshevik agitators" were at work. In response to this "Red Scare" of 1919, many states passed sedition laws with harsh penalties for those advocating revolution. Universities expelled radical students, and the federal government launched raids on centers of radical activity, arresting 6,000 people. In Britain, politicians such as Winston Churchill advocated military action to "crush Bolshevism in its cradle." In 1924 a forged letter, allegedly from a high Soviet official, called on British communists to create cells in the British army. The publication of the letter generated a wave of anti-communism in Britain. The fear of communism even penetrated the distant colonial world of East Africa, where a European missionary defending the interests of African people was denounced by one colonial official in 1927 as "an out and out Bolshevist."[1]

BECOMING "NORMAL."   Despite the fears and hostility of the capitalist world, the Soviet Union made considerable progress during the 1920s in defusing potential threats and in dealing, reluctantly, with the world as it was. Soviet representatives, dressed in regular business suits rather than the rough-and-ready clothing of revolutionaries, attended international conferences, assuring all of their country's peaceful intentions, their profound interest in disarmament, and their willingness to negotiate the debts that the czar's government owed to western countries. By the end of the 1920s, the Soviet Union had achieved diplomatic recognition from all the major powers except the United States, which waited to do so until 1933. They had also negotiated trade agreements and treaties of friendship and mutual nonaggression with a number of countries. The most important of these agreements, the Treaty of Rapallo in 1923, established an especially close relationship with Germany and subsequently led to cooperation in military training and the production of weapons. Both countries were outsiders to the network of established powers, both hated the Treaty of Versailles, and both had designs on pieces of Polish territory. All this represented "normal" balance of power politics in the international arena.

COMINTERN.   But the Soviet Union had not forsaken its revolutionary mission nor its belief in an eventual conflict with capitalist powers that would lead to the global victory of communism. But it chose to pursue that mission largely outside of the normal relationship of sovereign states through an organization called the Communist International or Comintern. Established in 1919, Comintern was an association of national communist parties from more than 40 countries, all committed to achieving socialism through revolution. Most had been established after the Russian Revolution as they broke away from more moderate socialist or "social-democratic" parties that sought to move toward socialism through peaceful political means. Thus, the Russian Revolution effectively split the world socialist movement between communist and social-democratic parties, creating a sharp and sometimes violent antagonism between them.

Theoretically independent of all governments, Comintern in practice was controlled by the Soviet Communist Party and served its purposes. Many member parties were financially dependent on the Soviet Union, which also had enormous prestige among communists as the home of the only successful socialist revolution. As a result, they closely followed the Soviet party line and, acting on Stalin's orders, ruthlessly purged those who deviated from these policies. For some western communists, an almost cultlike devotion to the Soviet cause persisted even after the barbarities of Stalinism became widely known. They remained "true believers" in the communist ideal, viewing it as a humanistic religion. Others, bitterly disillusioned with the "god that failed," turned against their old "religion" and contributed much to an emerging culture of anti-communism in the West.

Through an increasingly "Bolshevized" Comintern, the Soviet leadership called for revolution, offered encouragement to anticolonial movements, financed propaganda in various countries, trained foreign communists, and attempted to undermine the very governments with which the Soviet Union had begun to conduct normal relationships. It was the instrument through which the Soviet Union could infiltrate labor unions with local communists, stimulate strikes, interfere in elections, and publicize its policies throughout the world.

In terms of spreading communism, the Comintern was largely a failure because only in sparsely populated and remote Mongolia did a communist party come to power before the international organization was disbanded in 1943. Nonetheless, Comintern's activities complicated the more conventional diplomatic efforts of the Soviet Union, for during the 1920s and 1930s they suggested to many people and governments that "the specter of communism appeared to be stalking the globe."[2] The American unwillingness to accord the Soviet Union diplomatic recognition until 1933 was due in part to Comintern's actions, including its financing of the U.S. Communist Party.

In practice, however, the Soviet Union was careful not to allow the activities of foreign communists to get out of hand. Their primary function, in Stalin's view, was to defend the Soviet Union from the "imperialists" rather than to provoke capitalist powers by launching premature revolutions. Sometimes, Comintern directives turned out to be disastrous for local communist parties. In China, for example, Comintern advisors in the early 1920s insisted that the Chinese Communist Party join the Guomindang rather than launch its own revolution. This advice backfired badly when Chiang Kai-shek turned on his communist "allies" and massacred huge numbers of them in 1927, almost destroying the CCP. In general, Stalin was more interested in protecting the Soviet state than in immediately pushing communist-inspired revolutions around the world.

COMMUNISM, THE SOVIET UNION, AND THE NAZIS

HITLER'S ANTI-COMMUNISM.   Nowhere was the impact of communism and the role of the Soviet Union more important than in the rise of the Nazis in Germany during the 1930s. An important element of Hitler's appeal within German political life was his ferocious opposition to communism, Bolshevism, and Marxism. The internationalism of these revolutionary and class-based ideologies, appealing as they did to "workers of the world," deeply offended Hitler's intense German nationalism. Furthermore, he argued, they were all led by Jews. Ridding the world of this "Bolshevik-Jewish conspiracy" lay at the heart of the Nazi message. This kind of rhetoric attracted the support of conservative German elites—industrialists, bureaucrats, and military officers who despised communism—as well as small business owners, shopkeepers, and ordinary middle-class people, who feared its revolutionary implications. Furthermore, Hitler made no secret of his belief that Germany needed to expand to the east, to seize territory in the Slavic-speaking countries of eastern Europe and the Soviet Union in order to accommodate its growing population.

STALIN'S ANTI-SOCIALISM.   But as the Nazi influence in Germany rose during the early 1930s, the Soviet Union and Comintern did little to stop it, believing that the Hitler phenomenon would be temporary and that its radicalism would turn German workers toward communism. Furthermore, Stalin promoted an especially harsh and vitriolic campaign against the German Social Democratic Party, accusing it of abandoning revolutionary goals and being in league with German capitalists and even fascists. In retrospect, this proved disastrous, for it prevented German communists from cooperating with German socialists in resisting the rise of Hitler. This deep split and hostility between "left-wing" parties, enforced in large measure by Stalin and the Comintern, contributed to the Nazi's coming to power in Germany in 1933 and to the tragedies of the Holocaust and World War II, which followed. It also enabled Hitler to more easily destroy both the communist and socialist movements in Germany.

"COLLECTIVE SECURITY." It soon became apparent that Hitler and the Nazis were no temporary phenomenon and that they were pursuing an increasingly aggressive foreign policy. Furthermore in east Asia, Japan, increasingly dominated by its military, began moving aggressively against China and by 1931 controlled Manchuria, which directly bordered the Soviet Union. When Germany and Japan signed an agreement in 1936, Stalin's worst fears seemed to be coming true: a two-pronged threat to Soviet security—Germany in the west and Japan in the east. In response to this threatening global situation, Stalin and the Comintern made a sharp turn in their approach to the world. Talk of class war and anti-imperialism gave way to pleas for peace and "collective security." Attacks on Social Democratic parties ended, and communists were now instructed to form "popular fronts" with these formerly despised groups to fight fascism together. The Soviet Union joined the League of Nations to show its respectability as a responsible great power. And Stalin made major efforts to enter into agreements with France and Great Britain aimed at restraining German aggression.

It did not work. Despite Comintern's change in approach, western leaders remained deeply suspicious about dealing with a communist country, ideologically committed to the destruction of capitalism. The Soviet purges of the 1930s further horrified British and French officials. How could one trust the military capabilities of a country that had just destroyed its top military leadership? Feeling unprepared as yet to confront Hitler militarily, the western powers acquiesced when Germany introduced military forces into the Rhineland in 1936 in violation of the Treaty of Versailles and when it absorbed Austria into Germany and demanded territorial concessions from Czechoslovakia in 1938. To Stalin, it seemed as if the western powers were unwilling to confront seriously the growing danger of German aggression and were perhaps even try-ing to encourage a German-Soviet war in the hope that fascists and communists would destroy one another.

THE NAZI-SOVIET PACT.   In these increasingly desperate circumstances, the Soviet Union again changed course dramatically. In August 1939, to the amazement of the world, Stalin and Hitler, who had for years poured abuse on one another, signed a mutual nonaggression treaty, the so-called Molotov–Ribbentrop pact. In a late night dinner after the agree-ment was finalized, Stalin even raised a toast to the German dictator: "I know how much the German nation loves its Fuhrer. I should like to drink to his health." Though it represented a complete betrayal of communist principles and shattered the confidence of many faithful communists and Soviet sympathizers, the Nazi-Soviet Pact had tempo-rary advantages for the Soviet Union. When the Second World War in Europe began on September 1, 1939, the Soviet Union looked on, unin-volved. The agreement with Hitler delayed an impending clash with Germany for two years, giving the Soviet Union additional time to prepare. While Poland and France fell to the Nazi war machine and Britain was pounded by German bombing, the Soviet Union seized territory in Poland, Ukraine, and the Baltic region as the Nazi-Soviet Pact had stipulated. Stalin had gained both time and territory for the Soviet Union.

WORLD WAR II

THE NAZI INVASION.   But in other ways, Stalin had miscalculated badly. He had not anticipated the speed of Germany military success. Poland fell to the Nazi *blitzkrieg* (lightning war) within a month in 1939. And the following year, the German war machine quickly subdued most of western Europe as Norway, Belgium, the Netherlands, and France were quickly overrun. The fall of France, widely regarded as still a great mil-itary power, after only a month's struggle in 1940 astonished everyone. During all of this, Stalin remained faithful to the Nazi-Soviet Pact, even to the point of delivering raw materials to fuel the German military drive. The rapidity of German military success in Europe left Hitler free to turn his attention and his forces to the Soviet Union by 1941, far ear-lier than Stalin had expected. But Stalin refused to believe intelligence reports from Soviet, British, and American sources indicating an immi-nent attack, and so when the Germans launched their long-planned invasion of the Soviet Union on June 22, 1941, the country was caught unprepared. Stalin himself suffered something approaching a nervous breakdown and for 10 days was unable to exert strong leadership of his beleaguered country.

THE GRAND ALLIANCE.   The German invasion of the Soviet Union created an unlikely "grand alliance" against the Nazis. Great Britain, center of the world's largest empire, and the Soviet Union, the world's sole communist country, were now allies against a common enemy. In late 1941, the United States, the world's largest capitalist economy, joined that alliance after the Japanese attack on Pearl Harbor brought the United States into the war. The United States subsequently contributed some $11 billion (worth some $90–100 billion in contemporary dollars) in material aid to the Soviet Union during the war. To cement the Alliance, in 1943 Stalin disbanded the Comintern, so offensive to western countries. "The Grand Alliance," wrote one historian, "represented a triumph of interests over ideology in a moment of shared peril."[3] The British leader Winston Churchill put it more colorfully: "If Hitler invaded Hell, I would make at least a favorable reference to the Devil in the House of Commons."

The European theater of the war took place largely on the Soviet front, where some 6 million German casualties occurred, compared to 1 million in western Europe and the Mediterranean. For a year and a half, the Germans maintained the initiative and pushed deep into the Soviet Union, coming within a few miles of Moscow itself. Then in 1943, Soviet forces defeated the Nazis at the Battle of Stalingrad and slowly began to push the Germans back into central Europe. Defeat came finally in May of 1945 with the Soviet occupation of Berlin. The Grand Alliance had achieved its stated purpose—the destruction of German military power. The cost of this victory, especially to the Soviet Union, was staggering—some 27 million people were dead, millions more were homeless, thousands of towns and villages had been destroyed, and much of the country's industrial infrastructure had been devastated.

TENSIONS IN THE GRAND ALLIANCE.   The Grand Alliance of imperialists, capitalists, and communists held throughout the war, but not without many tensions. The ideological hostility of its members, though tempered in the interests of cooperation against the Nazis, surfaced in mutual suspicions by both the Soviet and British-American leaderships that each might make a separate peace with Hitler. A more concrete source of suspicion lay in the issue of a "second front." Stalin pleaded repeatedly for the British and Americans to launch a major attack on the western front to draw away some of the German forces concentrated against the Soviet Union. Delays in launching such an attack until June of 1944 struck many Russians as a deliberate effort to weaken or cripple the Soviet Union. United States' suspicion of the Soviet Union was reflected in the American refusal to share information about the atomic bomb project with the Russians.

As the tide of the war shifted in favor of the Allies after 1943, attention turned to questions about the postwar settlement. Which of the Allies should control particular countries such as Italy, Germany, Eastern Europe, and the Balkans? Should reparations be levied against a defeated Germany and should that country be dismembered? What kind of government should be established in postwar Poland? Would the western Allies recognize the territorial gains made by the Soviet Union as a result of the Nazi-Soviet pact? All of these questions were controversial and provided the subject matter for a series of high-level conferences at Tehran, Yalta, and Potsdam.

THE SOVIET PERSPECTIVE.   The most fundamental issue concerned the fate of eastern and central Europe. From Stalin's perspective, his country had twice in the twentieth century been invaded by Germany through eastern Europe, both times with devastating effect. He was determined, therefore, to permanently weaken German military capacity and to ensure "friendly governments" throughout eastern Europe to act as a buffer between the Soviet Union and a hostile West. Furthermore, because Stalin had demanded no role in postwar Italy and had accepted British control in Greece, he felt justified in insisting on Soviet dominance in eastern Europe. And beyond that, did the British not enjoy a worldwide empire? Did the Americans not have an uncontested sphere of influence in the Caribbean and Latin America? And did they not occupy Japan alone?

THE BRITISH-AMERICAN PERSPECTIVE.   The western Allies, not surprisingly, saw things differently. The British had gone to war to protect Poland's independence and were reluctant to see a communist government imposed upon it. The Americans had defined the war idealistically in terms of democracy and self-determination while seeking a postwar world open to trade and investment everywhere. All this ran counter to Stalin's insistence on an exclusive zone of Soviet control in eastern Europe. As the war ended in victory for the Grand Alliance, the great question was whether these issues could be resolved. Could the Alliance hold in the absence of a common enemy and in the very different circumstances of the postwar world?

EUROPE DIVIDED: THE ORIGINS OF THE COLD WAR, 1945-1950

Within five years, the answer was clear. The Grand Alliance was dead, replaced by a Europe sharply divided into an eastern bloc of communist nations dominated by the Soviet Union and a western bloc led by the

United States, facing one another with mutual fear and hostility across that imaginary barrier that Winston Churchill labeled the Iron Curtain. The Cold War had begun and was soon to become global as communism triumphed in China, North Korea, and North Vietnam as well. The term itself reflected the remarkable absence of outright military conflict between the two nuclear armed superpowers, despite the deep hostility and intense competition between them over the course of a half century. But there was no shortage of war and violence, as well as much mutual misunderstanding, as this East/West divide unfolded across the globe. The two sides even defined the conflict in different ways. To the West, it was a struggle between the "free world" and totalitarian communism; to the East, it was a struggle between an aspiring socialism and the greed, exploitation, and inequities of capitalism.

The Cold War's beginning in Europe was hardly surprising. Hostility between the Soviet Union and the West began with the Bolshevik Revolution and was interrupted only by the rise of Hitler and the Nazis, which posed a common threat to both. With that threat now removed, a resumption of that hostility between ideologically incompatible societies was perhaps inevitable.

But in 1945, many thought otherwise. Western leaders sought to accommodate the Soviet need for security in Eastern Europe while enfolding the Soviet Union into the emerging international economy. Stalin was eager for western economic assistance to help in the rebuilding of his shattered country. Furthermore, he did not immediately insist on fully "sovietized" communist governments in Eastern Europe, and as late as 1947, all of them had coalition governments in which communists shared power with other parties.

FRAGMENTATION OF THE GRAND ALLIANCE

But suspicions were growing, and whatever goodwill the Grand Alliance had generated was rapidly eroding. Soviet pressure on Turkey to gain access to the Mediterranean, along with Soviet reluctance to evacuate its troops from northern Iran and to hold free elections in Eastern Europe, increased doubts in the West as to whether the Soviet Union could be a partner in the postwar world. The temporary U.S. monopoly on nuclear weapons, until the USSR acquired them in 1949, encouraged American President Harry Truman (1945–1952) to take a more belligerent posture to the Soviet Union, particularly on the issue of Poland, which Soviet leaders resented as interference in their "sphere of influence." Furthermore, the question of how to treat postwar Germany remained perhaps an even more serious point of contention—such that no peace treaty formally ending World War II could be signed. The growth of local

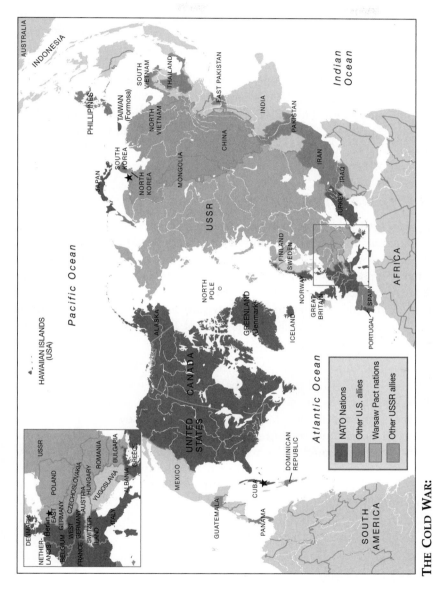

THE COLD WAR:
The rise of global communism sparked almost a half century of bitter division.

communist parties in Greece, France, and Italy, where they had gained prestige by actively opposing the Nazis, also worried western leaders and provided leverage for Soviet influence.

DECLARING THE COLD WAR.   On both sides, then, perceptions were hardening. In February 1946, Stalin made his famous "two worlds" speech, in which he asserted again the sharp difference between communism and capitalism, portrayed the world as divided into two hostile camps, and predicted inevitable war between them at some point in the future. A few weeks later, British wartime leader Winston Churchill, visiting the United States, declared that "an iron curtain has descended all across the Continent" [Europe] and called for Anglo-American cooperation against the Soviet threat. Both sides saw unlimited ambition and endless threat in the other.

ACTIONS AND REACTIONS

1947 and 1948 were the years that suspicions and declarations turned into concrete policies and actions that irrevocably launched the Cold War. A civil war in Greece pitted that country's communist forces against a conservative monarchy. American officials assumed, wrongly as it turned out, that Stalin was aiding Greek communists. Some feared that a communist victory in Greece would lead to communist control in Italy, France, and elsewhere. The fate of Europe seemed to hang in the balance.

TRUMAN DOCTRINE.   In response, the Americans launched two major initiatives that together catalyzed the division of Europe into belligerent camps. The first was the so-called Truman Doctrine, announced in mid-1947, that provided financial aid to Greece and Turkey to assist them in fending off communist pressures. In presenting this program to Congress and the American public, Truman framed it in dramatic terms. Every nation had to choose between freedom and tyranny, he declared, and the United States, as the "great arsenal of democracy," stood committed to supporting "free people" everywhere. Here was the beginning of the American policy for "containing communism," which characterized the U.S. global posture for the next 40 years.

THE MARSHALL PLAN.   The second American initiative was the Marshall Plan, a highly successful program of economic assistance for rebuilding the ravaged countries of Europe, designed in part to limit the appeal of communist propaganda by creating widespread prosperity. The Soviet Union and the countries of Eastern Europe were invited to take part. After briefly considering that possibility, Stalin rejected participation, fearing that becoming entangled in a web of capitalist economic relationships would undermine communist control and render the USSR and its allies dependent on the West.

THE SOVIET RESPONSE.   To Stalin, the Truman Doctrine and the Marshall Plan were signs of American aggression, aimed at pushing capitalism on a global basis and confirming that the United States was unwilling to accord the Soviet Union the security and benefits for which it had paid so dearly in World War II. The Soviet response, therefore, was to tighten its control over those territories that its army already controlled. Under Soviet pressure, coalition governments all across Eastern Europe were soon replaced by fully communist governments, loyal to Stalin and the USSR. A Council on Mutual Economic Assistance (COMECON) tied Eastern European economies decisively to that of the Soviet Union, while a new international organization of communist parties called Cominform served to tighten Soviet control over other communist parties. A failed attempt to force the western powers out of Berlin only hastened the creation of two Germanies: an East Germany linked to the emerging Soviet bloc and a West Germany tied increasingly to an American-led European alliance. With the formation in 1949 of the North Atlantic Treaty Organization (NATO), a western military alliance led by the United States, the world that both Churchill and Stalin had declared in 1946 began to take shape in Europe—a continent of two hostile camps divided by an iron curtain.

TWO EUROPES

World War II had ended the role of Britain, France, and Germany as truly "great powers" and had created a new balance of global power featuring the United States and the Soviet Union. The communist/capitalist divide prompted each of them to create a kind of "empire" in Europe. It was a strange reversal of fortunes for all concerned. Europeans, who had given birth to the world's modern empires, became themselves subjects of the American or Soviet empires. And the United States and the Soviet Union, both born in opposition to empire, became the leaders of competing, though quite different, empires of their own with their initial expression in Europe.

THE AMERICAN EMPIRE IN EUROPE.   The United States emerged from World War II as the world's strongest power, both economically and militarily. Its leaders were determined to avoid a retreat into isolationism as had occurred after the First World War. They viewed the United Nations, with strong U.S. participation, as a means of resolving international disputes without war. And they imagined a world open to American trade and investment as important in preventing another depression and in fostering global prosperity. The International Monetary Fund and the

World Bank were established to ensure such a world order. With these perspectives, the United States emerged as the dominant leader of the western alliance. Reflecting its own democratic traditions, the United States dealt with its European partners through negotiation and compromise. Coercion was largely unnecessary because European governments and their publics actively welcomed American leadership, American economic assistance, and American protection against the threat of Soviet aggression. It was, according to one historian, an "empire by invitation" rather than by imposition.[4]

THE SOVIET EMPIRE IN EUROPE. The Soviet empire in Eastern Europe was far different, reflecting the Soviet Union's own authoritarian character and its intolerance for competing views. Highly repressive Stalinist-style communist governments were imposed on Poland, East Germany, Czechoslovakia, Rumania, Hungary, and Bulgaria. The Soviet Union subsequently treated them as outright dependents, ordering massive purges of their communist parties in the early 1950s. Soviet leadership of this kind was clearly unwelcome and resented by most east Europeans. Thus the Soviet empire had to rely on force or the threat of it to periodically suppress anti-Soviet movements, most notably in Poland (1953, 1956, 1980), Hungary (1956), and Czechoslovakia (1968). Furthermore, unlike the wealthy Americans, the Soviets had little to offer their dependent allies in economic terms and in fact drew heavily on their resources for its own reconstruction.

But the Soviet empire did have some accomplishments and some support. Communists in many Eastern European countries had gained considerable prestige as vigorous opponents of the Nazis. In free elections of 1946, they gained 38% of the vote in Czechoslovakia. Many of the communist governments in Eastern Europe sponsored land reform programs that benefited small farmers. And in the early 1950s, planned economies carried out major programs of rapid industrialization in the previously backward countries of Eastern Europe. Most importantly from the Soviet point of view, their country's security had been enhanced by establishing Moscow's control over Eastern Europe. But this achievement came at a high price. It had provoked American hostility and an American-led system of alliances that virtually surrounded the Soviet Union, isolated it from the larger international community, and posed a continuing threat.

COMMUNIST BREAKTHROUGHS IN ASIA, 1949–1954

Although the Cold War began in Europe, it did not long remain confined to that region. A series of communist breakthroughs in Asia between 1949 and 1954 brought intense conflict—both hot and cold—to that part of the world. And as European empires in Asia and Africa crumbled in the aftermath of World War II, the "new nations" that emerged from their ruins provided still other arenas for the rivalries of the superpowers and their respective ideologies. Between 1950 and 1985, much of the world was caught up in these struggles as the Cold War assumed global dimensions.

CHINA

NEW ENEMIES FOR THE AMERICANS.   The globalization of the Cold War took shape first in Asia and most notably in China. With a speed that surprised both the United States and the Soviet Union, China's long-running civil war came to an end with a stunning victory for the Chinese Communist Party in 1949. It was an outcome that derived almost entirely from forces within China, owing very little to Soviet assistance or American actions. But its significance was enormous for both sides in the Cold War. Overnight it more than doubled the size of the communist world. Coming on the heels of communist expansion in Eastern Europe, it greatly exacerbated American fears of a steadily encroaching communist advance; it touched off an acrimonious debate about "who lost China?"—as though it were the Americans' property to lose; and it magnified a growing anti-communism in American public life. Furthermore, U.S. support solidified the remnants of Chiang Kai-shek's regime, now installed on the island of Taiwan, prevented communist China from invading the island, and created an enduring "little Cold War" between these two Chinas, which has lasted into the twenty-first century.

NEW ALLIES FOR THE SOVIET UNION.   For the Soviet Union, China's revolution meant an ally of major proportions, although one quite different from its dependent allies in Eastern Europe. Although communism had been largely imposed on Eastern Europe from outside, it was a wholly homegrown product in China, and that country entered into an alliance with the Soviet Union quite voluntarily and for its own reasons. One such reason was a common commitment to Marxism. Despite considerable differences over the years, Chinese and Soviet communists were comrades, fighting on the same side of a global struggle of historic dimensions. Mao in particular genuinely admired Stalin, had a great respect for his success in modernizing the Soviet Union, and looked forward to Soviet help in bringing China out of backwardness. Furthermore, Mao fully expected active American intervention in China to eliminate his fledgling revolution. Alignment with the Soviet Union, he hoped, would deter American aggression.

Stalin welcomed his new ally enthusiastically, seeing in the Chinese revolution a new opening for world revolution. He actually apologized for the bad advice and neglect with which the USSR had treated the Chinese Communist Party in the past and encouraged China to play the leading role in fostering communism in the colonial or semi-colonial countries outside of Europe. "I sincerely hope," he declared, "that the younger brother [China] will one day catch up with and surpass the elder brother [the Soviet Union]."[5] But not all was sweetness and light between the two communist giants. The slights and disagreements of the past were not easily forgotten. During a two-month visit to the Soviet Union shortly after seizing power, Mao and Stalin bargained hard, finally arriving at a mutual security agreement and promises of modest Soviet loans. Mao had hoped for more. Furthermore, Mao had to accept a Soviet-dominated Mongolia to the north of China, which he had hoped to incorporate within China itself. Here were some of the seeds of what became a decade later a serious split within the communist world.

KOREA

A DIVIDED PENINSULA. Korea represented a second communist breakthrough in Asia, but one that occurred quite differently than that of China. Korea had been a Japanese colony throughout the twentieth century. The sudden collapse of Japanese power at the end of World War II created a power vacuum, which was filled jointly by the Soviet Union and the United States by dividing the country at the thirty-eighth parallel. The Soviet Union imposed a communist regime on the northern half of the peninsula under the leadership of Kim Il-sung, while the Americans chose Syngman Rhee to create a very anti-Communist and authoritarian government in the south. But both superpowers withdrew their military forces from Korea by 1949, apparently agreeing not to compete further on the peninsula. Each of their client states, however, had ambitions to reunite the country.

THE KOREAN WAR. Within a year, the Korean peninsula exploded in war. That bitter conflict was initiated by the North Korean regime, demonstrating that small dependent states could sometimes pull the great powers themselves into unintended confrontations. Believing that he could unite a divided Korea under a communist government, Kim approached both Stalin and Mao, seeking their permission to launch an attack on the south. Both were skeptical but finally agreed, buoyed perhaps by the recent success of communism in Eastern Europe and China and believing that the Americans would not intervene. But when the North Koreans invaded the south in 1950, the Americans did respond, immediately and massively, acting under the authority of the United Nations. And when U.S. military success seemed likely to topple communist North Korea altogether, the Chinese, acting under intense Soviet pressure, entered the conflict with hundreds of thousands of "volunteers." A military stalemate ensued, and an armistice brought the conflict to a close in 1953. That brutal war with some 4 million casualties, most of them Korean, had ended with the peninsula still divided at close to the thirty-eighth parallel.

The international outcome of the Korean conflict was an extension and intensification of the Cold War. On the Korean peninsula itself, an enduring "little Cold War" followed, as North and South settled in for a tense and highly militarized standoff, lasting into the next century. The United States claimed to have saved South Korea from communist aggression, but it had failed to win the war outright. That experience, however, cemented American perceptions of a militant communism on the march. In its aftermath, the United States established a permanent military presence in South Korea and poured huge sums of money into rebuilding, rearming, and defending West Germany, Japan, and Taiwan as part of the western anti-communist alliance. These actions only heightened Soviet and Chinese suspicions and their sense of being threatened or encircled by the forces of capitalism.

VIETNAM

Ho Chi Minh.   Communism gained a third Asian foothold in Vietnam, a French colony since the late nineteenth century. The Japanese had chased the French out of Vietnam during World War II, but as the war ended, the French made plans to return. But in doing so, they encountered serious opposition in the form of a nationalist movement called the Vietminh, led by Vietnamese communist and former pastry chef Ho Chi Minh. Unable to defeat Ho's forces on their own, the French asked for American help by 1948. The United States was generally sympathetic to nationalist movements for independence from colonial rule. Had they not fought an anti-colonial war themselves? Furthermore, Ho had cited the American Declaration of Independence in proclaiming his resistance to the French. But the emerging Cold War and the fear of communism complicated the equation for the United States. So while encouraging the French to reform their colonial rule and to move Vietnam toward independence under a non-communist regime, the United States agreed to supply France with considerable military aid in their efforts to defeat the communist Vietminh. Fighting communism was more important than supporting nationalism.

Vietnam Divided.   But Ho and the Vietminh had an external ally as well. The Soviet Union was fully engaged in Europe and largely ignored the fate of the distant Vietnamese communists in the 1940s, but China, following the communist victory in 1949, was more than willing to help. With substantial Chinese military assistance, Ho wore the French down and finally defeated them at a decisive battle at Dien Bien Phu in 1954. The outcome, as in Korea and Germany, was a divided country, with North Vietnam under communist Vietminh control and the South independent under a corrupt anti-communist regime led by Ngo Dinh Diem with growing American support.

Thus, by the mid-1950s, communism had come to Asia, massively in the case of China and on a smaller scale in Korea and Vietnam. In all three cases the countries were divided, reflecting within particular states the larger global rift of the Cold War. These Asian developments made western fears of a steadily advancing communist menace even more acute and deepened the hostilities of the Cold War.

THE GLOBAL EXPANSION OF THE COLD WAR, 1955–1985

Paralleling the spread of communism in the postwar world was the collapse of European colonial empires in Asia, the Middle East, and Africa and the emergence of dozens of "new nations." Together with the countries of Latin America, they became the "Third World," distinct from the "first world" of the western capitalist countries and the "second," or communist, world. Despite vast differences among them in size, culture, history, and political system, they shared an intense desire to protect their fragile, recently won independence and a consuming interest in economic development and catching up with the more industrialized countries of the world.

Here lay, potentially, an attractive opening for the further spread of communism. The Soviet Union, after all, shared the anti-imperialist sentiments of the "new nations" believing, as Lenin put it, that imperialism was "the highest stage of capitalism." And had the Soviet Union not modeled an alternative and rapid path to industrialization through a state-planned economy? Furthermore, recent developments in China, Korea, and Vietnam demonstrated the appeal of communism in precisely such impoverished and ex-colonial settings. Many in the West feared that having stabilized the Cold War in Europe, it might yet lose the Cold War in the Third World.

THE SOVIET UNION AND THE THIRD WORLD

Until the death of Stalin in 1953, the Soviet Union had focused its attention on Europe and the communist states of East Asia and had paid little concrete attention to the regions that were becoming the Third World. But Stalin's successors, Nikita Khrushchev (1954–1964) and Leonid

Brezhnev (1964–1983), led their country into a much deeper engagement with the "new nations." Whereas Stalin had viewed the nationalist leaders of Asia and Africa with suspicion because they were not communists, Khrushchev saw them as potential allies who had a common interest in countering western imperialism and who might evolve toward socialism. In short, they were worth pursuing.

EXTENDING SOVIET INFLUENCE.   And pursue them he did! During his decade in power, Khrushchev traveled widely and often invited third-world leaders to Moscow. He began to extend economic aid to developing countries, and by 1981 the Soviet Union and its eastern European allies had contributed about $34 billion to well over 50 non-communist countries, mostly in low-interest loans. The Soviet Union also became a major arms supplier to the Third World, second only to the United States. Such assistance—both economic and military—allowed the Soviet Union to court Arab states, especially Egypt, and thus challenge western dominance in the Middle East. It also created a particularly close relationship with India. Tens of thousands of Soviet technical advisers were sent to the Third World, and large numbers of Asian and African students came to the Soviet Union for education. A People's Friendship University, catering to third-world students, was established in Moscow in 1960. In the United Nations, the Soviet Union generally supported third-world positions. In the 1970s, as Soviet military capacity increased and as a number of third-world countries evolved in a more radical direction, the Soviet Union found additional opportunities. In Ethiopia, Angola, Laos, and Cambodia, Soviet support helped to consolidate governments friendly to and dependent on the Soviet Union. The Soviet Union had become a global power with connections and interests around the world.

But Soviet extension into the Third World did little to spread communism itself. Countries with which the Soviet Union had friendly relations, Egypt and Iraq for example, routinely jailed or persecuted local communists. The militant atheism of Soviet practice had little appeal in the intensely religious cultures of Islamic, Hindu, Buddhist, and African countries. Furthermore, the Soviet Union had less to offer economically than the wealthier western capitalist nations. But Marxist ideas did spread, particularly among intellectuals in the Third World, and some in the West as well, providing some sympathy and support for the Soviet Union's position in world affairs.

CUBA: COMMUNIST TRIUMPH, COLD WAR CRISIS

THE CUBAN REVOLUTION.   But communism found a surprising foothold and the Soviet Union gained an unexpected ally in the early 1960s in an unlikely corner of the world and on the very doorstep of its American rival. The place was Cuba, economically dominated by U.S. corporations and a virtual American dependency since the end of Spanish rule in 1898. By the late 1950s, a revolutionary movement aimed at overthrowing Cuba's corrupt dictatorship took shape under the leadership of a fiery and charismatic Fidel Castro. With the victory of Castro's movement in early 1959, the new Cuban government began radical land reform and the expropriation of foreign-owned businesses. American hostility to these measures encouraged Castro to look to the Soviet Union for support and assistance, and gradually he began to think of himself and his new regime as Marxist.

A SOVIET WINDFALL.   For the Soviet Union, the Cuban Revolution represented a wholly unexpected plum that had fallen into its lap with virtually no effort. Here was an authentic and popular revolutionary regime, now espousing Marxism and seeking Soviet assistance, only 90 miles from Florida! Communism had breached the western hemisphere, long the exclusive preserve of American capitalism. A high Soviet official described the elation with which they greeted this remarkable development: "You Americans must realize what Cuba means to us old Bolsheviks. We have been waiting all our lives for a country to go communist without the Red Army. It has happened in Cuba, and it makes us feel like boys again."[6]

AMERICAN HOSTILITY.   What was elation for Soviet leaders became fear and loathing for the American government. The United States severed relations with Castro's Cuba, established an economic embargo on the country, and began planning to eliminate this offensive outpost of communism in its hemisphere. In 1961 an American trained force of anti-Castro Cuban exiles failed entirely to spark an expected uprising in Cuba, and the invaders were crushed. Subsequent American efforts to assassinate Castro likewise failed.

THE MISSILE CRISIS.   This was the context for the Soviet decision in 1962 to secretly place in Cuba missiles and nuclear warheads capable of striking the United States. It was the boldest Soviet effort of the Cold War to challenge the dominant position of the United States and to do so in its own back yard. To Soviet leader Khrushchev, it was primarily an effort to protect the Cuban revolution from demonstrated American hostility. To allow this new outpost of communism to be uprooted by the Americans would have been a serious blow to Soviet prestige and to world communism generally. It also served to correct the strategic imbalance of nuclear weapons, for the United States had recently installed similar missiles in Turkey on the southern border of the Soviet Union. "The

Americans had surrounded our country with military bases and threatened us with nuclear weapons," declared Khrushchev, "and now they would learn just what it feels like to have enemy missiles pointing at you; we'd be doing nothing but giving them a little of their own medicine."[7]

The American discovery of the missiles in October 1962 set off the worst crisis of the Cold War, bringing the world to the very brink of nuclear war. United States President John F. Kennedy ordered a naval "quarantine" of Cuba and made obvious preparation to invade the island. A direct clash of Soviet and American armed forces seemed imminent and nuclear war a probability. But after 13 days of intense negotiations, a compromise was arranged by which the Soviet Union agreed to remove the missiles, the Americans promised not to invade Cuba, and in a secret side agreement, pledged to dismantle its own missiles in Turkey a few months later. Both sides could claim to have won important concessions. The Cuban missile crisis was over and the world could breathe again.

AMERICA AND THE COMMUNIST THREAT IN THE THIRD WORLD

The communist phenomenon, interacting with the end of European empires and the growth of nationalism in the Third World, posed a serious challenge to the Western world in general and the United States in particular. How could the West maintain its dominant position in the Third World, even as its empires were rapidly fading? How could the United States counter the increasingly aggressive Soviet and Chinese interest in making allies in the Third World?

COUNTERING COMMUNISM.   One answer, of course, was aid. Beginning with the program to assist Greece and Turkey in combating communism in 1947, the United States funneled substantial sums of money and equipment to almost 100 countries in far larger amounts than the Soviet Union could afford. Its Peace Corps program, begun in the early 1960s, scattered tens of thousands of young Americans all across the Third World to assist in education and development projects and to win friends for the United States. Furthermore, private corporations and banks fostered trade and investment opportunities in many third-world countries, strengthening their ties to the West. So, too, did educational opportunities in the United States or western Europe. All of this was useful, many leading Americans believed, in enabling third-world countries to make the difficult and often destabilizing transition to modernity without succumbing to the "disease" of communism. Aid, trade, and investment in this view represented a kind of inoculation against that disease.

INTERVENTION, DICTATORS, AND ALLIANCES. But where the disease seemed to take root anyway, stronger measures—surgery in the medical metaphor—might be necessary. Covert American action and assistance to anti-communist forces helped to overthrow leftist governments in Iran (1953), Guatemala (1954), and Chile (1973) on the grounds that they might become beachheads for communism or Soviet penetration. More open military action was undertaken in Korea, the Dominican Republic, Grenada, and most famously in Vietnam (see below) to eliminate the threat of communism.

A further American strategy involved the active support of strongly anti-communist regimes, even though they might be corrupt, undemocratic, and brutal. The Shah of Iran, Zaire's famously corrupt dictator Mobutu Sese Seko, Ferdinand Marcos in the Philippines, and any number of conservative military regimes in Latin America were among U.S. client states. They were surely "bastards," commented one official, but they were "our bastards." A further American ally was the apartheid state of South Africa, where fear of instability and communist penetration were among the factors that inhibited U.S. willingness to strongly confront that country's racist policies.

A series of global alliances and military bases sought to create a barrier against further communist expansion and to provide launching points for military action should it become necessary. By 1970, one writer observed, "the United States had more than 1,000,000 soldiers in 30 countries, was a member of four regional defense alliances and an active participant in a fifth, had mutual defense treaties with 42 nations, was a member of 53 international organizations, and was furnishing military or economic aid to nearly 100 nations across the face of the globe."[8]

SUPERPOWER LIMITATIONS. But neither the Soviet Union nor the United States was able to completely dominate their supposed third-world allies in the Cold War. Many sought actively to remain "nonaligned" in the global rivalries of the Cold War or to play off the global superpowers against one another. India routinely took aid from both sides and criticized both of them while resolutely maintaining its neutrality. Indonesia, having received large amounts of Soviet and east European aid, destroyed the Indonesian Communist Party in 1965, butchering a half-million suspected communists in the process. Egypt turned decisively against the West in the mid-1950s, developing a close relationship with the Soviet Union, but in 1972, it expelled 21,000 Soviet advisers and aligned more clearly with the United States. Ethiopia, long a close ally of the United States with a large American communications base in its country, underwent a major change of government in the 1970s, becoming for a time a Marxist state and a Soviet ally. Neither side in the Cold War found it easy to impose its will in the Third World.

THE AMERICAN WAR IN VIETNAM

Nowhere was that reality more starkly demonstrated than in the long and unsuccessful American struggle to prevent communism from spreading from North Vietnam to the South. With the division of that country in 1954, its southern and non-communist half came to rely increasingly on American support in the face of growing and coordinated efforts by local communists (the Viet Cong) and the North Vietnamese government, armed and supported by the Soviet Union and China, to reunite the country under communist rule. A South Vietnamese government of bickering generals, often at odds with the country's Buddhists monks, was unable to counter the growing communist forces effectively. First, American military advisers and then growing numbers of American ground troops—some 550,000 by late 1967—were sent to South Vietnam to combat the communist offensive in what was becoming a protracted, brutal, and very well-publicized war. From the air, American forces dropped a greater tonnage of bombs than in all of World War II.

THE DOMINO THEORY. Why did the Americans make such a huge investment of manpower and resources in a small country in Southeast Asia? The core of the answer lies in the way the Cold War had shaped U.S. official thinking.[9] Communism in this view was a global movement, coordinated from the Soviet Union and China, an infinite peril to free societies and personal liberties everywhere, as well as to American economic interests around the world. A significant communist success, such as that which seemed imminent in Vietnam, could well trigger an escalating domino effect of further communist victories throughout Asia and beyond. Communist insurgencies in Burma, Indonesia, Malaya, and the Philippines represented the dominos waiting to fall. Only unwavering American commitment held the promise of containing that threat. "The aim [of the communists] in Viet-Nam is not simply the conquest of the South, tragic as that would be," argued President Lyndon Johnson in 1965. "It is to show that the American commitment is worthless. Once that is done, the gates are down, and the road is open to expansion and endless conquest."[10] For American leaders, the failure to oppose an expansionist Hitler in the 1930s had led to World War II; it was a lesson that had to be applied to containing communist expansion in the 1960s.

FIGURE 5-1   COLD WAR VICTIMS:
This Vietnamese woman, pleading with an American soldier while her home burns, was among the victims of the global conflict between communist world and the western capitalist world.

A COMMUNIST VICTORY.   The war in Vietnam had profound implication for all involved. That war had devastated Vietnam, killing some 900,000 of its people, smashing its infrastructure, and polluting its territory with land mines and chemicals. But the Vietnamese communists won the war. Their tenacity, the support from the Soviet Union and China, the weakness of the South Vietnamese regime, and bitter and growing opposition to the war within the United States drove American troops from the country by 1973 and allowed its reunification under communist control two years later. It was a remarkable victory over the world's greatest military power.

AN AMERICAN DEFEAT.   For the United States, it was a humiliating defeat, the first war the country had lost in its history. Some 58,000 Americans were killed. Bitter and divisive conflict about the war rent the fabric of American society as its often senseless brutality vividly entered American homes on the televised evening news. The war chased President Lyndon Johnson from political life, radicalized a generation of young Americans, generated enormous protests on the streets and university campuses, and divided the country as had nothing else since the Civil War.

It deeply shook the confidence of many Americans, and others, in the wisdom and moral sensibility of U.S. authorities and their policies.

INTERNATIONAL IMPACT.   In Vietnam, the Cold War rivalries and ideological hostilities of the superpowers had elevated a civil war between two parts of a small divided country into a major international conflict. In the process, it vastly magnified the destructiveness of that civil war. But the direct impact was primarily regional rather than global. The communist victory in Vietnam as well as American bombing in those countries contributed to the success of communists in neighboring Laos and Cambodia. Particularly in Cambodia it resulted in an extraordinarily murderous regime known as the Khmer Rouge, determined to implement communism almost overnight. This came to involve the emptying of the cities, the abolition of money, total collectivization, the elimination of entire groups of people, such as property owners, businessmen, and intellectuals, and the killing of perhaps a quarter of the country's population—all in the space of several years. Adding to the miseries was an extended war between the Vietnamese and Cambodian communists lasting through much of the 1980s.

But beyond Laos and Cambodia, the dominos did not fall as many Americans had feared. No further extension of communism in Asia or elsewhere followed the Vietnamese victory. Nor did the larger states become militarily involved with one another during the war. Neither the Soviet Union nor China contributed troops to the war, although they supported the communist North Vietnamese with substantial military aid, equipment, and training. The Soviets, of course, were pleased to see their American rival bogged down in a debilitating conflict, but they gained little from the communist triumph except a naval base in Vietnam and an impoverished ally needing endless assistance.

A SOVIET VIETNAM: AFGHANISTAN

Elsewhere as well, the Cold War projected local conflicts onto the global stage as the major contending powers got involved. The Arab-Israeli conflict, disputes between Somalia and Ethiopia, a civil war in Angola—all of these engaged the Soviet Union and the United States on opposite sides of local issues. The closest parallel to the situation in Vietnam took shape in Afghanistan, where a Marxist party had taken power in 1978. The Soviet Union was delighted at this extension of communism on its southern border. But radical land reforms and efforts to liberate Afghan women soon alienated much of this conservative Muslim country and led to a growing opposition movement under Islamic leadership that threatened to topple the new communist government. Soviet leaders decided that this would be an intolerable setback and might open the country to gathering forces of Islamic radicalism. Thus, they intervened militarily and by 1985 had more than 150,000 troops in Afghanistan.

Like the Americans in Vietnam, the Soviet Union became bogged down in guerrilla warfare, sustained growing numbers of casualties, and endured rising protests at home. It was "a bleeding wound" that alienated millions of Soviet citizens, the Americans, the Chinese, and the Islamic world. Under widespread international pressure, they withdrew in 1989, and by 1992 communism was gone from Afghanistan.

Even more than Vietnam, the Soviet invasion of Afghanistan brought the Cold War to a new level of intensity. Americans saw it as blatant aggression and possibly a Soviet move toward the Persian Gulf with its enormous and critical supplies of oil. President Jimmy Carter ordered an embargo on selling grain and high-technology goods to the Soviet Union, limited cultural and scientific exchanges, and withdrew U.S. athletes from the 1980 Olympics in Moscow. The United States provided substantial military assistance to the anti-communist *mujadeen* in Afghanistan, who wore away the Soviet forces. And the Americans, under the leadership of President Ronald Reagan, launched an across-the-board military buildup in yet another ratcheting up of the arms race. Although the war in Vietnam had seriously divided American society, the Soviet war in Afghanistan had an even more profound impact. It added to the growing disenchantment, even outrage, with Soviet communism and contributed to the collapse of the entire system by 1991. Not a few Soviet Afghan veterans, together with their friends and families, came to realize what that war had cost their country in terms of lives, money, widespread deception by political leaders, and the honor of the military. Many turned their backs on communism altogether in response. Afghanistan then was the last major crisis of the Cold War as that vast global conflict, together with one of its protagonists, faded away in the early 1990s.

THE COLD WAR AND THE NUCLEAR ARMS RACE

If the rise of the Soviet Union as a communist superpower touched off East/West rivalries in the Third World, it also generated another enduring feature of the Cold War—a massive buildup of military hardware, especially nuclear weapons. These weapons were destructive in a way hardly imaginable before 1945, threatening the extinction of human life, perhaps all life, on the planet. A few days after the Americans dropped an atomic bomb on Hiroshima in 1945, Stalin called some of the country's leading physicists together and told them: "Hiroshima has shaken the whole world. The balance has been broken. Build the bomb—it will remove a great danger from us."[11] The nuclear arms race had begun.

It continued for some 40 years. During that time, both sides acquired huge quantities of atomic bombs and far more powerful hydrogen bombs. They learned how to make these explosives lighter and smaller as well as ever larger and more destructive. They manufactured ingenuous ways of delivering these doomsday weapons to distant targets all around the world. Huge aircraft or manned bombers were the initial means of delivery, but rockets, especially intercontinental ballistic missiles (ICBMs), soon became the symbol of the arms race everywhere. These were terrifying weapons, for they could carry city-destroying bombs halfway around the world in 30 minutes. Both sides devised means of targeting these missiles with ever increasing accuracy and of loading single missiles with multiple warheads. Many such missiles found homes in underground silos from which they might be quickly launched; others were placed on submarines, scattered beneath the world's oceans where they were virtually invulnerable to attack; still others could be fired from airplanes in flight. All of this for 40 years and in ever growing numbers.

CAUSES AND CONSEQUENCES

MORE AND BETTER WEAPONS.   Underlying this enormous buildup in weapons of mass destruction were the elemental facts of technological possibility and the bitter rivalry of ideologically hostile superpowers. Twentieth-century nuclear physics, from which nuclear weapons were derived, could not be unlearned. That knowledge was available, and expanding it and applying it was a sweet task for scientists on both sides of the iron curtain, especially when that enterprise was lavishly supported by their governments. And if scientists and technicians could construct these weapons, governments could hardly resist acquiring them, for were their sworn enemies not already doing so? Advances on one side led to renewed efforts on the other as debates about who was ahead or behind with particular weapon systems spurred on both. When the Soviet Union successfully tested the first ICBM in 1957 and used it to launch a small satellite into earth orbit, a shaken American government poured additional resources into its own missile program, which soon surpassed that of the Soviet Union.

The interests of the various military forces—army, navy, air force—as well as those of the industries that supported them, provided additional momentum to the arms race. In the United States it was called the "military-industrial complex" and in the Soviet Union, the "metal eaters' alliance." Both President Eisenhower in the United States and Soviet leader Khrushchev favored nuclear weapons because they were less expensive than conventional forces, providing "more bang for the buck." In the American system of competing parties and elections, domestic politics played a role as Republicans and Democrats periodically accused one another of failing to keep up in the arms race.

GLOBAL MILITARIZATION. Nor was the arms race limited to nuclear weapons and the superpowers. The British, French, Chinese, Indians, and Pakistanis all became nuclear powers, though on a far smaller scale than the United States and the Soviet Union. As it became apparent that nuclear weapons were difficult, if not impossible, to actually use on the battlefield, the buildup of conventional forces—soldiers, navies, tanks, fighter jets, and all the equipment they required—also accelerated. Many Third World countries took part in this global militarization as well, supplied for the most part by the rival superpowers and their allies. Between 1960 and 1983, Third World spending on the military increased from $33 billion to $162 billion, growing at about twice the rate of military expenditures in the industrial world. Since World War II, 120 separate wars (civil and international) have occurred, almost all of them in the Third World and many fought with imported arms. Civil war in Nigeria in the late 1960s, the carnage in Cambodia, the Iran/Iraq conflict of the 1980s, several Arab/Israeli wars, the almost complete breakdown of civil order in parts of Africa—these are but a few of the many conflicts fought with imported weapons.

COSTS OF MILITARIZATION. Global militarization has clearly had economic consequences, for resources devoted to military spending were unavailable for other more productive purposes. The high price of militarization was particularly apparent in the poorer countries of the Third World, where the cost of a single modern tank could provide storage facilities for 100,000 tons of rice or build 1,000 classrooms for 30,000 children. The Soviet Union, too, suffered greatly from the need to keep up with its far wealthier American rival. While the United States typically invested between 5% and 8% of its GNP for defense during the Cold War, the Soviet Union found it necessary to devote 20% or more of its economy to military purposes. Here lay one source of Soviet economic stagnation, which contributed so much to the country's collapse in 1991.

HAUNTED BY NUCLEAR WEAPONS. The arms race also had profound psychic consequences, most visible in the more open societies of the West. Several generations of people since 1945 have lived their lives in the shadow of nuclear weapons, whose destructive power is scarcely within the bounds of human imagination. The public generally became aware that a single bomb in a single instant could obliterate any major city in the world. They learned that the detonation of even a small fraction of those weapons in the arsenals of the nuclear superpower could reduce the target countries to radioactive rubble and social chaos. Scientists warned that "nuclear winter" would likely follow a nuclear war— "prolonged darkness, abnormally low temperatures, violent windstorms, toxic smog, and persistent radioactive fallout." Under such conditions, they declared, "the extinction of many species of organisms—including the human species—is a real possibility."[12] Films such as *The Day After* vividly depicted the likely consequences of nuclear war to a wide audience. A widely read book of the 1980s, *The Fate of the Earth,* explored the meaning of extinction for those currently living. Many came to agree with Nikita Khrushchev's observation that in the event of nuclear war, "the living would envy the dead."

THINKING ABOUT NUCLEAR WEAPONS

The advent of nuclear weapons into the arsenals of the superpowers also occasioned a prolonged debate among strategists, defense intellectuals, political leaders, and others about the practical implications of these new devices. Was it possible to imagine actually using them without destroying the very things for which the war was being fought? Were they in fact weapons at all, in any ordinary sense of that term? What were they good for?

MUTUAL ASSURED DESTRUCTION (MAD).   One answer to the question was deterrence. Upon contemplating the possibility of massive retaliation by the other side, the argument went, no rational leader would start a war. The purpose of nuclear weapons, then, was wholly psychological— to prevent a war from beginning by persuading one's opponent that doing so would result in his utter destruction. Mutual Assured Destruction, as it was called, was simply a fact of life by the early 1960s. It was also the declared policy of the United States. On the Soviet side, it caused a change in the long-held Marxist doctrine of "inevitable war" between communism and capitalism. The military strength of the peace-loving "socialist camp" would prevent the "imperialists" from unleashing all-out war against an advancing communist tide.

NUCLEAR UTILIZATION STRATEGIES (NUTS).   But there were problems with the MAD idea. One was moral. Was it morally permissible to base American security on a threat to kill untold millions of noncombatants? There was also the issue of credibility. If confronted by a conventional attack or a political provocation, would any nuclear power actually unleash its nuclear weapons, knowing full well that it would mean mutual suicide? If not, was MAD a believable policy against anything other than an all-out nuclear attack? Such thinking highlighted the importance of building up conventional forces as well. It also led to the idea of designing smaller and highly accurate nuclear weapons and actually planning to use them on the battlefield. This kind of "limited nuclear war-fighting capability" would provide political leaders with alternatives to either surrender or suicide in the event of enemy attack and thus make deterrence more credible. But critics argued that it also made the use of nuclear weapons seem reasonable and offered no way to assure that "limited nuclear war" would not escalate into a massive exchange. In the fog of war, was this kind of rational control and gradual escalation really likely? Or were nuclear weapons simply too immense and overwhelming to be entrusted to fragile hands of leaders, always prone to error and misjudgment?

ARMAGEDDON AVOIDED: A REMARKABLE NONEVENT

Fortunately, and amazingly, none of this was ever put to the test, for during the four decades of the Cold War, despite numerous crises, bitter hostility, and ever-growing arsenals, no nuclear weapons were ever used. Furthermore, the military forces of the Soviet Union and the United States never engaged one another in conventional war. Much blood was spilled during the Cold War, but the entire East/West conflict passed without a single shot being fired directly between the two major protagonists. It was a remarkable and quite unexpected feature of the Cold War.

EXPLAINING THE SUPERPOWER PEACE. The most obvious explanation for absence of war between the superpowers is that nuclear deterrence worked. The sure knowledge of what nuclear weapons could do, demonstrated so vividly at Hiroshima and Nagasaki and at numerous test sites, certainly sobered leaders on both sides and induced a greater caution than might otherwise have prevailed. Particularly after the Cuban missile crisis in 1962, that sense of horror at what might have been generated efforts to negotiate some stability in the relationship of the United States and the Soviet Union. The two sides established a "hot line" between the White House and the Kremlin to facilitate communication in a crisis. They agreed to halt the testing of nuclear weapons in the atmosphere. And in the 1970s, they adopted some modest limitations on the number of nuclear weapons that each side might possess. None of this did much to slow down the arms race, but it reflected a recognition of the dangerous situation into which they had both stumbled.

Furthermore, some scholars have argued that a bipolar international system with only two major powers was inherently more stable than one with many equal powers jockeying for position. With separate economies and relatively equal military forces, the two great powers learned to live with one another, despite frequent quarrels and fundamental distrust. Earth-orbiting satellites, cameras in the sky, helped them to do so, providing accurate information as to the capabilities of their opponent. With this kind of information, misjudgments were less likely. Because neither really had designs on the territory of the other, they waged their global struggles using other people—Koreans, Vietnamese, Cubans, Afghans—as cannon fodder and thus avoided direct conflict between themselves.

DISSENSION IN THE COMMUNIST WORLD

COMMUNIST ACHIEVEMENTS, COMMUNIST WEAKNESSES

In the course of the Cold War, communism gained a global presence. From its initial outpost in the Soviet Union, it had embraced China, Eastern Europe, North Korea, much of Southeast Asia, Cuba, and briefly Afghanistan. The Soviet Union in particular had gained a much sought-after security buffer zone in Eastern Europe. It had established a worldwide network of political and economic relationships, and it had emerged by the 1970s as the full military equal of the United States and a global superpower.

On the other hand, the global spread of communism had provoked a powerful anticommunist alliance to combat it. The western, or the "free world," was far wealthier and apparently more successful economically than the communist world, and the western capitalist democracies, despite their association with an older and despised imperialism, proved more attractive in many parts of the world. Certainly few Third World people found migration to the Soviet Union an appealing prospect, whereas millions sought entry to west European countries or the United States. The oppression, brutality, and violence that accompanied the building of socialism almost everywhere badly tarnished the image of world communism.

A further weakness of the communist world lay in the bitter divisions between its various states. Here was a wholly unexpected outcome of the spread of communism. Many in the West saw world communism as a monolithic force whose disciplined members meekly followed Soviet dictates. And Marxists everywhere contended that revolutionary socialism would erode national loyalties, as the "workers of the world" found solidarity among themselves in common opposition to global capitalism. How strange, then, that the communist world experienced far more bitter and divisive conflict than the western alliance, composed of supposedly warlike, greedy, and highly competitive nations. When France largely withdrew from the North Atlantic Treaty Organization (NATO) in the mid-1960s, no one in the western alliance even imagined invading their recalcitrant ally. But the Soviet Union did invade its Hungarian and Czecho-slovakian allies and came to the very brink of war with Poland, Yugoslavia, and China. These bitter disputes played a major role in the international politics of the Cold War, while undermining the credibility and strength of the communist world in its 40-year struggle with capitalism.

TITO AND YUGOSLAVIA

The first site of major dissension within the communist world was Yugoslavia. In that country, local communists, led by Joseph Broz, or Tito, had led the resistance to the Nazis, gained considerable popular support, and came to power after World War II on their own without much Soviet help. Although he was a loyal supporter of the Soviet Union and Stalin, Tito also believed in various roads to socialism and that "everyone [should] be master in his own house." Here was the sticking point, for Stalin was determined to be master of the communist house, particularly in Europe. Disagreements over economic ties with the Soviet Union, over aid to Greek communists, and over plans for a proposed federation of Balkan states soured the relationship. In behaving like an independent communist state, Yugoslavia threatened Soviet control over the other communist parties of eastern Europe and enraged Stalin. "I shall shake my little finger," he declared, "and there will be no Tito." Soviet plans for an invasion of Yugoslavia were never implemented, but Stalin did expel it from the communist bloc and purged Tito's support-ers in the other Eastern European countries. Yugoslavia went on to develop its own form of communism and retained its independence within the communist world.

EASTERN EUROPE

The communist-governed states in Eastern Europe were in a different position, for most of them shared a common border with the Soviet Union and their communist parties came to power with substantial Soviet help and enjoyed little grassroots popular support. They were anything but independent. Nonetheless, in Hungary, Czechoslovakia, and Poland, reform-minded communists sought internal change and greater inde-pendence from Soviet dictates. They found support for these aspirations in the Soviet Union after Stalin's death in 1953. There the new Soviet leader Khrushchev initiated a wave of reforms aimed at "deStalinizing" the Soviet Union, and in a famous speech in 1956, he bitterly denounced the crimes of the Soviet dictator.

HUNGARY, 1956–57. These events had echoes in Eastern Europe and especially in Hungary, where they triggered a major uprising in Budapest that briefly brought to power a popular reform-minded communist, Imre Nagy. As the revolt spread and became more openly anti-communist, Nagy abolished the one-party system in Hungary and withdrew the country from the Warsaw Pact, the communist bloc's military alliance. In response to this open defiance of standard communist practice and Soviet control, Khrushchev ordered an invasion of Hungary to crush the "counterrevolution." To the Soviet leadership, the success of the Hungarian revolt meant that "we would have capitalists on the frontier of the Soviet Union." Nagy himself was arrested and executed, and some 200,000 Hungarians fled the country into exile. The image of Soviet troops shooting Hungarian students and workers provided further evidence of communist brutality in the minds of already anti-communist westerners.

CZECHOSLOVAKIA 1968. A decade later, something similar took shape in Czechoslovakia, when reformers within the Party came to power in the midst of serious economic difficulties. Led by Alexander Dubcek, they initiated far-reaching changes. Censorship diminished, newspapers explored previously forbidden topics such as the purge trials of the 1950s, and provocative theatrical productions played to packed houses. The country came alive politically in hundreds of meetings where matters of public policy were openly discussed. Talk of multiparty democracy and "market socialism" swept the country. This was the "Prague Spring" and it aroused enormous hope in millions of Czechoslovaks and many others around the world who saw in it the possibility of what Dubcek called "socialism with a human face."

But the Soviet Union increasingly saw it otherwise. Dubcek sought to reassure his Soviet overseers that, unlike in Hungary, the Party remained in control of the reform process and would not take the country out of the Warsaw Pact. To Soviet leader Brezhnev and his conservative colleagues, however, it was a dangerous precedent that could well infect other communist bloc countries, including the Soviet Union itself. Thus, in late August of 1968, almost a half-million Soviet and Soviet-bloc troops occupied Czechoslovakia, crushed the Prague Spring, and installed a conservative and pro-Soviet government on the country. Accompanying the invasion was the so-called Brezhnev Doctrine, which proclaimed the right of the Soviet Union to intervene in Soviet-bloc countries to "save socialism" and prevent "the restoration of a capitalist regime." It was a mirror image of the earlier Truman Doctrine, which committed the United States to defending democracy and "free people" everywhere.

POLAND, 1980.   Yet another breach in the Soviet bloc threatened in Poland in 1980. In response to rising food prices and deteriorating living standards, Polish workers spontaneously created an independent trade union called Solidarity, led by the charismatic shipyard electrician Lech Wolesa. Solidarity soon had millions of members, including many communists, and the support of Poland's Catholic Church. In a series of strikes and peaceful demonstrations, Solidarity demanded official recognition by the state as well as a range of democratic political reforms and economic concessions to workers. Here was a mass grassroots challenge to the Communist Party, led by workers themselves. The Soviet Union mobilized its forces for another military intervention, but the Polish government, acting to forestall this disaster, itself declared martial law, outlawed Solidarity, and brought Poland, temporarily, back into the Soviet fold.

These movements of protest in Hungary, Czechoslovakia, and Poland illustrate the continuing resistance in Eastern Europe to Soviet-style socialism and Soviet domination. Even within Stalinized communist parties, impulses toward reform and independence periodically surfaced. But within Soviet-dominated Eastern Europe, such "separate roads to socialism" had very limited room for expression, and the penalty for going beyond those limits was severe indeed. The brutal suppression of the Hungarian revolt, the Prague Spring, and Solidarity gave credibility to western perceptions of the Cold War as a struggle between tyranny and freedom, and it badly tarnished the image of Soviet communism as a reasonable alternative to capitalism.

THE GREAT DIVIDE IN THE COMMUNIST WORLD: CHINA AND THE SOVIET UNION

"CATS AND MICE."   The most serious and consequential dissension within the communist world occurred between its two giant states— China and the Soviet Union. Despite the initial warmth with which Stalin greeted the Chinese revolution and the alliance between the two countries, that relationship deteriorated badly during the 1950s and 1960s. The Chinese were surprised and frustrated at the modest aid that the Soviets offered and the strenuous conditions attached to it. And Mao complained that relations between the two communist parties were hardly "brotherly," but more like those "between father and son or between cats and mice."[13]

IDEOLOGY AND NUCLEAR WEAPONS.   More serious, perhaps, was the growing ideological divide—almost a theological dispute—between the two countries, which expressed their growing rivalry for leadership within the communist world. After the death of Stalin, Khrushchev dramatically discredited the Soviet dictator, revealing his crimes and removing his body from the vault he had briefly shared with Lenin. Furthermore, he declared that nuclear weapons had made the idea of inevitable war between capitalism and communism outmoded and proclaimed instead the doctrine of "peaceful coexistence." To Mao, this smacked of betrayal and represented a deviation from the true faith of revolutionary socialism. With the Soviet success in acquiring nuclear weapons and in launching ICBMs, Mao believed the communist bloc could pursue revolution throughout the world and confront the capitalists vigorously. He sharply criticized the Soviet Union for backing down in the Cuban missile crisis and for signing a Test Ban Treaty with the United States In Mao's view, the Soviet Union was appeasing imperialists.

Mao's views on nuclear war stunned and appalled Soviet leaders. Khrushchev recalled Mao saying: "We shouldn't be afraid of atomic bombs and missiles. No matter what kind of war breaks out—conventional or thermonuclear—we'll win. As for China, if the imperialists unleash war on us, we may lose more than three hundred million people. So what? War is war. The years will pass and we'll get to work producing more babies than ever before."[14] To Soviet leaders, this was dangerous and irresponsible thinking of the highest order. Furthermore, they viewed Mao's Great Leap Forward as an unMarxist effort to create communism before industrialization. As a result of the growing conflict and bitterness, Khrushchev reneged on a promise to provide a prototype atomic bomb to the Chinese and in 1960 quite suddenly withdrew all the Soviet advisors and technicians who had been sent to assist Chinese development. The breach between them was now out in the open.

ALMOST AT WAR.   Adding to the enmity were territorial disputes. The world's longest border—some 4,500 miles—ran between China and the Soviet Union in Central Asia and the Far East. During the nineteenth century, China had lost considerable territory to the Russian empire as part of the imperialist assault on China. In 1964, Mao claimed that those lost territories should be returned. Tension along the border caused the Soviets to increase their military forces from 15 divisions in 1967 to 44 divisions in 1972. A major though brief military clash broke out in 1969, during which the Soviets broadly hinted that nuclear weapons might be used if the conflict escalated. Here were the two major communist powers virtually at war with one another.

COMPETITION IN THE THIRD WORLD.   A further expression of their rivalry lay in the Third World where Chinese-style communism based on peasants and oriented toward rural life sometimes seemed more appealing than the Soviet Union's urban-based proletarian revolution. China's strong stand against the Americans in Korea, its commitment to rural development, and its economic success all attracted attention. In a few places—North Yemen, Tanzania, Vietnam—Chinese aid competed with that of the Soviet Union. At stake was which country would become the leader of world communism in the vast and complicated domain of the Third World.

COURTING THE UNITED STATES.   The bitter hostility between China and the Soviet Union led to one of the most remarkable developments of the Cold War. In the late 1960s and early 1970s, both communist countries began to explore the possibility of closer relations with the United States, each hoping to use an American connection in their struggles with the other. Even more remarkably, this slow and tentative courtship of the great capitalist enemy was occurring even as the United States continued to pound communists in Vietnam. On the Soviet side, this process gave rise to "détente," a temporary easing of Cold War tensions and a 1972 arms control agreement that acknowledged the Soviet Union as a military equal with the United States. On the Chinese side, it led to the famous visit to China by Richard Nixon, the arch anti-communist American president, also in 1972, followed by the formal opening of diplomatic relations in 1979. From the American point of view, playing on the enmity of the two communist powers made good geopolitical sense, particularly while trying to extricate itself from the war in Vietnam. But the advent of this "triangular diplomacy" illustrated how deep was the hostility between the Soviet Union and China and how fragile was the unity of the communist world.

CONCLUSION: THE COMMUNIST WORLD IN THE 1970s

The communist experiment had an enormous impact on the world of the twentieth century, creating what was surely the deepest global divide of a conflicted century. It had contributed to both the rise and the defeat of the Nazis. It had occasioned bloody revolutions in Russia, China, Cambodia, and elsewhere and destructive wars in Korea, Vietnam, and Afghanistan. It had divided both continents and countries. It had elevated to the global stage regional conflicts in the Middle East, South Asia, and Africa and kept the world on edge as superpowers confronted one another across the world. It precipitated an arms race of unprecedented dimensions and danger, confronting humankind with the prospect of annihilation and extinction. It prompted a realignment of global power into two competing blocs and occasioned the creation of a culture of anti-communism, particularly in the United States.

Despite its many internal conflicts, world communism remained a powerful force in the world of the 1970s. It had reached the greatest extent of its global expansion. China was emerging from the chaos of the Cultural Revolution. The Soviet Union had achieved its long-sought goal of military equality with the United States, so much so that the Americans launched a major buildup of their own military forces in the early 1980s, during what became known as the second Cold War. Despite American hostility, Cuba remained a communist outpost in the western hemisphere with impressive achievements in education and health care for its people. Communism triumphed in Vietnam, dealing a major setback to the United States. A number of African countries affirmed their commitment to Marxism. Few people anywhere expected that within two decades most of the twentieth century's experiment with communism would pass into history. The end of the Cold War, the abandonment of communist economic policies in China, the abrupt overthrow of communist regimes in Eastern Europe in 1989, and the total collapse of the Soviet Union—these were the major expressions of the demise of world communism, and they were among the great surprises of the late twentieth century.

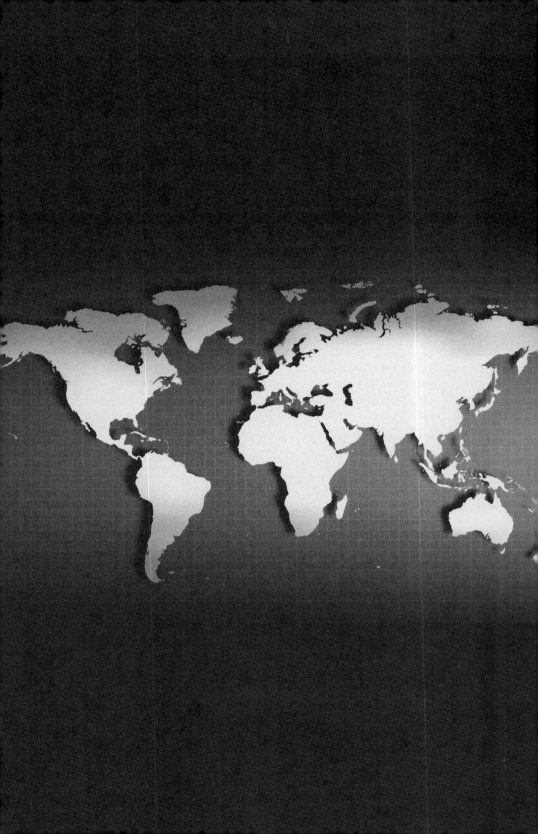

CHAPTER SIX

THE END OF THE
COMMUNIST ERA

GETTING READY FOR CHAPTER SIX: In the 1980s, both the
Soviet Union and China set out to reform their ailing communist
economies. How can you explain the great differences in these two
processes? Why did the Soviet Union disintegrate entirely, while
China largely abandoned Maoist approaches to communism without
collapsing? Was the end of communism a product of external pressures or of developments within the major communist states? And
how did the end of the communist era affect the rest of the world?

In the early evening of Christmas Day, 1991, an unknown official lowered the red flag of the Soviet Union for the last time from its accus-
tomed place high above Moscow's Kremlin. That event marked the
collapse of the Soviet Union as a unified state as its 15 republics became
independent nations. It also symbolized the final erosion of communism
as an appealing or effective idea in the modern world, and it was accompanied by the disintegration of the political party that had given birth
to that idea and sustained it for more than 70 years. It was a stunning
conclusion to the communist era in world history. But that process
involved much more than the Soviet collapse. China, the other communist giant, had already abandoned almost everything that had characterized Maoist socialism, except the domination of the Chinese Communist
Party. And in a single year—1989—popular movements all across Eastern Europe unceremoniously overthrew their despised communist
governments, while East Germans with hammers and picks broke holes
in the Berlin Wall, which had long symbolized the division of Europe.
World communism, and with it the twentieth century's global rift
between East and West, was effectively over.

All of this occurred in scarcely more than a dozen years, the blink of an eye in world history, between 1978, when China began its dramatic turn away from Maoism, and 1991, when the Soviet Union expired. Historians are inclined to probe for the deeper roots of such unexpected developments. But how far back should we go in seeking to understand the end of the Communist era? Some historians, especially those with strongly anti-communist views, have answered in effect, "all the way back to the beginning." They have argued that the communist enterprise was unrealistic, unworkable, and fatally flawed from the start and that its demise was inevitable and only a matter of time. Efforts to engineer the human soul and human society into the straightjacket of Marxist ideology were, in this view, a mission impossible.[1] Such an approach, although provocative, does little to explain why communism lasted for more than seven decades and why it collapsed in the 1980s, rather than, say, in the 1960s or 2010s. It runs the danger of turning hindsight into inevitability, and it discounts the sense of stunned surprise with which much of the world greeted these dramatic developments. To understand the end of the communist era, we will need to look more carefully at the contrasting examples of communism's demise in the Soviet Union and China and then to assess the impact of these events on the larger world of the late twentieth century.

THE COLLAPSE OF COMMUNISM IN THE SOVIET UNION

CRACKS IN THE FOUNDATION

The implosion of the Soviet Union was clearly the centerpiece of the drama that marked the end of the communist era, as the birthplace of communism now became the site of its funeral. For most historians, the beginning point for understanding that collapse lies in the three decades following Stalin's death in 1953. During those years, a number of the supports that had sustained both communism and the USSR began to weaken, though almost no one at the time imagined that the end was in sight.[2]

DeStalinization and the Erosion of Fear.   One of those supports was widespread fear, born of Stalin's terror. The new leadership under Nikita Khrushchev (1954–1964) recognized that terror, the secret police, and the absolute authority of one man provided no secure foundation for the continued rule of the country's communist elite. Rebellions in the Gulag and growing public demands for the release of its many prisoners added to the pressure for change. Khrushchev responded by denouncing the dictator's many crimes to a stunned audience of party leaders, by releasing millions from the Gulag, and by exonerating millions more, long dead, from crimes they had never committed. Artists, writers, and academic specialists benefited as greater freedom of expression was granted. So did party officials, who could now debate policies, within limits, without fear of the executioner. Ordinary people could also speak more freely—if not in public, at least in their own kitchens. This was Khrushchev's "thaw." One young woman who experienced this "deStalinization" recorded its impact on her thinking:

> My generation became . . . more critical towards the country's new leadership . . . For whereas Stalin, who had been put forward as the "genius of all time" turned out to be a common criminal, the people who had taken his place had far more ordinary biographies . . . There was, therefore, no reason to regard their decisions as "the last word in truth."[3]

In addition to lifting the pervasive fear of the Stalin era, Khrushchev's reforms in politics, culture, and the economy provoked an enduring conflict between reformers and conservatives within the Soviet establishment. The central issue was change itself. Was it, as the reformers argued, a means of fulfilling the promise of the revolution and of Lenin's ideals, from which Stalin had led the country astray? Or was change, as the conservatives feared, a threat to the stability and functioning of essentially sound institutions and socialist values that had modernized the country in record time and brought it through the horrors of war to superpower status? Thus, the Khrushchev years established lines of controversy and debate that endured for two decades and reemerged vigorously during the 1980s.

SOVIET CONSERVATISM.   After a decade of Khrushchev's often impulsive reforms and the country's humiliating withdrawal of its missiles from Cuba, his more conservative and staid colleagues engineered his peaceful replacement by the more predictable Leonid Brezhnev (1964–1983). In Brezhnev's overriding concern with stability, little that was revolutionary or seriously reformist survived, but his years in power provided considerable security and privileges for an aging communist elite. A widely told joke had Brezhnev's mother visiting him at the Kremlin. Upon seeing his many cars, servants, and luxurious surroundings, she said, "I'm worried about you, Leonid. What will happen to you when the communists take over?" In this prolonged reluctance to tackle the country's growing problems lay another source of its later collapse.

ECONOMIC STAGNATION.   The most serious of those problems was a slowing economy. For twenty-five years after World War II, the Soviet economy had grown impressively by world standards—about 5–6% per year—and standards of living for ordinary people had clearly improved.

Millions happily left the communal apartments where they had shared a kitchen and bathroom with other families and moved into newly constructed apartments of their own. But by the 1970s, growth rates had fallen to 3% a year and even lower by the 1980s as Soviet citizens stood in longer lines and complained endlessly about the poor quality and declining availability of consumer goods. For a system that had long boasted a more effective strategy for modern development, it was highly embarrassing to fall even further behind the western capitalist countries. In 1987, when the United States had some 25 million microcomputers, the Soviet Union had only 200,000. Why was a communist system that had industrialized in record time performing so poorly now?

In large measure, it was because a state-controlled economy was ill-equipped to make the transition from "extensive growth," based on adding more land, labor, and capital to the production process, to "intensive growth," depending on technological improvements to increase output. It was possible to command the replication of steel mills in the 1930s, based on a known technology; it was not possible to order into existence a computer industry based on a new and rapidly evolving technology in the 1970s. Doing so required greater flexibility, incentives to innovate, and more freedom for factory managers than the Soviet system was able to provide. All kinds of reforms were tried, but those that involved decentralization, market prices, and a weakening of party authority felt like a restoration of a hated capitalism and represented an unacceptable threat to the Soviet elite. Furthermore, enormous investments in the military amounting to 15–25% of GNP robbed the civilian economy of investment capital. The growing complexity of an economy with some 50,000 enterprises producing more than 24 million separate products overwhelmed a system designed to operate as a single unit directed from the top.

LOSING CONTROL.   While the economy weakened badly, Soviet society was changing rapidly, and parts of it slowly slipped outside of the control of the state and party. The continued growth of industry in the post-Stalin years created a primarily urban society in the Soviet Union, and the expansion of secondary and higher education made it a far more educated society. Members of this growing urban educated class had ideas of their own, had been enthused by Khrushchev's "thaw" and disappointed by the more conservative and restrictive policies of the Brezhnev years. They were not so easily governed as the rural and largely illiterate society that Stalin had dominated. A handful among them became open "dissidents" publicly repudiating Soviet values and practice. Larger numbers, operating from the relative safety of academic institutions, developed independent and critical views of the Soviet system.

BLACK MARKETS. In other ways as well, state control was eroding. A flourishing "black market" or "second economy" allowed millions to obtain otherwise scarce goods and services as practically everyone wove a web of private and illegal contacts to supplement what was available in the official economy. Laced with corruption, bribes, and payoffs, it fueled popular cynicism and justified the small scale illegalities of ordinary people. "Of course we steal from them [the state]. Don't they steal from us on a far larger scale?"

SOVIET ROCK. An alternative cultural arena likewise emerged, as popular singers and poets focused attention on private life—love affairs, neighborhood streets, nostalgic recollections—or on the bitter unspoken realities of Soviet life such as widespread drunkenness and poverty. While not directly anti-communist, such music and poetry was certainly at odds with the official optimism and collectivism of party propaganda. By the 1970s a growing fascination with western popular culture—blue jeans, T-shirts, and above all, rock-and-roll music—also challenged official values. The Beatles, the Rolling Stones, and Stevie Wonder became wildly popular, and dozens of Soviet rock bands sprang up to play in cafes and university dormitories. In its individualism, its open sexuality, and its embrace of the West, rock-and-roll became the music of youthful protest.

ENGAGING THE WEST. Nor was rock-and-roll the only opening to the West. More and more people had shortwave radios, which enabled them to tune into BBC, Radio Free Europe, or the Voice of America. Growing numbers were able to travel outside the Soviet Union. Awareness of the larger world often had an unsettling impact on those who experienced it. One woman reported on her first trip abroad, to Sweden, in 1957:

> It made a very great impression on me; before me was another, a different way of life . . . [It] shattered the idea I had been given that the working life of people in the West consisted mainly of suffering. We saw that, in fact, the countries of the West had in many instances overtaken us and we had lively discussions about ways of overcoming our weaknesses . . .[4]

NATIONS IN THE MAKING. A final crack in the foundation of the Soviet Union lay in a growing sense of nationality among the country's many and diverse ethnic groups. In its early years, the Soviet Union had recognized the reality of this cultural diversity by encouraging the use of local languages and by dividing the country administratively into territorial units based on ethnicity—Ukraine, Georgia, Armenia, Kazakhstan, Uzbekistan, and many others. But they fully expected that these cultural distinctions would soon merge into a new Soviet and socialist identity.

It did not happen. Repeated efforts to push Russian as the national language of the Soviet Union only created resentments and fears that local languages and cultures were in danger. Furthermore, some 25 million Russians migrated to other regions of the country where their more advanced education landed them better jobs, creating further resentments and sharpening cultural identities on both sides.

In the more relaxed atmosphere of the post-Stalin years, this growing national consciousness found expression in various ways. In a number of non-Russian republics, national elites consolidated their control, established connections with the black market, and developed extensive networks of corruption and patronage that gave them a measure of independence from Moscow. Their intellectuals defended national languages, fostered national literatures, and created national histories. The Ukrainian poet Vasyl Symonenko spoke for many others when he declared in verse: "My people exist! My people will always exist! No one can blot out my people!"[5] More public protests occasionally erupted. Lithuanians signed petitions by the tens of thousands demanding respect for their rights as Catholics. Some 100,000 Armenians demonstrated in 1965 to obtain the return of Armenian territory in the neighboring republic of Azerbaijan. Here were the fault lines along which the Soviet Union eventually disintegrated.

THE DISEASE OR THE TREATMENT?   But none of these cracks in the foundation seemed very wide, and few observers—either within or outside the Soviet Union—anticipated major changes when Brezhnev died in 1983. The party was in firm control of the country. No street demonstrations disrupted public order; the economy provided at least the basics for almost everyone. Whatever the country's many problems or weaknesses, it was the effort to fix them—rather than the problems themselves—that threw the entire Soviet system into crisis and brought down the original citadel of world communism. The patient died, not directly from her several diseases, but from the unexpected outcome of the treatment that the doctor prescribed.

THE GORBACHEV PRESCRIPTION

The doctor in this case was Mikhail Gorbachev, who emerged as Brezhnev's successor and Soviet leader in 1985. For the next six years he led an increasingly far-reaching effort to rescue the Soviet Union from its assorted ills. His program was a Soviet "New Deal," designed to save socialism by reforming it, much like Franklin Roosevelt's effort to reform and preserve American capitalism in the 1930s. An enthusiastic communist since his youth, Gorbachev had risen rapidly within the Party hierarchy as a part of its moderate reformist wing and ascended to the top job in the country, General Secretary of the Communist Party, at the young age of 54. His selection as Party leader reflected the growing influence of party reformers, people who perceived the country's increasingly serious problems and foresaw a crisis in the making. A stagnant economy, pervasive corruption, public apathy, bureaucratic inertia, an arms race that drained the country's resources—all of this needed to change. "Everything is rotten," Gorbachev commented to a friend. "We can no longer live this way." Nonetheless, few people expected a reform program as radical as Gorbachev shortly delivered.

PERESTROIKA. The centerpiece of Gorbachev's program was an effort to restart economic growth. It was called *perestroika,* or restructuring. Without a revived economy, the country's status as a superpower and the credibility of socialism itself could hardly be sustained. After two years of modest tinkering with existing economic structures, the pace of reform picked up. The 1987 Law on State Enterprises sought to free Soviet factories from the heavy hand of central government ministries, which had traditionally controlled every detail of their activities, and to make them operate more like private firms, seeking profits, becoming self-financing, and catering to consumer demand. In support of this effort, Gorbachev drastically cut the state and party bureaucracy charged with economic oversight. *Perestroika* also opened up some space for small-scale private enterprises, called cooperatives, that were permitted to hire workers and sell their goods and services for whatever price they could get. By early 1991, some 245,000 businesses with 6 million employees were involved in catering, restaurants, auto and apartment repair, construction, software design, and many other activities. Opportunities for private farming also opened up, although few people took advantage of it. Foreign investment in "joint enterprises" was also permitted, but not many western capitalists were prepared to make a commitment to what was still a socialist economy. Nonetheless, *perestroika* had challenged the idea that state had to control everything and had provoked much discussion about how to combine the market with socialism.

GLASNOST. Gorbachev soon encountered enormous opposition to even modest reforms and found it necessary to seek allies outside the official party and state establishment. The vehicle for widening his circle of support was *glasnost,* or "openness," a policy of permitting a much wider range of cultural and intellectual freedoms in Soviet life. It was also intended to overcome the pervasive distrust between society and the state that had long characterized the Soviet Union and to energize Soviet society for the tasks of *perestroika.* "We need *glasnost,*" Gorbachev declared, "like we need the air."[6]

In the late 1980s, *glasnost* hit the Soviet Union like a bomb. Newspapers and TV exposed social pathologies once presented solely as the product of capitalism. Crime, prostitution, child abuse, suicide, corruption, homelessness—all this and more flooded the public media. Viewers learned that the abortion rate in the Soviet Union was the highest in the world, and they discovered something of the degrading process of obtaining one. Films broke the ban on nudity and explicit sex. TV reporters climbed the wall of a secluded villa to film the luxurious homes of the party elite. Soviet history was also reexamined as revelations of Stalin's crimes poured out of the media. Mass graves were uncovered, and a former executioner described on camera precisely how he had shot people. The Bible and the Koran became more widely available, atheistic propaganda largely ceased, and thousands of churches and mosques were returned to believers and opened for worship. Plays, poems, films, and novels that had been long buried "in the drawer" were now released to a public that virtually devoured them. "Like an excited boy reads a note from his girl," wrote one poet, "That's how we read the papers today."[7] Many people echoed the sentiments of the Soviet academic who declared, "For me now my country is the most interesting place in the world."[8]

Gorbachev hoped that a grateful public would recover its faith in socialism and drive his plans for economic reform. And for several years he did enjoy a wide popularity. But before long, *glasnost* slipped beyond Gorbachev's intentions. Attacks on Stalin turned into criticism of Lenin, Marx, and the revolution itself. Non-Russian nationalists began to talk of independence, and some activists mused about political alternatives to a one-party state. For many the revelations of *glasnost* shattered whatever remained of their belief in the sustaining myths of the Soviet Union and the credibility of the Communist Party.

DEMOCRATIZATION. Political reform was likewise on Gorbachev's agenda. Like *glasnost,* a measure of democracy was intended to demonstrate public support for Gorbachev's reforms and thus nudge a reluctant bureaucracy into accepting more substantial changes. The key element of his *democratization* program was a new parliament with real powers whose members were chosen in competitive, though still one-party, elections. It was a dramatic change from decades of single-candidate balloting for a parliament that rubber-stamped the decisions of the party leadership. When those elections took place in the spring of 1989, the results were stunning. Dozens of leading communists, including the mayors of Moscow and Kiev, were decisively rejected at the polls. Some lost even though running unopposed, because more than half of the voters scratched their names from the ballot! Even though the vast majority of elected deputies were party members, the party leadership had been badly humiliated.

When the new parliament, called the Congress of People's Deputies, met for the first time, its sessions were televised to a live audience of 100 million or more. The country was transfixed as long-standing taboos were shattered and real political debate sprang to life before the cameras. One deputy decried the continuing role of the secret police despite its murderous past. Others openly criticized the war in Afghanistan. Another called for the embalmed Lenin to be removed from his public tomb and reburied as an ordinary mortal. Nothing like this had occurred in the Soviet Union in living memory. A year later an important constitutional change made it possible for other non-communist political parties to be established. All of this demoralized the Communist Party, and growing numbers withdrew their membership.

Here was the irony, and tragedy, of Gorbachev's *democratization*. To enact his reforms, he felt forced to attack and weaken the party, for its powerful conservative wing obstructed those reforms at every turn. Yet in doing so, he fatally undermined the single institution that had held the country together for 70 years.

NEW THINKING ABOUT THE WORLD.   Early on, Gorbachev recognized that the success of his domestic program demanded a less-threatening international environment. When he took power in 1985, the Soviet Union was confronted by a new and expensive round in the arms race, led by the strongly anti-communist American President Ronald Reagan. The Soviet invasion of Afghanistan had deepened the rift with China and alienated the Islamic world. The Soviet Union was largely isolated in world affairs. Every nuclear weapon not in the Soviet Union was pointed at the Soviet Union.

Gorbachev acted quickly to defuse this hostile environment and in doing so repudiated long-held communist ideas about the world. He set aside the notion of socialism and capitalism as locked in a ceaseless struggle of "two camps" and began to speak about "common human problems" such as pollution, poverty, famine, and avoiding nuclear war. National security, he declared, was not entirely military and had to be mutual. "It is either equal security for all or none at all."[9] Repeatedly, he articulated "freedom of choice" as a principle of Soviet foreign policy.

New thinking soon led to new actions. Unilateral cuts in Soviet conventional forces and military spending accompanied arms-control negotiations with the United States that resulted in substantial reductions in the nuclear arsenals of the superpowers. It was a striking reversal of an arms race that had spiraled steadily upward for 40 years. When Eastern European countries decisively rejected their communist governments in 1989, no Soviet intervention followed, and the Soviet Union's security buffer zone vanished. Gorbachev also withdrew Soviet forces from Afghanistan and worked cooperatively with Americans to resolve regional conflicts elsewhere throughout the world. Aid to Cuba likewise diminished. By the time his country disintegrated in 1991, its long estrangement from the West had ended and the Cold War had passed into history.

UNEXPECTED CONSEQUENCES

Almost nothing worked out as Gorbachev had intended. He had initiated surprising, even radical, changes in every aspect of Soviet life, but far from strengthening socialism and reviving the country, those changes led to its further weakening and collapse.

THE UNRAVELING OF THE SOVIET ECONOMY.   The most obvious failure was economic, as the Soviet economy spun into a sharp decline that lasted for well over a decade. Both food and consumer goods were in short supply, requiring people to hunt for ordinary products and to wait in endless lines. Rationing coupons, not used since the desperate days of World War II, reappeared in many places. Furthermore, prices skyrocketed as inflation leaped out of control, jumping by 10% in 1989, 53% in 1990, and 650–700% in 1991.[10] More and more people found themselves impoverished, spending 60–80% of their income on food alone. The quality of that food declined as well. One newspaper fed sausage to 30 cats and found that 24 of them rejected it altogether![11] Many others began to fear the loss of their jobs. Employment security, long a taken-for-granted benefit of socialism, now seem threatened. Gorbachev's reforms had substantially dismantled a centralized and planned economy before a functioning market system had emerged to replace it. Furthermore, the Chernobyl nuclear accident in the Ukraine in 1986, a massive earthquake in Armenia in 1987, and temporarily declining world prices for gas and oil only added to the country's problems. The result was economic crisis.

By 1990, this crisis produced an embittered and angry population, most of whom saw themselves as victims of *perestroika* rather than its beneficiaries. Nostalgia for the stability and predictability of the Brezhnev era, and even for the strong hand of Stalin, surfaced amid the growing desperation. Adding fuel to the fire was the rise in crime on streets once widely regarded as safe, the emergence of open prostitution and pornography, and growing and more visible inequality as a small elite of "new Russians" paraded their recently acquired private wealth in the face of mass impoverishment.

THE DEMOCRACY MOVEMENT. While the economy contracted sharply, Soviet society awakened from decades of fear and apathy. One expression of this awakening was the emergence of a democracy movement. Hundreds of "unofficial" or "informal" groups or parties, previously forbidden in a society where all such organizations were state sponsored, now sprang to life. They wanted a "normal" western society with complete civil liberties, full multiparty democracy, and, increasingly, a capitalist economy with private property and market-based prices. While Gorbachev sought to reform communism, much of the burgeoning democracy movement became committed to ending it. The May Day parade of 1990 featured openly anti-communist placards and chants of "down with the party."

LABOR AWAKENINGS. Allied with the democracy movement after 1989 were growing numbers of workers who began to organize independent unions and to go on strike. Such a thing was virtually unheard of earlier, for was the entire Soviet system not a "workers' state?" Now the actions of workers themselves undermined that founding myth of the Soviet Union. Coal miners were especially militant. Health, safety, and housing conditions had long been appalling. Now bonuses were reduced, supplies were more difficult to obtain, and rumors circulated that mines might close. Even soap had become scarce. "Can you imagine," demanded one outraged worker, "what it's like for a miner without soap?"[12] By 1991, miners and other workers had become almost totally disillusioned with socialism and the Soviet regime, and they had clearly demonstrated their capacity for independent action.

NATIONAL AWAKENINGS. If the democratic and labor movements challenged communism, the various nationalist movements that exploded in the late 1980s called into question the continuation of any Soviet state at all. Virtually all of Gorbachev's reform efforts backfired badly in the non-Russian republics. *Glasnost* allowed intellectuals, journalists, and activists to recover their own histories, to protest openly the "russification" of their cultures, and to highlight the environmental degradation that flowed from Soviet-style industrialization. The weakening of central economic control encouraged the republics to act independently, sometimes withholding tax revenues or goods from the rest of the country. Real elections provided incentives for politicians to seek support on nationalist grounds. To various degrees, nationalist movements demanding autonomy or even independence erupted quickly all across the country. They were especially prominent in the Baltic republics of Latvia, Lithuania, and Estonia, where in 1989 a human chain some 370 miles long linked the three countries and sent the word "freedom" along the line of a million people. Even in Russia, long the center of the Soviet Union, separatist feeling mounted as anti-Russian sentiment in the rest of the country created a backlash in Russia itself. Perhaps the Soviet Union was a burden to be shed, thought growing numbers of Russians, rather than a benefit to be enjoyed. None of this growing demand for separation from the Soviet Union was evident when Gorbachev came to power. The speed and power of its growth surprised everyone.

EASTERN EUROPEAN AWAKENINGS.   Events in the Soviet Union had spill-over effects in the East European communist countries. Imposed from the outside, communism had never connected with the national traditions of these countries. They, too, were experiencing severe economic problems that were highlighted by comparison with the much more prosperous and nearby states of Western Europe. In these circumstances, Gorbachev's reformist agenda lit a fuse. If the Soviet Union was holding competitive elections and permitting open discussion of public policies, why not in Eastern Europe as well? Furthermore Gorbachev made it clear that the East European communist regimes were on their own and would not be rescued by Soviet invasion as in the past.

This was the background to the "miracle year" of 1989. Massive demonstrations, elections, last-minute efforts at reform, the breaching of previously closed borders—all of this and more took place to varying degrees throughout Eastern Europe. The end result was the same everywhere—the overthrow of communist governments, first in Poland and then, like falling dominos, in Hungary, East Germany, Bulgaria, Czechoslovakia, and Romania. Now Eastern Europe was the example for democrats and nationalists in the Soviet Union. If they had thrown off communism and Soviet domination, why could the same not happen in the Soviet Union itself?

A STRANGE DEATH

CONSERVATIVE BACKLASH.   While the democracy, labor, and nationalist movements pressed Gorbachev for further and more rapid change, others wanted to turn back the clock: upper-level party and government officials, military officers, still-committed communists, and Soviet patriots. They too used the new freedoms of *glasnost* to organize politically and to publicize their views. By 1990, a conservative movement took shape arguing that Gorbachev's ill-considered changes were ruining the country. The Communist Party, which had made the revolution in 1917 and brought the country to a position of a global superpower, had been attacked, criticized, and weakened by its own leader. Overt anti-communism was daily fare in the media, and the country's glorious

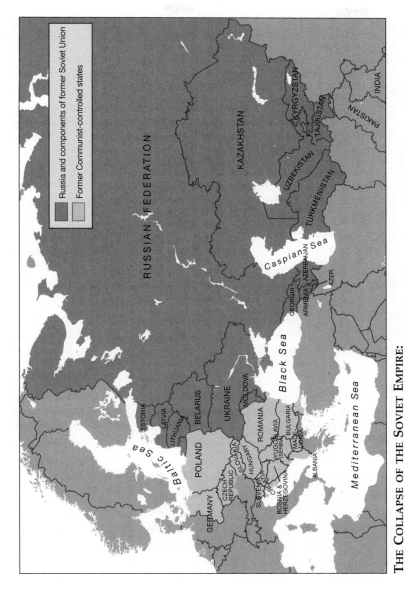

THE COLLAPSE OF THE SOVIET EMPIRE:

The end of communist control in Eastern Europe and the disintegration of the Soviet Union marked the end of the communist era in world history.

history was subjected to endless slander. The explosion of crime, prostitution, and pornography represented cultural pollution from the West. The economy was close to collapse and poverty had increased dramatically. A despised capitalism was making a comeback in the country that had first built socialism. The very survival of that country was threatened by mounting nationalist demands for autonomy or independence. And in Eastern Europe, communist governments had been overthrown and a unified Germany was part of the western alliance. The political gains of World War II, for which the Soviet Union had paid in rivers of blood, had vanished without a fight and with Gorbachev's permission. To Gorbachev's most conservative critics, all of this was the tragic outcome of *glasnost, perestroika,* and *democratization,* and it was little short of treason.

POLARIZATION.   In its last several years, the Soviet Union increasingly polarized. Gorbachev came under growing pressure from the democracy movement to abandon the Communist Party and socialism altogether and to move quickly to a full-market or capitalist economy with openly competing parties. Nationalists pressured him to negotiate a new "union treaty," which would greatly weaken the central government while granting far more power to the individual republics. On the other side, a bitterly hostile conservative movement demanded that Gorbachev halt the slide toward anarchy and chaos and declare a "state of emergency." The head of the country's secret police said publicly that *perestroika* was a blueprint for the country's destruction and declared that "we have had about as much democracy as we can stomach."[13]

THREE DAYS IN AUGUST.   In this increasingly tense and polarized situation, the conservatives struck first. A secret committee of leading state and party officials launched an attempted takeover of the Soviet state on August 18, 1991. When Gorbachev refused to cooperate with them, they detained him at his vacation home on the Black Sea. The next morning, astonished Muscovites awoke to find tanks and armored personnel carriers taking up positions throughout the central city. The committee declared a six-month state of emergency, banned all strikes, demonstrations, and political parties, shut down liberal newspapers, and imposed strict censorship on the media. They also prepared arrest warrants for several thousand people and ordered 250,000 pairs of handcuffs. Clearly, a major crackdown was planned. Here was the action that democrats had feared and conservatives had longed for.

But in only three days, this attempt to reimpose a repressive order on the Soviet Union fell apart. Boris Yeltsin, a reformist politician and by now the acknowledged leader of the democracy movement, narrowly avoided arrest and dramatically summoned the country to resist the illegal coup. Tens of thousands of Muscovites responded, flocking to the Russian "White House" where Yeltsin and his supporters had established their headquarters. There they built barricades, tracked the movement of troops, confronted soldiers and tanks, and waited for what they expected would be a deadly assault. One participant described the mood:

> [T]his was the Pepsi generation under threat. Our very existence was in jeopardy. The bikers feared for their motorcycles. The young businessmen worried about their markets. The racketeers even thought about their bottom line and came to defend the White House. Prostitutes, students, scholars, everybody had an interest in this new life, and we were just not willing to give it all up to these old men. And also, it was like being in a great movie.[14]

Equally important were divisions within the various military and security forces on which the committee depended. Some defected to the Yeltsin camp, and others refused orders to attack. Soon the emergency committee was ready to retreat, its members divided, dispirited, or drunk. The coup was over and Gorbachev returned to Moscow.

COMING APART.   But he came back to a different country. The August coup badly discredited the conservative movement, and the Communist Party, in the country of its origin no less, was defined as a "criminal organization," legally banned, and its property seized. Democrats, politically strengthened by their brave resistance to the coup, roamed the streets, toppling statues of Lenin, while the museum dedicated to the Soviet founder was closed "pending reconstruction." Perhaps most important, the coup had emboldened those who sought to end the Soviet Union as a single state. In early December the leaders of three republics— Russia, Belarus, and Ukraine—cobbled together, virtually overnight, an agreement terminating the existence of the Soviet Union and forming in its place a wholly voluntary Commonwealth of Independent States with virtually no powers whatever. Fifteen new independent states now replaced the defunct Soviet Union. On December 25, Gorbachev formally resigned, transferring his control of Soviet military forces and the "nuclear briefcase" to Yeltsin, the president of the now-independent Russian state. That evening, with both pride and sadness, Gorbachev addressed his now vanishing country for the final time as the Russian tricolor replaced the hammer and sickle atop the Kremlin. The Soviet Union had passed into history.

A PEACEFUL PASSING.   Unlike the end of communism in Eastern Europe, where it had been quickly overthrown by popular movements,

in the Soviet Union it had collapsed from within. Beneath the calm sur-
face of the Brezhnev years, the economy had seriously weakened, the
credibility and control of the Communist Party had eroded, and nationalist consciousness had grown. Gorbachev's efforts to address these
issues had only made them worse and polarized the country sharply.
Then a brief and incompetent effort to turn back the clock tumbled the
fragile structure of Soviet communism altogether. Among the most
remarkable features of this collapse was the relative absence of blood-
shed with which it occurred. The disintegration of a huge multiethnic
empire and the demise of an entrenched communist system occasioned
no bloody wars of liberation such as those in Algeria, Zimbabwe, Kenya,
or Vietnam during their decolonization; no civil war of the kind that
accompanied secessionist movements in the United States or more
recently in Ethiopia, Nigeria, Sudan, or Sri Lanka; no revolutionary violence against the old order such as that which scarred the fall of communism in Romania; and except for the Armenian-Azeri conflict, no
ethnic cleansing or massive, uncontrolled, and violent movement of
population like that which occurred at the breakup of British India and
at the disintegration of Yugoslavia. The August coup notwithstanding,
the defenders of the established system, including an entrenched party
elite, a fearsome KGB, and the military forces of a global superpower,
put up an amazingly modest resistance against those who sought to end
their power and their privileges. How should we explain this strange
feature of the Soviet collapse?

One answer lies perhaps in the declining "self-legitimacy" of the
Soviet elite. Over the several decades preceding Gorbachev's accession
to power, a harsh Stalinist order had become a "corrupt and sloppy
bureaucracy, full of cynicism and self-seeking" in which real commitment to Marxism-Leninism was increasingly rare.[15] Many among the
Soviet elite simply ceased to believe in communism. The revelations of
the Gorbachev era only diminished that belief further. Until virtually the
end, defenders of the old order had the means to halt the reform process,
for the structures of the party, the secret police, the internal security
forces, and the military remained in place. What they lacked was the will
to use them decisively.

Perhaps the need to use them was diminishing as well, for opportunities as well as threats beckoned in the new order. Not a few communist officials rapidly became nationalists and emerged as leaders of
the new independent states. Those states needed skilled managers, and
the party/state apparatus was virtually the only place to find them.
Directors of state enterprises frequently became owners of those valu-
able assets as a largely uncontrolled and corrupt process of privatization

continued throughout the 1990s. Not a few former communist officials gained great wealth, while many in the Soviet elite wound up on top of the new society that was emerging.

Gorbachev, too, deserves some credit for his country's peaceful demise. His unwillingness to authorize large-scale violence, his desire to humanize and democratize Soviet socialism and make it consistent with western values, his "freedom to choose" rhetoric, and the success of *glasnost* in discrediting the brutalities of Soviet history—all this served to discredit the use of force as the basis for political action. It set a new standard for Soviet political behavior, which apparently affected even the leaders of the August coup.

Finally, the surge of separatist sentiment within Russia, particularly among the triumphant democrats, certainly eased the way to a peaceful divorce. Many of the dominant Russians had come to feel their empire as a burden and a drain, which they sought to discard to their own advantage. After the coup, little resistance to the dissolution of the Soviet Union in Russia, its dominant republic, stood in the way of the country's collapse. In sharp contrast to its birth and to much of its life, the Soviet Union died a peaceful death.

THE ABANDONMENT OF COMMUNISM IN CHINA

China's role in the "end of communism" story has been dramatically different from that of the Soviet Union. While both countries undertook major efforts to reform their communist societies in the 1980s, the Chinese state emerged strengthened, with its Communist Party intact and its economy booming. In sharp contrast, the Soviet state disintegrated, its Communist Party was temporarily banned, and its economy spiraled downward into the twentieth century's worst peacetime depression. In short, the Soviet Union "fell" and China "rose" as the communist era in world history came to an end.[16]

Chinese efforts at reforming communism began in 1978, well before those of Gorbachev in the Soviet Union, and served as one model for the Soviet program. Whereas the Chinese reform process continued into the twenty-first century, Soviet reform under communist control lasted but six years (1985–1991). After that, Russia and the other post-communist states continued their transitions toward market economies and at least semi-democratic societies, but Communist parties no longer directed that effort.

Here is surely the most distinguishing feature of China's recent history, for as a communist China "rose," it abandoned almost everything that had been associated with Maoist socialism. Agriculture was "decollectivized" as private family farming swept the country. All kinds of private or semiprivate enterprises were encouraged. Foreign investment was actively and successfully courted. Commitment to social equality largely vanished and the regime exhorted its people that "to get rich is glorious." Mass campaigns to mobilize the country for building socialism vanished. Even Mao himself was subjected to serious criticism. In an amazing reversal, an essentially capitalist society emerged in China during the 1980s and 1990s, but it was led and encouraged at every step by none other than the Chinese Communist Party itself! Who could have imagined in 1949 . . . or in 1970 . . . that a communist party would give birth, not to socialism, but to a modern and flourishing capitalism, long despised by communists of all stripes? Mao's worst fears during the Cultural Revolution—that the Communist Party itself was "taking the capitalist road"—seemed to be coming true. How had this happened? And why was the "end of communism" story in China so different than in the Soviet Union?

AFTER MAO: THE RISE OF DENG XIAOPING

The death of Mao Zedong in 1976 raised serious questions about China's leadership and policies. Who would—or could—succeed the towering figure of Mao? And would his commitment to mass mobilization, to social equality, and to realizing socialism quickly continue? A two-year struggle for power answered those questions quite clearly. The person who emerged from that struggle as China's "paramount leader" was Deng Xiaoping. He was a longtime communist of Mao's generation, a veteran of the "long march," and a leading figure in the party until he was purged, twice, during the Cultural Revolution and in the final years of Mao's life. Long a spokesman for a more moderate and stable communism, Deng attracted a great deal of support among the party elite and among millions who had suffered grievously during the Cultural Revolution. He was committed to ending the periodic upheavals of the Maoist period, to creating a more effective, better educated, and technically competent Communist Party, and especially to promoting economic growth. The "four modernizations"—in agriculture, industry, science and technology, and national defense—became the slogan that summed up Deng's priorities. Though he declined the top position in either the state or party structures, Deng was the acknowledged leader of China from 1978 until his death in 1997. It was under his leadership that communism in practice was largely abandoned in China, even as the Communist Party maintained clear and exclusive political control of the country.

MOVING AWAY FROM MAOISM.   Even before Deng Xiaoping had fully consolidated his power, authorities began to discard important elements of Maoism. Major leaders of the Cultural Revolution, the so-called Gang of Four including Mao's widow, were arrested and later put on trial. Previously banned plays, operas, films, literary journals, and translations of western classics reappeared. A "literature of the wounded" exposed the sufferings of the Cultural Revolution. Some 100,000 political prisoners, many of them high-ranking communists in disgrace or detention for years, were released and restored to important positions. A crash program for training scientific research workers was announced with rigorous academic standards for admission rather than class background. The heavy hand of Party control was partially lifted from Chinese society.

EVALUATING MAO.   Much as the Soviet Communist Party had to confront Stalin's legacy, the Chinese Communist Party felt compelled to evaluate Mao, both to address the enormous suffering that his policies had caused and to secure the legitimacy of the Party itself. In the Soviet Union, the Party could condemn Stalin unequivocally, while holding fast to the image of Lenin, who had led the revolution. But in China, Mao had been both Lenin and Stalin, both the leader of the revolution and the architect for the building of socialism. So the party's final verdict, issued in 1981, was a mixed judgment—great praise for his role in the revolution and in the early years of socialist construction, but severe criticism for his "mistakes" during the Great Leap and the Cultural Revolution. By some strange mathematical calculation, he was judged to have been 70% correct and 30% wrong.

THE DEMOCRACY MOVEMENT.   The rise of Deng, the repudiation of the Cultural Revolution, and the open criticism of Mao himself persuaded some people that political democracy would soon follow. Deng himself had spoken about "socialist democracy" and "political reform." And so young activists, mostly former Red Guards in their 20s and 30s, began to write posters, create semipolitical organizations, and publish mimeographed journals advocating "the holding of power by the laboring masses themselves," rather than by a corrupt and dictatorial party. "What is true democracy?" asked Wei Jingsheng, who became the most well known of these activists. "It means the right of the people to choose their own representatives . . . [and] to replace their representatives any time . . . "[17] Democracy, Wei declared, must become China's "Fifth Modernization." But to Deng Xiaoping, political reform meant modernizing the Communist Party, not surrendering its political monopoly. A wave of arrests and the banning of offensive magazines and organizations showed the limits of Deng's reforms and ended the embryonic democracy movement by 1981, though it soon reappeared in a much larger and more dramatic form.

THE END OF SOCIALIST AGRICULTURE

"DECOLLECTIVIZATION." Economic growth, certainly not democracy and not even socialism, was Deng's highest priority. China's economy, he insisted ambitiously, must quadruple in size by the year 2000. The first breakthrough occurred in agriculture, where 70–80% of the labor force worked. If the country's overall economy was to grow rapidly, as Deng intended, Chinese agriculture had to become more productive. His initial reforms, announced in late 1978, raised prices for farm products and authorized small "work groups" of a few families to lease land from the commune and farm it as they saw fit. Over the next few years, China's peasants spontaneously and massively rushed through these limited openings and pushed them much further than the reformers had anticipated or desired. Although party policy had actually forbidden individual family farming, that is in fact what developed as collectivized agriculture, a signature of communism everywhere, largely vanished in China. What began as limited household contracts with the commune became something close to private property as peasants built houses on collective land, rented out portions of it, hired labor, and even bequeathed family plots to their children. A vast array of rural entrepreneurial initiatives, most operated by local governments, soon followed.[18] In the wake of all this, agricultural and industrial output boomed in the rural areas, and peasant standards of living jumped dramatically. What made this experiment so successful and why would the Communist Party agree to dismantling its socialist agriculture?

PEASANT MOTIVES. China's peasants had compelling motives for seizing the moment, for they were extremely poor. The government itself admitted in 1978 that 100 million peasants did not have enough grain to eat. And most rural areas had experienced little material improvement, despite generally impressive growth rates, as the state siphoned off much of the rural surplus for the benefit of urban industries.[19] Furthermore, Chinese peasants were excluded from the welfare provisions available to urban dwellers: pensions, medical care, child care, sick leave, maternity leave.[20] Because only two decades had passed since collectivization, powerful family obligations and attachment to the ideal of family farming remained strong.[21]

Although these peasant initiatives far outran the original intentions of the reformers, Deng and the party leadership generally acquiesced and approved, persuaded by the enormous boost in rural production that the end of socialist agriculture had generated. Furthermore, the process involved no direct political challenge to the Party and even provided the government with new allies in the form of successful farmers and rural entrepreneurs. Quite a number of rural party cadres, originally opposed to decollectivization, soon found opportunities for personal enrichment in the process.[22]

A SOVIET COMPARISON.   All this contrasted sharply with the situation in the Soviet Union. There, agricultural reform had a lower priority because the country had just 14% of its labor force in agriculture.[23] But even more impressively, little rural response greeted the reform openings that were available. The authorization of small rural work units and agricultural leasing opportunities of up to 50 years (more generous than the initial 15-year leases in China) prompted nothing remotely similar to the spontaneous and mass surge toward quasi-private farming in China. By the end of 1992, only 3% of Russia's agricultural land was in the hands of private farmers and by mid-1997 only 6%.[24] Why did Russian farmers not jump at the chance to farm their own land as Chinese peasants did?

In the first place, massive political opposition emerged from a small army of rural party officials, collective and state-farm chairmen, and their administrative and technical staffs, who had a vested interest in the existing system. Few of them smelled opportunity in the new possibilities as did numbers of rural cadres in China. They argued that only corrupt officials, the "mafia," and foreigners would be able to take advantage of private agricultural opportunities, thus dooming the majority of rural residents to ruin.

Perhaps even more important, few Soviet collective or state-farm workers themselves—only 10% according to polls—were inclined to seriously consider a plunge into private farming.[25] Soviet agriculture, after all, had been collectivized for 60 years. Its practitioners had become specialized agricultural workers with no direct experience or memory of what private farming meant. Furthermore, most of the energetic younger people had long ago fled to the cities, leaving an older, conservative, and heavily female labor force behind in the villages. Since the 1960s, most collective farmers had become salaried employees whose wages and social benefits had substantially improved. Unlike the impoverished Chinese peasants, who operated outside of the socialist welfare system, Soviet farmers were reluctant to forgo their newly won security for the uncertainties of commercial farming. The few who did often encountered hostility from their neighbors and opposition from the collective farms that continued to dominate the Russian countryside.

INDUSTRIAL REFORM

GRADUALISM IN CHINA.   In dealing with state-owned industrial enterprises, Deng moved more slowly. Here gradualism was the key. The managers of these enterprises were given greater authority and encouraged to act like private owners, making many of their own decisions and seeking profits. But fearing the reaction of their workers, few were actually closed, nor did many workers lose their jobs when these firms continued to lose money. Gradually, state authorities permitted some prices to be set by the market while continuing to determine many others centrally. Not until the mid-1990s did China begin to privatize its major state-owned industries and even then, privatization occurred very slowly. Furthermore, Chinese authorities directed much of their new investment toward light industries, producing consumer goods—TVs, refrigerators, washing machines—which were eagerly snapped up by a Chinese population whose incomes were growing rapidly.

"Shock Therapy" in Russia.   In the Soviet Union, by contrast, all of this occurred much more abruptly. By 1991 when the country collapsed, the central planning mechanism had already been largely dismantled, leading to economic chaos. The newly independent Russian state then freed most prices virtually overnight in early 1992, sending prices through the roof, and it soon undertook an extremely rapid and largely corrupt process of privatizing many state industries—a process that came to be known as "shock therapy." Capitalism came to Russia as it did to China, but the most dramatic changes occurred after communism had collapsed. They took place in a much more abrupt and chaotic fashion, and they were associated with a contracting economy and great hardship for most people.

Opening Up to the World Economy.   Two other features of China's industrial reform process distinguished it from the Soviet/Russian case. One was the extent and rapidity with which China opened itself to the world economy. Abandoning two decades of Maoist "self-reliance," China's international trade boomed in the 1980s with Japan, Hong Kong, and the United States as its primary trading partners. Even more important were the "special economic zones" (SEZs), where foreign investment was welcomed. There China's communist government offered to build plants to the specifications of foreigners, to provide trained, cheap, and nonunion workers, and to give tax breaks and other financial inducements to capitalist investors. Begun in 1979, SEZs grew up dramatically along China's coast, attracting by 1993 some $22 billion in investment funds, compared to only $1.5 billion in Russia.[26]

Despite their impressive economic success, SEZs worried the conservative wing of China's Communist party. They seemed hauntingly similar to the nineteenth century "treaty ports" in which foreigners had humiliated and exploited Chinese people. Had imperialism returned to China? Furthermore, the SEZs were points of entry for western culture and political ideas. To conservative communists this was "spiritual pollution" and "bourgeois liberalism," and they launched periodic educational and media campaigns to combat these threats in the 1980s. Finally, SEZs created regional conflicts between rapidly growing and technically advanced coastal areas and more backward and slower-growing interior provinces.

RURAL INDUSTRY.   A second source of rapid industrial growth, not paralleled in the Soviet Union, lay in numerous "township and village enterprises" (TVEs), which sprang up throughout the rural areas of China's vast countryside. Owned and managed jointly by local governments, private entrepreneurs, and various collective groups, TVEs were a unique form of industrial enterprise, located largely in the rural areas and drawing on the traditions of decentralization and of rural industrialization during the Maoist era. Producing processed food, clothing, building and construction materials, and much more, TVEs became, during the 1980s and 1990s, the most rapidly growing sector of China's exploding economy, able to compete effectively with larger state-owned enterprises and contributing 43% of China's exports by 1995.

CHINA'S TRANSITION TO CAPITALISM.   Here, then, was the Chinese approach to economic reform as it evolved over several decades with many fits and starts and amid much controversy within the Communist Party. It was rooted in an explosive development of essentially private family farming, abandoning decades of collectivized agriculture. It featured very gradual changes in the large, state-owned industrial enterprises while allowing a variety of private businesses, foreign firms, and TVEs to grow up around the state-owned sector. By the time Deng died in 1997, this set of policies had created a largely capitalist economy from what had been a thoroughly state-controlled socialism only a few decades earlier. And it had done so while maintaining relative stability in the country and the continuing political control of the Communist Party. Why was China able to accomplish this remarkable feat while Soviet Communism and the Soviet Union itself had perished amid Gorbachev's efforts at reform?

THE FATE OF TWO COMMUNISMS

DIFFERENT COUNTRIES

One clear difference between the Soviet Union and China lay in their ethnic composition. The Soviet Union was both highly diverse and organized in ethnically based republics such as Ukraine, Lithuania, Kazakhstan, and many others. The dominant Russians represented a little less than half of the population. Here was the cultural basis for many aggrieved "nations in the making." When Gorbachev's reforms allowed them to express their grievances, nationalist sentiments grew dramatically, and a weakened Soviet Union fragmented along ethnic lines. China, by contrast, was far more culturally homogeneous. Though it recognized more than 50 ethnic minorities, they constituted only 8% of the total population. Far in the interior, in Tibet, Xinjiang, Inner Mongolia, and elsewhere on the country's northwest border, separatist movements did emerge during the 1980s and 1990s, but they were not sufficiently large or widespread to seriously threaten the state. Regional conflicts, caused by differing levels of economic growth and competition for scarce resources, generally lacked the explosive nationalist dimension that proved the undoing of the Soviet Union.

CONTRASTING APPROACHES TO COMMUNIST REFORM

THE SOVIET UNION: ECONOMICS AND POLITICS.   Equally important were the very different reform strategies that the two countries pursued. Almost from the start, Gorbachev linked economic reforms with much greater freedom of expression and especially with democratizing political change. By 1990, the Soviet Communist Party had legally lost its political monopoly and dozens of other parties and informal groups entered the political arena. Openly competitive elections had already ousted many leading communists and created a parliament ready to challenge Gorbachev's regime. *Glasnost* and *democratization,* in short, opened the door for the expression of growing anti-Soviet and anti-communist sentiments.

CHINA: ECONOMICS ONLY.   In China, by contrast, the reform agenda was much more limited. It focused almost wholly on the economy. It did ease censorship and permit intellectuals greater freedom of expression, but then periodically cracked down when they went beyond permissible bounds. And nothing like the Soviet opening to democracy took place in China. For the new Chinese leadership under Deng Xiaoping, democratizing political reform at the national level threatened the strong state and party structures believed to be absolutely necessary for successful economic reform. "Talk about democracy in the abstract," Deng declared, "will inevitably lead to the unchecked spread of ultra-democracy and anarchism, to the complete disruption of political stability, and to the total failure of our modernization program . . . China will once again be plunged into chaos, division, retrogression, and darkness."[27] But why did China and the Soviet Union adopt such different reform strategies?

EXPLAINING ALTERNATIVE STRATEGIES. Gorbachev's answer would likely be that he had no choice. It was, he wrote in his memoirs, like "cutting . . . through jungle undergrowth" to get anything accomplished.[28] Opposition to even modest economic reform was so great that he felt compelled to build pressure on a reluctant state and party bureaucracy. *Glasnost* and *democratization* were the means of doing so. In China, despite disagreements about specific issues, there was a wider consensus in favor of reform and thus little need to create public pressure for it. Furthermore, the Cultural Revolution in China had traumatized the party and much of the country, giving rise to a widespread desire to repudiate its practices. It also created an obsession with order and an inclination among many in the party elite to identify democracy with potential chaos and division. Democracy, potentially at least, was the Cultural Revolution revisited! But in the Soviet Union, Gorbachev's reforms had been preceded by a generation of post-Stalinist stability that provided few warnings of the dangers that democratization might unleash.

Furthermore, a large number of Soviet leaders had almost completely lost their belief in communism. Alexander Yakolev, perhaps the most influential of Gorbachev's early advisors, referred to Bolshevism as "social lunacy" and described it as "an anti-human precept, hammered in with the ruthlessness of an ideological fanaticism that conceals its intellectual and economic nullity."[29] Few, if any, leading Chinese communists would have spoken in similar terms. They were more ready to defend their Communist Party as still standing for something important, whereas growing numbers of Soviet communists were more than willing to let it go.

CHINESE SUCCESS, SOVIET FAILURE

DRAMATIC CONTRASTS. A further, and perhaps decisive, factor that enabled China to avoid the fate of the Soviet Union was its astonishing economic growth, a process that greased the skids of reform and eased the tensions of that process. Growth rates averaging 10% a year, sustained for more than two decades, represent the most impressive record of economic performance of modern world history. Rising standards of living, improved incomes, better diets, declining poverty, lower mortality rates, and a diminished rural-urban gap—all of this surely contributed to the legitimacy of the communist regime, despite regional inequalities and widespread corruption among officials. Initial economic success confirmed China's leadership in a strategy that separated economic from political reform. But in the Soviet Union, the sharp contraction of the economy by 1990 led to massive shortages, out-of-control inflation, fear of unemployment, declining life expectancies, and lower standards of living for most. All of this discredited the Communist Party as incompetent as well as corrupt and oppressive. But why were Chinese economic reforms so much more successful than those of the Soviet Union?

EXPLAINING THE DIFFERENCE.   Some scholars have pointed to a variety of Chinese advantages, suggesting that its socialist economy was "more reformable" than that of the Soviet Union. China was located near the growing economies of East Asia (Japan, South Korea, Taiwan, Hong Kong), and the presence of a large Chinese overseas community provided a ready source of money, entrepreneurial experience, and technical knowledge that had no counterpart in the Soviet Union. Furthermore, China's largely agrarian economy and relative "backwardness" was perhaps an advantage, allowing it to make a quick agricultural breakthrough with little investment and to draw upon a large pool of rural and cheap labor as a source of economic growth unavailable to an "over-industrialized" Soviet Union.[30] China's Maoist legacy with its decentralized administration and history of rural industrialization may likewise have provided a better environment for private initiative, once reforms began, as compared to the more rigidly centralized and more completely state-run Soviet economy. China had a long tradition of private trade and entrepreneurial initiative that had little parallel in old Russia, where the state, rather than private enterprise, had long been the primary motor of economic change.

Others have credited Chinese reform strategy as simply more effective than that of the Soviet Union/Russia. The Chinese approach, characterized by one economist as "growing out of the plan," permitted the market to emerge gradually outside of the state-controlled sector in decollectivized farms, in township and village enterprises, in small-scale private businesses, and in SEZs that welcomed foreign investment, all the while maintaining the planning process and keeping the state sector intact.[31] The more abrupt Soviet/Russian approach of dismantling the planned economy very quickly, before economic growth and the market had really kicked in, proved disastrous.

THE OTHER SIDE OF SUCCESS.   But China's overall economic success generated serious social tensions, similar to those of other countries in the early stages of capitalist development. Rapid economic growth spawned environmental destruction on a massive scale, shrinking the amount of cultivated land and making Beijing's air quality among the worst in the world. Periodic surges of inflation and the decontrol of some prices and rents badly frightened urban consumers. So did the requirements of capitalist "efficiency" that threatened the benefits and even the jobs of workers, especially in the state-run industries. Urban vices such as street crime, prostitution, gambling, drug addiction, and a criminal underworld, largely eliminated after 1949, surfaced again in China's cities. In the countryside, successful farmers, private businesspeople, and party officials formed an interlocking and wealthy elite, while many millions of displaced peasants became a "floating population" roaming from city to city in search of temporary work. Their impoverished lives contrasted sharply with those of China's new urban elite, who wore the latest in western fashion, talked on cell phones, and drove imported luxury automobiles. Such inequalities were common across the world in developing countries, but in China they emerged with stunning suddenness from what had very recently been a socialist society of relative equality. "To get rich is glorious," one of the slogans of the reform era, was a far cry from "serve the people," a common exhortation of Maoist China.

Accompanying these inequalities was rampant corruption among Communist Party officials and their families. Particularly in the "special economic zones" along the coast, children of high officials, including Deng Xiaoping's son, easily took advantage of their connections to benefit personally from the exploding opportunities in import/export businesses. A Communist Party whose reputation for honesty and simple living had gained it great respect in the 1940s now lost much of that esteem. One of the party's own newspapers in 1988 reported on the dramatic decline in public confidence in the party:

> The decay of party discipline, bribery and corruption, covering up for friends and relatives, deceiving and taking advantage of good cadre and party members, open violations of the law . . . being covered up through "special connections" of various kinds . . . —all these types of flagrant misconduct have produced such harmful social results and led to such deterioration of the party's image that the damage done is inestimable.[32]

THE DEMOCRACY MOVEMENT: RENEWED AND CRUSHED

TIANANMEN SQUARE.   All this was grist for the mill of a renewed democracy movement that took shape in China's cities in the late 1980s. Spearheaded by university and secondary school students, it found the solution to many of these problems in a more open, democratic, and western political system. One of its leading spokesmen, the physicist Fang Lizhi, repeatedly toured university campuses where he urged students to "break all barriers." "I am here to tell you," he declared publicly in 1985, "that the socialist movement, from Marx and Lenin to

FIGURE 6-1   THE GODDESS OF LIBERTY:
This plaster figure, similar to the American Statue of Liberty, was constructed by students during the Tiananmen Square upheaval and symbolized the eroding commitment to Maoist style communism among China's youth.

Stalin and Mao Zedong has been a failure ... I think that complete Westernization is the only way to modernize."[33] In the spring of 1989, students in Beijing began leading rapidly swelling marches into the capital city's central plaza, Tiananmen Square, the site of the ancient "Forbidden City" of the emperors and currently the headquarters of China's communist government. There in an atmosphere of growing radicalism, they erected a "tent city," supported a small group of hunger strikers, created a plaster "goddess of democracy" in the likeness of the American Statue of Liberty, and paraded before the TV cameras of the world, calling for democracy and denouncing official corruption. They danced, sang, chanted, debated politics, and ridiculed party leaders.

As if this was not threatening enough to a shaken Communist Party leadership, soon growing numbers of workers and ordinary citizens joined the movement. Entire factories and government offices openly supported the students. Frightened communist leaders, witnessing the rise of a powerful independent trade union organization in Poland, saw the possibility of another Solidarity movement or even the renewal of another Cultural Revolution. By late May, demonstrations in the square attracted a million or more people, and neighborhood groups began to erect barricades to defend against the military forces—some 250,000 troops—that had begun to assemble around the city.

REPRESSION.   For seven weeks, the standoff continued while a divided Communist Party leadership debated what to do—negotiate and compromise with the students or crush them. The rapid growth of independent workers' organizations in many major cities and the increasing number of political and military officials siding with the students seemed to Deng and others to threaten the very survival of the communist regime. By early June, hardliners had won the internal debate and ordered the military to take Tiananmen Square. In the violence that ensued, perhaps a thousand people were killed, mostly workers in their neighborhoods rather than students. Severe repression followed with many thousands more arrested and a small number executed. The democracy movement had been crushed and the limits of Chinese reform clearly demonstrated. But economic reform persisted and even accelerated in the decade that followed, as the emergence of an essentially capitalist economy within a highly authoritarian state dominated by the Communist Party continued to unfold.

THE SOVIET DIFFERENCE.   Here was another major difference with the Soviet experience. The Chinese communist leadership was willing to use overwhelming force to defend its power, privileges, and policies. In the Soviet Union, neither Gorbachev nor the leaders of the August 1991 coup unleashed the military or police forces at their disposal to preserve the Soviet system. Because the Soviet reform package had included *democratization* from the beginning, cracking down decisively was more difficult than in China, where the reformist leadership had rejected democracy from the start. Furthermore, belief in communism had eroded far further in the Soviet Union, and its democracy movement probably had a wider base of support than in a still largely rural and peasant China.

THE QUESTION OF SOCIALISM

What remained of socialism amid China's reforms and the emergence of a market economy? It was a question that deeply troubled many in the Communist Party leadership. Reformers recalled Marx's assertion that real socialism had to be preceded by a long period of capitalist development. In this view, China's current condition represented a "primary form of socialism" with "fully developed socialism" pushed into the distant future of 50 to 100 years ahead. To Deng Xiaoping, almost anything that contributed to rapid economic growth now was, by definition, a contribution to "socialism." To Deng's more orthodox critics, such thinking stretched the meaning of socialism too far. They wanted to reassert the central government's control over the economy and to heighten the party's ideological struggle against "bourgeois liberalism" or capitalist values. Some conservative communists urged that all the SEZs should be shut down immediately. The collapse of communism in the Soviet Union and Eastern Europe seemed to them a dire warning of what might befall China if reform continued unchecked. These debates among party leaders continued even as the death of Deng in 1997 brought to power a new generation of Chinese communists.

NATIONALISM.   As commitment to socialism weakened, party authorities increasingly pushed nationalism and patriotism as the primary ideology of the state. "The purpose of socialism," Deng declared, "is to make the country rich and strong." Great emperors were now publicly praised rather than condemned. Confucianism, long damned as the embodiment of "feudal" China, made a comeback. Confucian teachings were reintroduced into school curricula, and the country hosted a large international conference in 1994 to celebrate the 2,545th birthday of China's ancient sage. Many Chinese, and not just communists, viewed the 1997 recovery of Hong Kong, under British control for 150 years, as a triumph of Chinese nationalism. Then only Taiwan stood in the way of China's complete reunification, and the fate of that island, an issue of great sensitivity within China, continued as a source of international tension and of potential war.

CONSUMERISM.   For many millions of newly prosperous Chinese, socialism had given way to an unabashed materialism. A popular slogan suggested that life in modern China required the "Eight Bigs": color TV, refrigerator, stereo, camera, motorcycle, a suite of furniture, washing machine, and electric fan. In addition, a man needed the "three highs" to attract a suitable wife: high salary, advanced education, and a height of over five feet six inches. The pursuit of such a life was encouraged in the media by stories celebrating individual entrepreneurs who took advantage of the new opportunities to become wealthy. Chinese writers and filmmakers, like their counterparts the world over, explored the tension between prosperity and mindless consumerism and asked penetrating questions about the loss of older values of simplicity, family, and nature in the rush to achieve and consume.

TRADITION.   If nationalism and consumerism helped fill the void of a declining socialism, so too has a marked revival of traditional Chinese practices. In the freer environment of contemporary China, more people have openly participated in burial rituals for the dead and in venerating their ancestors by making offerings and tending their tombs. Buddhism, too, has experienced a revival, as well as traditional Chinese arts such as shadow plays. Perhaps the most dramatic expression of this trend was expressed in the enormous growth of the Falun Gong movement. Created only in 1992 by former grain clerk and trumpet player Li Hongzhi, Falun Gong combined Buddhist and Daoist beliefs with *qigong* exercises and aimed at the physical and moral improvements of its practitioners. Its tight structure and explosive growth in the 1990s frightened Communist Party officials, who saw it as a rival organization and ideology. It has been harshly suppressed with more than 10,000 people arrested. Nonetheless, Falun Gong represents a continuing search for meaning, drawing upon ancient Chinese traditions, as a discredited Socialism no longer provided the sense of purpose and solidarity that it had earlier in the century.

As China entered the twenty-first century, its communist experiment remained in question. The Communist Party continued to dominate China's political life, as did state control over major areas of the urban economy such as chemicals, metals, electrical power, and oil production. Even this was threatened as the party made plans in the late 1990s to sell off many of the remaining state-owned firms, permitting them to join the rest of China's essentially capitalist economy. A real commitment to creating socialism anytime soon was vanishingly rare among most ordinary Chinese as well as among many high-ranking party officials. Socialism by 2000 was a far more diluted, tenuous, and contested affair than it had been even a quarter century earlier. Mao would hardly have recognized it.

THE WORLD AND THE END OF THE COMMUNIST ERA

The end of communism took place largely in the Soviet Union and China, but its impact was felt around the world. The most dramatic and even stunning of these changes was the end of the Cold War, which had structured international life throughout the second half of the twentieth century. As the Soviet Union reformed and then collapsed, the often tense and fearful antagonism between the two superpowers melted away. The arms race between them now ended as the USSR/Russia was economically unable to pursue it. A variety of arms control agreements sharply reduced the nuclear arsenals of both sides and the world breathed more freely as the threat of a nuclear holocaust receded. In Europe, where the Cold War began, entrenched divisions between eastern and western blocs dissolved as the Berlin Wall fell and Germany was reunited and brought within the NATO alliance. Early in the twenty-first century, other former communist states—Hungary, Poland, and the Czech Republic—were also admitted to NATO, and the European Union enlarged to include even parts of the former Soviet Union, such as Latvia, Lithuania, and Estonia. The sharp ideological division of Europe, a prominent feature of European life for a half century, was over.

CAPITALISM TRIUMPHANT.   So, too, was the great global debate about capitalism and socialism as distinct and rival social systems. Controversies continued, of course, about the precise mixture of state action and the market in fostering economic growth, but by the end of the twentieth century, virtually all of the world's nations operated on the assumption of a prominent role for the free market. All of them, including China, eastern European countries, and the states of the former Soviet Union sought to participate actively in a single world economy. Capitalism, in short, had triumphed, at least for the moment.

TRANSITIONS TO DEMOCRACY.   Democracy as well seemed to get a global boost as communism faded. Many of the post-communist states of eastern Europe and the former Soviet Union joined the swelling ranks of new democracies in Latin America, Africa, Asia, and southern Europe in the last quarter of the twentieth century. Elections, constitutions, and competing political parties proliferated. But previously communist states had a uniquely difficult transition to democracy because their societies had been almost totally controlled by the state and lacked the kind of civic organizations and private property that were the basis for democratic revival elsewhere. Theirs was a double transition—to democracy and to capitalism at the same time.

A SINGLE SUPERPOWER.   The collapse of the Soviet Union left the United States as the world's sole superpower with unprecedented economic and military power. The apparent victory of capitalism and democracy over communism left many Americans feeling triumphant and confident that their culture, economy, and politics were the wave of the global future. But the exercise of their power—in Iraq, in Afghanistan, in global trade negotiations, in refusing to join a Global Warming agreement—created accusations of an American empire in the making and gave rise to widespread though uncoordinated opposition to the dominant position of the United States in world affairs. For many Americans, the assertive forces of Islamic revivalism seemed to replace Communism as the global enemy, especially after the attacks on the World Trade Center and the Pentagon in September 2001.

DEVELOPING COUNTRIES.   The role of the Third World likewise changed as the Cold War came to an end. Fewer opportunities for playing off the great powers against one another presented themselves. Foreign aid and investment that had previously flowed toward Africa and Asia now was more often directed toward eastern Europe. The international significance of the Third World declined as that of the former communist countries increased in the calculations of western powers and their investors. Long-standing conflicts within the Third World continued—between Arabs and Israelis, India and Pakistan, for example—but without the added pressure of Soviet/American rivalry to fuel them.

In many places the end of the Cold War seemed to allow simmering ethnic tensions to explode into open conflict. Beyond the disintegration of the Soviet Union, Yugoslavia and Czechoslovakia fragmented in the post-Communist years, the former amid horrendous violence and the latter peacefully. Chechens in Russia, Abkhazians in Georgia, Tibetans in China, Kurds in Turkey and Iraq—all of these "minority" peoples found themselves in bitter opposition to the states in which they lived. Elsewhere terrible civil wars, rooted in ethnic conflict, raged in Rwanda, Bosnia, Congo, Liberia, and Afghanistan.

THE NORTH AND THE SOUTH.   As the Cold War faded, other global conflicts took on greater prominence. The North/South division between the more wealthy and developed countries and the poorer "developing" nations came to occupy center stage in the global arena. Issues of debt relief, environmental policies, global trade, and the role of the World Bank and the International Monetary Fund complicated this relationship. The rise of a militant Islam and "terrorism" likewise took on global dimensions that affected the United States, Russia, China, India, Indonesia, the Philippines, the Middle East, and Algeria, among others. Concerns about the proliferation of nuclear, biological, and chemical weapons—especially in the arsenals of less stable countries—worried governments and peoples around the world. The end of the Cold War certainly did not bring peace and stability, but new kinds of conflicts and disorders.

CONCLUSION: THE COMMUNIST WORLD IN 2000: SHRUNKEN AND DILUTED

As the twenty-first century dawned, the communist world had shrunk considerably from its high point just three decades earlier. In the Soviet Union and Eastern Europe, it had disappeared entirely as the governing authority and dominant ideology, although communist parties continued to play a role in some countries. China had considerably diluted its communist economic policies as a market economy took shape. Vietnam and

Laos remained officially communist while pursuing Chinese-style reforms, although more cautiously. Even Cuba, beset by economic crisis in the 1990s after massive Soviet subsidies ended, allowed small businesses, private food markets, and tourism to grow, while harshly repressing opposition political groups. An impoverished North Korea remained the most unreformed and Stalinist of the remaining communist countries.

International tensions born of communism remained only in east Asia and the Caribbean. North Korea's threat to develop nuclear weapons maintained a state of crisis on the peninsula and presented the United States, China, and Japan with a difficult problem. Continuing tension between China and Taiwan as well as between the United States and Cuba were enduring hangovers from the Cold War era. But either as a major source of international conflict or as a compelling path to modernity and social justice, the communist era was over.

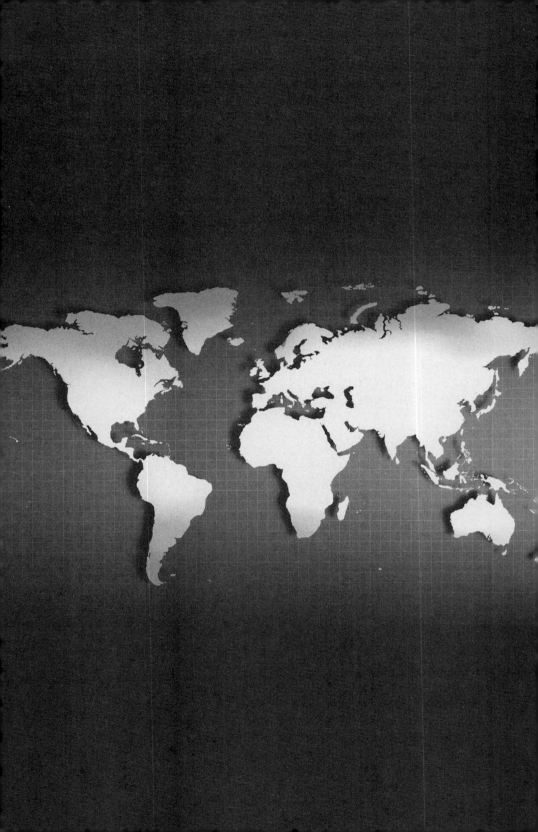

COMMUNISM AND REFLECTIONS ON HISTORY

The study of history—any kind of history—invites us to reflect on some of the larger questions of human life and society. As we conclude this examination of modern communism, it might be useful to ponder a few of these issues as they relate to what we have just learned. In doing so, we are unlikely to find clear answers to profound questions, but we may perhaps sharpen the questions we ask and probe a little more deeply into the rich and tragic history of revolution, socialism, and global conflict in the twentieth century.

UNDERSTANDING AND FORGETTING

Is historical understanding across cultural boundaries really possible? If many men and women profess difficulty in understanding even their own mates, how can we ever hope to understand entire cultures different from our own? Separated by both time and culture, can we grasp the ways other people have lived? The question becomes more pointed as we realized that virtually all important historical discussion is forever laced with controversy and dispute. The earlier notion of scientific objectivity in historical analysis—the idea that detached and trained observers might reconstruct the past "as it really happened" and come to final consensus about it—has largely vanished. Most scholars now recognize controversy as an inescapable and enduring part of the historian's craft, even while they struggle to sift the evidence with care and put aside obvious bias. But the various perspectives associated with differences in class, gender, nation, ethnic group, ideology, and generation provide no common vantage point for understanding the past and ensure that lively debate continues on virtually every historical

189

question imaginable. History is society's memory, but it is at virtually every point contested memory.

Studying communism while living in the Western world, and particularly in the United States, illustrates the point. American historical experience has been uniquely hostile to socialism, and unlike many western European countries, no large-scale popular socialist movement ever developed in the United States. American individualism, the frontier experience, a preoccupation with race and ethnicity, cold war fears—all of this and more has made anything remotely socialist virtually taboo in American public life. Furthermore, we now know that communism failed and that it generated some of the most appalling barbarities of the twentieth century. In light of all this, can we understand how many people were, for a time at least, genuinely enthusiastic about making socialist revolutions and constructing socialist societies?

Historical understanding sometimes comes from forgetting. To enter into the experience of those who were once enthusiastic about socialism, we need to set aside—or temporarily forget—much of American political culture and our knowledge of the Stalinist or Maoist outcomes of the communist experiment. Russian and Chinese revolutionaries did not know what was coming. But they did know something about the brutal exploitation of workers in capitalist factories, about the wretched poverty of peasants subjected to the whims of their landlords, about China's humiliation in the face of western and Japanese imperialism, and about the terrible war among capitalist states in which Russia was tragically entangled in 1914. And they learned that many progressive Europeans were rallying around the ideas of Karl Marx. These ideas seemed then the most advanced thinking from the most advanced part of the world. They claimed to be scientific at a time when science seemed a sure path to truth, and they promised a way out of intolerable conditions by means of a revolution that would renew human society and restore justice and prosperity for all.

Furthermore, communist regimes, once in power, dealt decisively with many of the injustices of the past—expropriating land from the wealthy, distributing it to the poor, providing new educational and work opportunities for many who could never have dreamed of such things before, and ending their countries' subjugation to foreign imperialists. Communism also projected a compelling social vision—that the lives of previously downtrodden and impoverished people could be different, that their work could contribute to a grand enterprise of world historical significance, that their societies could become places of freedom, equality, prosperity, and community. Can we capture something of the appealing quality of the socialist vision, so different from the individualistic, acquisitive, and competitive spirit of capitalism?

INTENTIONS, OUTCOMES, AND SURPRISES

But visions, or human intentions generally, frequently do not turn out as expected, and the historical record is littered with surprising twists and turns. Looking backward and knowing what happened, those of us living in the present are perhaps less aware of the unexpectedness of the historical process than were the actual actors in the story. Certainly the Russian and Chinese reformers, who sought to bolster the Romanov and Qing dynasties in the early twentieth century, never expected that their efforts would lead to vast revolutionary upheavals sweeping away forever the societies they struggled to preserve. More recently, Mikhail Gorbachev's program to revitalize a declining Soviet Union backfired at virtually every point, and in just a few years triggered the collapse of everything he had intended to strengthen.

But the greatest discrepancy between intention and outcomes surely lies in the evolution of communist revolutions themselves. Intended to create humane socialist societies free of the oppression and cruelty of the past, they instead gave rise to some of the most horrendous brutalities of a bloody twentieth century—Stalin's terror and the Gulag, Mao's Cultural Revolution, Cambodia's mass executions. Even in milder forms, communist regimes displayed a blatant disregard for the kind of political and cultural freedoms common in western democracies. How are we to understand this vast chasm between intention and outcome in the history of twentieth-century communism?

One answer has been that the vision itself was fatally flawed. Perhaps any effort at such a radical transformation of human society and human consciousness runs up against the intractability of human nature. Meeting resistance and blinded by the beauty of the vision, revolutionaries resort to force and violence, persuading themselves that short-term sufferings, even cruelties, are made bearable by the loveliness of what is to come. The ends, in short, justify the means. To their opponents and critics, of course, the pursuit of perfection becomes the enemy of the possible.

Another answer has been that the revolutions occurred in the wrong place. As economically backward countries with no tradition of democratic practice, Russia and China offered no fertile ground for the realization of Marx's vision. He had assumed, after all, that socialism would flourish in countries where capitalism had already created great wealth, waiting to be redistributed justly, and where democracy had already established a tradition of mass participation in public life. The tragedy of socialism in this view was that it took root prematurely where conditions were not ripe rather than in the more advanced parts of the world. Would a British or a Swedish socialism have generated the kind of evil that took place in Stalin's Soviet Union?

A third answer focuses on the enemies of socialism, both internal and external. Were the socialist countries virtually forced into harsh measures to defend themselves against those who sought to preserve their unjust privileges? Could a Soviet Union, surrounded by hostile powers who hated the very idea of socialism, have survived without a powerful state to manage its industrialization and the military forces required to protect the revolution? Should a newly communist China have permitted landlords and Guomindang supporters to operate freely in their efforts to reverse the revolution? The enemies of socialism, as well as its advocates, perhaps deserve some of the responsibility for its deformities.

Finally, particular leaders and policies may help to explain the gap between intention and outcome. Stalin's narrow conception of socialism, his inclination to see enemies everywhere, his drive for absolute power—all of this surely shaped and deformed Soviet socialism. Had Lenin lived another 20 years or had he been replaced by a less-fearful person, might the Soviet Union have avoided the horrors of the terror? Or if Mao had been replaced by Deng Xiaoping after the disaster of the Great Leap Forward, could China have escaped the Cultural Revolution?

Whatever the explanation for the vast gap between communist promise and communist performance, it might serve as a caution about easy acceptance of grand schemes for human regeneration. And reflecting on the unexpected in history might make us more careful about predicting the future and especially about assuming that the future will be an extension of the past. Contrary to popular opinion, history seldom repeats itself. The only certainty is that we will be surprised.

MAKING HISTORY

Who—or what—shapes the process of historical change? It is perhaps the most fundamental of all historical questions. One of the most succinct and cogent answers has come from, of all people, Karl Marx. "Men make their own history," he wrote, "but not exactly as they please nor under conditions of their own choosing." In asserting that "men (and women) make their own history," Marx was claiming that human beings have a measure of freedom to determine how their lives and societies shall be ordered. In our examination of twentieth-century communism, we have witnessed various ways in which people made their own history through their own voluntary actions. Major public figures such as tsars and emperors, Lenin, Stalin, Mao, Gorbachev, and Deng Xiaoping, certainly put their stamp on the events of their time. Without Lenin's drive and persistence, it seems unlikely that a reluctant Bolshevik Party would have undertaken the October Revolution of 1917. More than 40 years of Fidel Castro's leadership in Cuba has certainly marked that communist island in distinctive ways.

Beyond prominent individuals, ordinary people, when acting in concert with one another, have likewise driven historical change. Russian workers who marched in the face of tsarist troops in 1917, citizens who denounced others during the Soviet Terror, Soviet democrats who rallied against the August 1991 coup, East Germans who stormed the Berlin Wall in 1989, Chinese peasants who confronted their landlords in thousands of villages during the 1940s, millions of Red Guards who made China's Cultural Revolution, students who occupied Tiananmen Square in defiance of Chinese authorities—all of these groups, and the individuals who chose to join them, surely made history, for better or worse.

But they did not make history "as they pleased," for their own pasts limited and constrained their actions in the present, even if they were wholly unaware of it. Those pasts largely determined the issues they were required to confront. Russian industrialization and World War I set the agenda for Russian revolutionaries much as foreign imperialism and China's rural inequalities did for their Chinese counterparts. The reform programs of both Gorbachev and Deng were responses to the legacies of Stalinism and Maoism. And the Stalinist era surely was shaped by the heritage of tsarist Russia, which preceded it, while Maoism bore the marks of imperial China and Confucianism. Growing populations, international conflicts, slow economic or ecological change—these large-scale forces likewise set boundaries to human action.

Here then are two useful reminders. The first affirms our freedom and urges us to use it responsibly in the pursuit of a better world. If others have acted in the past, so can we! The second highlights the constraints under which all of us operate in both our public and private lives and emphasizes the limits of human freedom. It cautions us that not everything desirable is possible, and that action sometimes makes things worse. Together, they remind us of the famous prayer of St. Francis in which he asked for the courage to change the things he could, the capacity to accept what could not be changed, and the wisdom to know the difference.

AMBIGUOUS JUDGMENTS

Historians not only describe what happened and try to explain why things turned out as they did, they also evaluate the events and people they study and make judgments based on their own particular values.

This reality has both distorted and enriched the study of communism virtually from the beginning, for few observers were neutral in their assessment of the phenomenon. Were the Russian and Chinese revolutions a blow for human freedom and a cry for justice on the part of oppressed people, or were they a replacement of one tyranny by another? Was Stalinism a successful effort to industrialize a backward country or a ferocious assault on the moral and social fabric of that country? Do Chinese reforms in the late twentieth century represent a return to sensible policies of modernization, a continued denial of basic democratic rights, or an opening to capitalist inequalities, corruption, and acquisitiveness?

Clearly, there is something to be said for all sides of these questions. How can we balance and integrate their competing and apparently contradictory truths? How can we hold in our minds both the genuine achievements of communism—the righting of past inequalities; new opportunities for women, workers, and peasants; rapid industrial development; the end of imperialist domination—as well as the mountains of crimes which can be clearly attributed to communist regimes—millions killed and wrongly imprisoned; massive famines predictably caused by radical policies; human rights violated on an enormous scale; lives uprooted and distorted by efforts to achieve the impossible? Sometimes efforts to note anything positive about communism, or even to understand its horrors, brings the charge of whitewashing its crimes. And in most communist countries most of the time, even modest criticism was held to be "counterrevolutionary" and was forbidden. Holding the tension and making balanced judgments is never an easy task.

Communism, like many human projects, has been an ambiguous enterprise. Studying it challenges our inclination to want definitive answers and clear moral judgments. It forces us to hold contradictory elements in some kind of tension and to become less uncomfortable with ambiguity. But that is also true for most of human history and it is perhaps an important part of growing up and of achieving intellectual maturity. That is the gift, both painful and enormously enriching, which the study of history offers to us all.

SUGGESTIONS FOR
FURTHER READING

Chang, Jung. (1991). *Wild Swans: Three Daughters of China*. New York: Anchor Books.

Chen, Yuan-Tsung. (1980). *The Dragon's Village: An Autobiographical Novel of Revolutionary China*. New York: Penguin Books.

Chukovskaya, Lydia. (1999). *Sofia Petrovna*. Evanston: Northwestern University Press.

Dommen, Arthur J. (2001). *The Indochinese Experience of the French and the Americans: Nationalism and Communism in Cambodia, Laos, and Vietnam*. Bloomington: Indiana University Press.

Ferdinand, Peter. (1991). *Communist Regimes in Comparative Perspective*. Savage, MD: Barnes and Noble Books.

Figes, Orlando. (1997). *A People's Tragedy: The Russian Revolution, 1891–1924*. New York: Penguin Putnam.

Fitzpatrick, Sheila. (1982). *The Russian Revolution, 1917–1932*. Oxford: Oxford University Press.

Fowkes, Ben. (1993). *The Rise and Fall of Communism in Eastern Europe*. New York: St. Martin's Press.

Goldstone, Jack. (2002). *Revolutions: Theoretical, Comparative and Historical Studies*. Belmont, CA: Wadsworth.

Grass, June, Corrin, Jay, and Kort, Michael. (1997). *Modernization and Revolution in China*. Armonk, NY: M.E. Sharpe.

Heng, Liang and Shapiro, Judith. (1983). *Son of the Revolution*. New York: Vintage Books.

Hinton, William. (1966). *Fashen: A Documentary of Revolution in a Chinese Village*. New York: Vintage Books.

Hinton, William. (1984). *Shenfan: The Continuing Revolution in a Chinese Village*. New York: Random House.

MacFarquhar, Roderick. (1997). *The Politics of China: The Eras of Mao and Deng.* New York: Cambridge University Press.

Meisner, Maurice. (1999). *Mao's China and After.* New York: The Free Press.

Perez-Stable, Marifeli. (1998). *Cuban Revolution: Origins, Course, and Legacy.* New York: Oxford University Press.

Read, Christopher. (2001). *The Making and Breaking of the Soviet System.* New York: Palgrave.

Rosenberg, William G. and Young, Marilyn. (1982). *Transforming Russia and China: Revolutionary Struggle in the Twentieth Century.* New York: Oxford University Press.

Spence, Jonathan. (1999). *The Search for Modern China.* New York: W.W. Norton.

Strayer, Robert. (1998). *Why Did the Soviet Union Collapse?* Armonk, NY: M.E. Sharpe.

Suny, Ronald Grigor. (1998). *The Soviet Experiment.* New York: Oxford University Press.

Ward, Chris. (1993). *Stalin's Russia.* London: Edward Arnold.

◄ NOTES ►

CHAPTER ONE

1. Karl Marx and Friedrich Engels, *The Communist Manifesto* (New York: Appelton-Century-Crofts, 1955), p. 12. (Originally published in 1848).

2. Ibid., p. 32.

3. Antoine-Nicholas de Condorcet, *Sketch for a Historical Picture of the Progress of the Human Mind*, trans. June Barraclough (London: Weidenfeld and Nicolson, 1955), pp. 199–201.

4. Richard Stites, *Revolutionary Dreams* (New York: Oxford University Press, 1989), p. 49.

5. Stites, p. 38.

6. Barbara Evans Clement, *Daughters of Revolution: A History of Women in the USSR* (Arlington Heights: Harlan Davidson, Inc., 1994), p. 58.

7. Samuel P. Huntington, *The Third Wave* (Norman: University of Oklahoma Press, 1991), p. 17.

8. Stephane Courtois et. al., *The Black Book of Communism* (Cambridge: Harvard University Press, 1999).

CHAPTER TWO

1. For a helpful summary of various theories, see Jack Goldstone, *Revolutions: Theoretical, Comparative and Historical Studies* (New York: Harcourt Brace Jovanovich, 1986), pp. 1–17.

2. Quoted in E. P. Young, "Problems of a Late Ch'ing Revolutionary," in *Revolutionary Leaders of Modern China*, ed. Chun-tu Hsueh (New York: Oxford University Press, 1971), p. 220.

3. John Lust, "Secret Societies, Popular Movements, and the 1911 Revolution," in *Popular Movements and Secret Societies in China, 1840–1950*, ed. Jean Chesneaux (Stanford: Stanford University Press, 1972), p. 167.

4. Geoffrey Hoskings, *Russia: People and Empire* (Cambridge: Harvard University Press, 1996), p. 459.

CHAPTER THREE

1. Maurice Hindus, *Red Bread* (Bloomington: Indiana University Press, 1988), p. 1.

2. Hindus, p. 25.

3. Quoted in Sheila Fitzpatrick, *Stalin's Peasants* (New York: Oxford University Press, 1994), p. 67.

4. V. Kravchenko, *I Choose Freedom* (Robert Hale: London, 1947), p. 113.

5. Quoted in Fitzpatrick, p. 316.

6. Joseph V. Stalin, *Works*, vol. 13, *July 1930–January 1934* (Moscow: Foreign languages Publishing House, 1955), pp. 40–41.

7. From the *New York Times*, May 3, 1996, p. 10.

8. John Scott, *Behind the Urals* (Bloomington: University of Indiana Press, 1989), pp. 5–6.

9. Quoted in Ronald Suny, *The Soviet Experiment* (New York: Oxford University Press, 1998), p. 242.

10. Eduard Shevardnadze, *The Future Belongs to Freedom* (New York: Free Press, 1991), p. xiv.

11. Quoted in Sarah Davies, *Popular Opinion in Stalin's Russia* (New York: Cambridge University Press, 1997), p. 139.

12. Quoted in Stephen Kotkin, *Magnetic Mountain: Stalinism as a Civilization* (Berkeley: University of California Press, 1995), pp. 221–222.

13. Irina Kakhovskaya, "Our Fate," in *An End to Silence*, ed. Stephen F. Cohen, trans. George Saunders (New York: Norton, 1982), pp. 81–90.

14. Eugenia Semyonovna Ginzburg, *Journey into the Whirlwind* (New York: Harcourt Brace Jovanovich, 1967), pp. 366–67.

15. Anna Akhmatova, *Poems*, selected and translated by Lyn Coffin (New York: Norton, 1983), p. 82.

16. *Poems of Anna Akhmatova*, selected and translated by Stanly Kunitz (Boston, 1967), p. 99.

17. Geoffrey Hosking, *The Awakening of the Soviet Union* (Cambridge: Harvard University Press, 1991), p. 8.

18. Theodore von Laue, "A Perspective on History: The Soviet System Reconsidered," *The Historian* 61:2 (Winter, 1999), p. 383.

CHAPTER FOUR

1. Mao Tse-tung, "On the People's Democratic Dictatorship," in *Selected Works of Mao Tse-tung* (Peking, 1967), 4:422. *Li* is a unit of measure, about two kilometers, or 1.2 miles.

2. Maurice Meisner, *Mao's China and After* (New York: The Free Press, 1986), p. 118.

3. Yuan-tsung Chen, *The Dragon's Village* (New York: Penguin Books, 1980), p. 85.

4. Kay Ann Johnson, *Women, the Family and Revolution in China* (Chicago: University of Chicago Press, 1983), pp. 235–239.

5. Judith Stacey, *Patriarchy and Socialist Revolution in China* (Berkeley: University of California Press,1983), Ch. 4.

6. Quoted in Chao Kuo-chun, *Agrarian Policies of Mainland China* (Cambridge: Harvard University Press, 1957), pp. 85–86.

7. William Hinton, *Shenfan* (New York: Random House, 1983), p. 151.

8. Hinton, *Shenfan*, p. 89.

9. Stuart Schram, *The Political Thought of Mao Tse-tung* (Harmondsworth: Penguin, 1969), pp. 351–2.

10. Roderick MacFarquhar, *The Hundred Flowers Campaign and the Chinese Intellectuals* (New York: Praegar, 1960), p. 87.

11. Robert R. Bowie and John K. Fairbank, *Communist China: 1955–1959: Policy Documents with Analysis* (Cambridge: Harvard University Press, 1962), pp. 337–41.

12. Liang Heng and Judith Shapiro, *Son of the Revolution* (New York: Random House, 1983), p. 9.

13. Hinton, *Shenfan*, p. 205.

14. Quoted in William G. Rosenberg and Marilyn B. Young, *Transforming Russia and China* (New York: Oxford University Press, 1982), p. 311.

15. Roxane Witke, *Comrade Chiang Ching* (Boston, 1972), p. 310.

16. Ken Ling, Miriam London, and Lee Ta-ling, *Red Guard: From School Boy to 'Little General' in Mao's China* (London: Macdonald, 1972), pp. 18–19.

17. Harry Harding, "The Chinese State in Crisis, 1966–1969," in Roderick MacFarquhar, *The Politics of China* (Cambridge: Cambridge University Press, 1997), pp. 239–47.

18. Gordon A. Bennett and Ronald N. Montaperto, *Red Guards: The Political Biography of Dai Hsiao-ai* (New York: Anchor Books, 1972), pp. 222–24.

19. Maksim Gorky, *Lenin: A Biographical Essay* (London: Morrison and Gibb, 1967), pp. 31–32.

CHAPTER FIVE

1. Robert Strayer, *The Making of Mission Communities in East Africa* (London: Heinemann, 1978), p. 107.

2. Kevin McDermott and Jeremy Agnew, *The Comintern: A History of International Communism from Lenin to Stalin* (New York: St. Martin's Press, 1997), p. xvii.

3. John Lewis Gaddis, *Russia, the Soviet Union and the United States,* (New York: McGraw Hill, 1990), p. 173.

4. John Lewis Gaddis, *We Now Know: Rethinking Cold War History* (Oxford: Oxford University Press, 1997), p. 52.

5. Zhe Shi, "With Mao and Stalin: The Reminiscences of Mao's Interpreter: Part II: Liu Shaoqi in Moscow," trans. Chen Jian, *Chinese Historians* (Spring, 1993), pp. 82–86.

6. Richard Rusk, *As I Saw It* (New York: Norton, 1990), p. 245.

7. Nikita Khrushchev, *Khrushchev Remembers*, trans. and ed. Strobe Talbot (New York: Bantam, 1971), p. 547.

8. Ronald Steel, *Pax Americana* (New York: Viking Press, 1970), p. 254.

9. See Robert McNamara, *In Retrospect* (New York: Random House, 1995).

10. Quoted in Ralph B. Levering, *The Cold War, 1945–1987* (Arlington Heights: Harlan Davidson, 1988), p. 105.

11. Quoted in Gaddis, *We Now Know*, p. 96.

12. Richard Turco et. al., "The Climatic Effects of Nuclear War," *Scientific American*, 251:2 (August, 1984), p. 33.

13. Quoted in Gaddis, *We Now Know*, p. 214.

14. Nikita Khrushchev, *Khrushchev Remembers: The Last Testament*, trans. and ed. Strobe Talbot (Boston: Little Brown, 1971), pp. 255–57.

CHAPTER SIX

1. See, for example, Martin Malia, *The Soviet Tragedy* (New York: The Free Press, 1994), Ch. 13.

2. Parts of this section are drawn from Robert Strayer, *Why Did the Soviet Union Collapse?* (Armonk, NY: M.E. Sharpe, 1998). Reprinted with permission.

3. Tatyana Zaslavskaya, *The Second Socialist Revolution* (Bloomington: Indiana University Press, 1990), pp. 28–29.

4. Zaslavskaya, pp. 28–29.

5. Bohdan Nahaylo and Victor Swoboda, *Soviet Disunion: A History of the Nationalities Problem in the USSR* (New York: The Free Press, 1990), p. 143.

6. Mikhail Gorbachev, *Perestroika: New Thinking for our Country and the World* (New York: Harper and Row, 1987), p. 64.

7. Quoted in Abraham Brumberg, *Chronicle of a Revolution* (New York: Pantheon Books, 1990), pp. 225–26.

8. Quoted in Andrei Melville and Gail Lapidus, *The Glasnost Papers* (Boulder: Westview Press, 1990), p. 1.

9. Gorbachev, p. 128.

10. William Moskoff, *Hard Times: Impoverishment and Protest in the Perestroika Years* (Armonk, NY: M.E. Sharpe, 1993), p. 89.

11. Stephen White, *Communism and Its Collapse* (London: Routledge, 2001), p. 79.

12. Moskoff, *Hard Times*, p. 190.

13. David Remnick, *Lenin's Tomb* (New York: Random House, 1993), p. 398.

14. Remnick, *Lenin's Tomb*, p. 479.

15. Vladislav Zubok, "The Collapse of the Soviet Union: Leadership, Elites, and Legitimacy," in *The Fall of the Great Powers*, ed. Geir Lundestad, (New York: Oxford University Press, 1994), pp. 154–74.

16. See Peter Nolan, *China's Rise; Russia's Fall* (New York, St. Martin's Press, 1995).

17. James Seymour, *The Fifth Modernization: China's Human Rights Movement, 1978–1979* (Stanfordville, NY, 1980), p. 52.

18. See Daniel Kelliher, *Peasant Power in China: The Era of Rural Reform, 1979–1989* (New Haven: Yale University Press, 1992).

19. Kelliher, *Peasant Power*, p. 89. Mark Selden, "Post-Collective Agrarian Alternatives in Russia and China," in *China After Socialism*, eds. Barrett L. McCormick and Jonathan Unger (Armonk, NY: M.E. Sharpe, 1996), pp. 22–23.

20. Kate Xian Zhou, *How the Farmers Changed China* (Boulder: Westview Press, 1996), p. 38.

21. Martin K. Whyte, "The Social Roots of China's Economic Development," *China Quarterly*, 144 (December 1995), pp. 999–1019.

22. David Zweig, *Freeing China's Farmers* (Armonk, NY: M.E. Sharpe, 1997), p. 16.

23. Anders Aslund, *How Russia Became a Market Economy* (Washington, D.C.: The Brookings Institution, 1995), p. 14.

24. Minxin Pei, *From Reform to Revolution* (Cambridge: Harvard University Press, 1994), p. 131; Stephen K Wegren, *Agriculture and the State in Soviet and Post-Soviet Russia* (Pittsburgh, University of Pittsburgh Press, 1998), p. 13.

25. Mark Selden, "Russia, China, and the Transformation of Collective Agriculture," *Contentions*, 3:3 (Spring, 1994), p. 81.

26. Nolan, *China's Rise; Russia's Fall*, p. 288.

27. Deng Xiaoping, "The Necessity of Upholding the Four Cardinal Principles in the Drive for the Four Modernizations," in *Major Documents of the People's Republic of China* (Beijing: Foreign Language Press, 1991), p. 54.

28. Mikhail Gorbachev, *Memoirs* (New York: Doubleday, 1995), p. 230.

29. Alexander Yakolev, *The Fate of Marxism* (New Haven: Yale University Press, 1993), p. 79.

30. Minxin Pei, "The Puzzle of East Asian Exceptionalism," *Journal of Democracy* 5:4 (October 1994), pp. 96–100; Jeffrey D. Sachs and Wing Thye Woo, "Structural Factors

in the Economic Reforms of China, Eastern Europe and the Former Soviet Union," *Economic Policy* 18 (April 1994), pp. 101–45.

31. Barry Naughton, *Growing Out of the Plan: Chinese Economic Reform, 1978–1993* (New York: Cambridge University Press, 1995).

32. Quoted in Richard Baum, "The Road to Tiananmen" in Roderick MacFarquhar, *The Politics of China* (Cambridge: Cambridge University Press, 1997), p. 422.

33. Baum, "The Road to Tiananmen," p. 394.

 CREDITS

Page 42: © Hulton-Deutsch Collection/Corbis; **65:** © sovfoto/eastfoto; **73:** RUSU 650, Poster Collection, Hoover Institution Archives; **86:** © Bettmann/Corbis; **107:** AP/Wide World Photo; **138:** © Camera Press/Retna; **180:** AP Photo/Jeff Widener

◀ INDEX ▶